AFRICANITY REDEFINED

In solidarity
Ali A. Mazrui

Feb 2003

AFRICANITY REDEFINED

COLLECTED ESSAYS OF ALI A. MAZRUI VOLUME I

EDITED BY
RICARDO RENÉ LAREMONT
TRACIA LEACOCK SEGHATOLISLAMI
MICHAEL A. TOLER
FOUAD KALOUCHE

TOYIN FALOLA
SERIES EDITOR
CLASSIC AUTHORS AND TEXTS ON AFRICA

Africa World Press, Inc.

| P.O. Box 1892 | | P.O. Box 48 |
| Trenton, NJ 08607 |  | Asmara, ERITREA |

Africa World Press, Inc.

P.O. Box 1892
Trenton, NJ 08607

P.O. Box 48
Asmara, ERITREA

Copyright © 2002 Ali A. Mazrui
First Printing 2002

Cover design: Ashraful Haque

Library of Congress Cataloging-in-Publication Data

Mazrui, Ali Al Amin.
   Africanity redefined / edited by Ricardo René Laremont ...[et al.].
     p.cm. -- (Classic authors and texts on Africa) (Collected
essays of Ali A. Mazrui ; v. 1)
Includes bibliographical references and index.
   ISBN 0-86543-993-1 -- ISBN 0-86543-994-X (pbk.)
   1. Africa--Civilization. 2. Pluralism (Social sciences)--Africa. 3.
Afrocentrism. I. Laremont, Ricardo René. II. Title. III. Series.

DT14 .M388 2002
960--dc21

               2002003940

TABLE OF CONTENTS

EDITORS' NOTE

This collection of essays, *Africanity Redefined: Collected Essays of Ali A. Mazrui, Volume I*, is the first volume of a three-volume set of books that will provide readers with a broad spectrum of Ali A. Mazrui's scholarly writings during his four decades as both scholar and public intellectual. This first volume is a collection of essays that reexamines the definition of Africanity. Africanity as Mazrui defines it is not to be misconstrued with being born on the African continent or being a descendant of Africans. His concept of Africanity is broader and more inclusive: it involves a cosmology, a way of thinking about the world that shatters epistemological and geographical boundaries. As these series of essays will demonstrate, Ali A. Mazrui redefines Africanity across geographical spaces, time, and academic disciplines. He challenges preestablished notions both of the definition of Africans and Africanity, forcing us to reject imperialist and neo-imperialist paradigms and encouraging us to think more creatively about "African" social realities. Reading these essays is a liberating process.

The second volume in this series will deal with cultural exchanges between global Africa and the rest of the world, and the third will focus primarily on politics and power. The second volume logically follows this collection of essays because it deals with how Africa as redefined by Professor Mazrui's concept of "Global Africa" has exchanged, negotiated, and confronted ideas with other cultures and civilizations.

The third volume deals with politics and power. While focusing principally on Africa and its diaspora, Mazrui examines politics globally, analyzing the disequilibrium of power between the developed world and the developing world, between tyrants and toilers, and between princes and peasants. His critiques are sharp, his examination of power relationships can be startling, but in the end, his recommendations and suggestions are most often humanitarian. We hope you enjoy this collection of essays.

TOYIN FALOLA
RICARDO RENÉ LAREMONT

ACKNOWLEDGEMENTS

This book was made possible by the assistance of three graduate students at the State University of New York/Binghamton: Fouad Kalouche, Tracia Leacock Seghatolislami, and Michael A. Toler. They labored diligently to scan and correct the text. They should be recognized for their extraordinary efforts.

The support staff at the Institute of Global Cultural Studies at SUNY Binghamton also contributed significantly, all in their own ways, to the success of this project: Nancy Levis, Barbara Tierno, and Anna Maria Palombaro.

As always, our longstanding editor, Grace Houghton, did her best to catch our last typographical and editing mistakes. To her we give final thanks for the completion of this book.

TOYIN FALOLA
RICARDO RENÉ LAREMONT

PART I

THE (MULTI)CULTURAL PARADIGM

ONE

IN SEARCH OF AFRICA'S PAST

In 1963, in a special series of television lectures on The Rise of Christian Europe,[1] the Oxford historian, Hugh Trevor-Roper, dismissed the history of Africa as meaningless. "Perhaps in the future," he argued, "there will be some African history. . . . But, at present, there is none; there is only the history of Europeans in Africa. The rest is darkness . . . and darkness is not a subject of history." Trevor-Roper's interpretation was part of a long-standing European school of thought, going back to Hegel and beyond.

The latest phase of Africa's rebuttal of this view was, perhaps, initiated by the first president of the first black African country to win independence from European rule, President Kwame Nkrumah. Nkrumah took Ghana to independence in 1957, and continued in power until he was overthrown in February 1966. Part of his greatness for Africa lay in a capacity to identify significant sensibilities underlying the major aspirations of African peoples in the twentieth century. Nkrumah understood that a people denied history was a people deprived of dignity.

The UNESCO project on the history of Africa, surveying the entire span of Africa's past, was in itself a refutation of the proposition that Africa is a continent without history. But let me consider Trevor-Roper's contention in more detail. One problem with the English word "history" is that it tends to be used in three different senses. Sometimes, by the word "history," we mean the actual events of the past. Sometimes we are referring to the type of evidence that may be available to tell us about those events. This second meaning, based on the nature of the evidence, is what we use to distinguish history from "prehistory." The third meaning of "history" is the actual account worked out scientifically by historians.

When Hegel or Trevor-Roper asserts that Africa has no history, do they mean that the continent has no past events? Clearly, that is an absurd proposition. Any society, or any culture, must have a historical background, in the sense of past events which lead to its present dimensions. Trevor-Roper did not mean that nothing occurred in Africa before the Europeans came, but he may have meant that nothing occurred which was worth the attention of a historian. According to him, we can not afford "to amuse ourselves with the unrewarding gyrations of barbarous tribes in picturesque but irrelevant corners of the globe."

Trevor-Roper was denying Africa a history by referring to the things which he thought went on in Africa. He was using the *content* of Africa's past as a way of deciding whether or not Africa had a history. That kind of approach is, basically, either subjective or ethnocentric. In Trevor-Roper's case, it also reveals a certain cultural arrogance.

The second sense of "history" concerns the nature of the evidence available about the society's past. Is that evidence comprehensive enough, and verifiable enough, to give us a historical account of past events? Under this definition of history, the majority of African societies were supposed to be "unhistorical" partly because they were pre-literate. Historical evidence was documentation, and a document was equated with the written word.

In the face of such a conception of history, three lines of defense were open to Africa. One was to accept the paramount position of written documents and then proceed to demonstrate that Africa does have documentary testimony for much of its precolonial history. The second line of defense was to establish the validity of oral evidence for historical work. The third line of defense was to try to cast doubts on the validity of written evidence, in an attempt to show that countries which have massive written documentation of their history are no more certain about their past than those which do not have such evidence.

The first defense — trying to prove that Africa is well endowed with written documentary evidence about its pre-colonial past —

has been more important for West Africans and North Africans than for Africans to the east and to the south. For one thing, in many countries south of the Sahara, Arabic was used as an official and literary language. Much of this material still exists, and has yet to be fully analyzed. Then there is the material written in African languages, like Swahili and Hausa, which use the Arabic script. Much of this has not even been collected. Then again, it is not widely known that before the colonial period, many private citizens in Africa used European languages in their written accounts of their lives and experiences. And, beyond that, there are the private papers of African families in both West and East Africa that have not yet been studied and analyzed by historians.

The second line of defense concerns the validity of the oral tradition as historical evidence. By the "oral tradition" I mean two things: on the one hand, the handing down, by word of mouth, from one generation to the next, of details of specific past events, such as the causes and outcomes of wars, outbreaks of epidemics, etc.; and, on the other hand, the romantic versions of the past which take the form of legends, ballads, and stories of ancestry. Clearly, it is more difficult to gauge the accuracy and reliability of these oral stories — but that is simply a new challenge for the African historian. It does not destroy the validity of the material.

The third line of defense goes well beyond the others. It takes the form of an attack on the written word itself, as a kind of superstition among those who accept it uncritically. Our understanding of Africa and its past has been bedeviled by reports written by imaginative European travelers throughout the continent. In many ways, the recollection of past events, passed on by word of mouth in Africa today, may be a better guide than the vivid and romantic accounts of some of the European explorers. It is worth recalling the Spekes and Burtons of African historiography, with all their colorful descriptions of the "avarice," "savagery," "selfishness," and "proficiency for telling lies" that they claimed to have discovered among Africans.

It may be, though, that the proposition that Africa has no history rested on the assertion that, until recently, much of sub-Saharan Africa had no trained historians. The argument here is that there is a form of analysis, conducted by professional students of the past, governed by specific rules of deduction and verification, without which there can be no history in this scientific sense.

The oral tradition in Africa is a form of reporting. It is often better than a newspaper account of a particular event, but it belongs to the same category. If history were merely reporting, oral tradition, sanctified by time, and journalism, inspired by speed, would both be history. But if the study of history requires particular rules of assembling data, deducing meaning, and verifying conclusions, then oral tradition and journalism are both material for the historian, rather than history itself.

But does the reality of Africa's history depend upon the historians' being African? The UNESCO project on the history of Africa was based on the principle of the primacy of the *view from within.* By the statutes of the project, two-thirds of the members of the supervising International Scientific Committee had to be Africans. The main editor of each volume also had to be an African, though associate editors could be drawn from other parts of the world. The majority of the authors in each volume are Africans.

I remember discussing with the late, distinguished British social anthropologist of the University of Manchester, Professor Max Gluckman, the issue of whether African societies had been, until then, excessively studied by outsiders. Gluckman suggested to me that a culture shock was a necessary qualification for an effective social anthropologist. He seemed to suggest from this that Africa was fortunate to have had a number of outsiders to study its societies, for these outsiders had undergone the culture shock necessary for true scientific understanding, whilst retaining their basic empathy with the people they were studying. An Ibo studying Ibo society might so easily overlook, or undervalue, the significance of certain social facts about his own society.

My response to Max Gluckman was that a Western-trained Ibo going back to study his own society has already undergone this culture shock because he has been exposed to Western academic culture and its ideas. He has already acquired a firm basis for comparison.

The question which now arises is whether, like the social anthropologist, the historian also needs a culture shock in order to appreciate the relevance of certain aspects of the past. Or is the very fact that a historian is writing about a period other than his own enough of a comparative factor? On balance, the UNESCO project assumed that there should be a preponderance of Africans studying Africa, but it also seemed to accept the need for the moderating influence of non-African scholars, representing the "view from without," to supplement and moderate the dominant view from within.

Some scientists and historians are already familiar with the notion of participant observation, whereby a scholar lives with the community he is studying in order to understand it more intimately. What I am suggesting here by the phrase "the view from within" is a good deal more than that. What I am saying is that, in order to understand fully *some* aspects of a society, it is not good enough simply to observe it; you have to be a member of it.

I have already indicated that one of the great milestones in our approach to studying African history has been the recognition of the values of oral evidence and the sophisticated ways in which it can be used. We are also tackling the problem of linguistic evidence. Sometimes, the evidence is necessary in order to assess the history of migration from one part of the continent to another. For example, there has been a major debate about the migration of the Bantu, a composite of races and tribes scattered through a large portion of sub-Saharan Africa. Where did these groups sharing Bantu languages come from? What route did they take? A sophisticated analysis of words and language becomes an important tool in trying to work out historical movement and change.

Then there is archaeology, or, rather, the lack of it. The poets of Africa and of the African Diaspora have sometimes reveled in this fact. As Aimé Césaire, the black poet of Martinique who invented the word "negritude," once put it,

> My negritude is no tower and no cathedral,
> It delves into the deep red flesh of the soil.
>
> Hurray for those who never invented anything,
> Who never discovered anything.
> Hurray for joy, hurray for love,
> Hurray for the pain of incarnate tears.

Aimé Césaire was romanticizing the sparsity of physical monuments in African civilization south of the Sahara. As it happens, because so little has been done, and because African archaeology south of the Sahara is relatively underdeveloped, there is still a substantial amount to explore. Even so, archaeologists will have to recognize the poet's exaltation, "My negritude is no tower and no cathedral . . ."

African historians have to find new ways of taking advantage of what archaeology has to offer. They have to do so while recognizing that the discipline can tell us much less about how ancient Africans lived than it can about many aspects of Greek civilization, for example.

But, in the end, history is not just about methods and techniques of research. It is primarily concerned with assessing past events and discovering how people lived. Here, an African historian has to decide what aspects of Africa's past deserve special attention. I have been reflecting on a number of questions about selection and balance in writing a definitive history of Africa. For example, should a despised continent emphasize its great civilizations? Should we pay special attention to the civilizations of Songhai, Mali, Ghana, and ancient Zimbabwe? On the other hand, should the despised continent attempt to enhance our understanding of its own despised classes?

Who makes history, in any case? Is it the great figures like Shaka, the Zulu, or Akhenaton, the Egyptian? Or is history to be explored among the masses? And, if so, how do we go about it, given that they are nameless?

How far should we aim to correct what we see as a distorted view of our history? Given that previous foreign historians have exaggerated the role of non-Africans in Africa's history (Semites, Hamites, Cushites and Europeans), should African historians themselves deliberately play down the role of foreigners? Given, too, that foreign historians have emphasized the shortcomings of African social and political life in the past, should modern African historians, as a corrective device, give special attention to African achievements?

When it comes to dealing with the whole historical span of Africa's existence, should emphasis be placed on shared experiences among Africans in different parts of the continent? Should "unity across space" be accepted as a principle? Alternatively, should we stress the continuities of African history, challenging the assumption that European colonialism brought millennia of African life to an end? Should colonialism be regarded only as an episode in a grand panorama of African experience? Should there be stress on unity across time?

I want to finish by quoting some remarks by the historian and philosopher Christopher Dawson:

Happy is the people that is without a history, and thrice happy is the people without a sociology, for as long as we possess a living culture we are unconscious of it, and it is only when we are in danger of losing it or when it is already dead that we begin to realize and to study it scientifically.

There is an echo, there, of the Hegelian concept of the owl of Minerva, spreading its wings at dusk. We begin to understand our societies only when the characteristics we have comprehended are about to come to an end. Both Hegel and Dawson exaggerate the issue, but the message has some relevance for African historians today. African students of the past, like Dike and Ogot, and the younger generation of African scholars probably constitute Africa's owl of Minerva, emerging from the dusk of the continent's past.

Christopher Dawson emphasizes that it is only when we are about to lose a culture that we discover what it is in an intellectual sense, and large parts of Africa have, indeed, been in the process of losing great slices of their own culture. Hugh Trevor-Roper was right in saying that a substantial part of the history of the world in the last five centuries has been "European history." This has arisen partly out of Europe's leadership in the industrial revolution, Europe's triumph in exploring different parts of the world, and its more ambiguous achievements in colonizing and ruling other people.

The impact of this aspect of world history includes a substantial Europeanization of Africa in the last one hundred years. Among those especially Europeanized are precisely those Africans who sat on the International Scientific Committee for the UNESCO General History of Africa. They, and many of those who will be writing the chapters of Africa's history, are products of Europe's cultural impact on Africa. The initial languages in which the UNESCO *General History of Africa* was published were, in fact, English and French, though translations into Arabic and selected indigenous African languages were also envisaged.

Trevor-Roper is wrong in seeing virtually the entire history of the world in the last five hundred years as Eurocentric. But if he had limited himself to saying that the academic and scientific culture of the world in the last three hundred years had sprung out of Western civilization, he would have been closer to the truth. African historians are products of this Eurocentric intellectual tradition.

For me, as an African scholar, the process of writing the history of my own continent is a profound and sometimes agonizing experience. My first exposure to Western culture included a sense of shock at the West itself, but, as I got partially assimilated into the alien culture, the shock became directed at my own roots. In addition, two fears began to haunt me: one, the fear of my being part of a lost generation of Africans, culturally severed from their own societies; the other is the fear of a situation where all future generations of Africans would be culturally lost, like mine.

Christopher Dawson may have been wrong in the claim "happy is the people that is without a history," but he is persuasive when he says that only in a true crisis of identity do we stand a chance of recognizing ourselves. Partly because of the impact of Europe, Africa is currently in such a crisis of identity. It may well be on the edge of self-discovery. And what is self, after all, if not primarily the product of its own past?

NOTES

A version of this essay appeared in BBC London's *The Listener* 100, no. 2573 (August 17, 1978): 194–196.
1. Delivered as a series of lectures to the University of Sussex in October, 1963, and relayed by BBC Television. As delivered, they were printed in *The Listener* in November and December, 1963.

TWO

THE STUDY OF AFRICA
GENESIS, SUBSTANCE,
AND CULTURAL BOUNDARIES

W hen did African studies begin? There are those who would trace it to ancient Egypt and the Nile Valley as areas of Africa's first grand civilization. The systematic study of the customs and traditions of a people is associated with a sophisticated culture of scholarship. Ancient Egypt may be identified not only as the cradle of monotheism in Africa (the legacy of Akhenaton, in the 14th century B.C.E.) but also as the birthplace of the systematic study of an African civilization.

Another defensible starting point of African studies lies in the observations about West and East Africa by the medieval North African traveller, Abu Abdallah Muhammad Ibn Battuta (1304–1368 C.E). Born in Tangier, Morocco, this Maghrebi traveller became the greatest African explorer of medieval times, covering some 75,000 miles (more than 120,000 km). He wrote one of the most famous of all travel books — *Rihlah (Travels)* — chronicling encounters with cultures in Africa, the Muslim world, and as far as China and Sumatra. His information about East, West, and North Africa can be regarded as the ultimate pioneer work in African studies.

A third starting point for African studies can be traced to the time when Africa began to be truly identified as a continent in its own right. Such a phase is much more recent than many people assume. After all, it was as recently as 1656 that the Geographer

Royal of France described Africa as "a peninsula so large that it comprises the third part, and this the most southerly, of our [European] continent."[1]

We may therefore assume that the concept of Africa as a whole continent did not crystallize before the eighteenth century — although the concept of "Land of the Blacks" was much older for sub-Saharan Africa on its own. Curiously enough, the word "Africa" (probably etymologically Berber) was originally applied only to North Africa, the land of Ibn Battuta. Indeed, the term "Africa" was once even more narrowly focused only on Tunisia. But its application expanded with the centuries, and eventually encompassed the whole continent.

There were many people in the following three centuries who still did not regard Africa as a single continent, and even fewer who regarded the term "Africans" as applying to inhabitants of the whole continent. Paradoxically, although the term "Africa" originated as applying only to North Africa, by the twentieth century the term "the Africans" had become disproportionately associated with inhabitants of only the sub-Saharan part of the continent. To the present day many Centers of African Studies in the Western world are in reality Centers about the study of Africa south of the Sahara.

But what is an "African"? There are two main types — those who are "African" in a continental sense (like Egyptians and Algerians) and those who are "African" in a racial sense (like Nigerians, Ugandans and Senegalese). Egyptians and Algerians are Africa's children of the soil. Sub-Saharan Blacks are Africa's children of the blood. In reality all those who are natives of Africa are children of the soil (called *wana-nchi* in the Swahili language). But sub-Saharan Blacks are in addition Africa's children by racial blood.

Former UN Secretary General Boutros Boutros-Ghali is a continental African of the soil. Present UN Secretary General, Kofi Annan, is an African in both the continental and the racial sense — both son of the soil and son of Africa's racial blood. In the position of Secretary-General and its two last incumbents of the twentieth century, Africa itself has been defined and redefined. Significant in a different sense is the simple fact that Boutros-Ghali was an Africanist long before he became a statesman. As a professor at Cairo University, his research interests at one time focused especially on African studies. As a Copt, he represents some symbolic continuity with scholarship from ancient Egypt. As an Arabic-speaking, travelling North African, Boutros-Ghali symbolizes some continuity with the legacy of Ibn Battuta. And as a scholar who has written both in French and in English about Africa, Boutros-Ghali symbolizes the more recent phase of Westernized African studies, in which there has been a triple heritage: indigenous, Islamized, and Westernized. There has also been a triple mode of articulation — oral, written, and increasingly, electronic.

BETWEEN AFRICAN STUDIES AND ISLAMIC STUDIES

The more purely indigenous legacy of the study of Africa has on the whole been mainly of the oral tradition. It ranged from praise songs in honor of heroes to the wider gamut of oral history. The full significance of this contribution was not adequately appreciated until the second half of the twentieth century when scholars like Belgium's Jan Vansina and Kenya's Bethwell Alan Ogot blazed a trail to lend legitimacy to history based on oral transmission. These two were in the forefront of this methodological revolution, of major relevance to the rest of the world. Even countries with extensive written documentation have been gradually learning the need to tap the oral evidence which is always part and parcel of human communication. African studies led the way in developing techniques for using the oral tradition and oral history as documentation for modern historiography.

The oral tradition was also an invaluable source for those who were trying to understand African traditional religion. For centuries the West had treated Africa's sacred beliefs as heathenism and superstition. It was not until the twentieth century that any serious effort was made to treat those beliefs as religious at all, as distinct from pagan superstition. A meticulous study of the oral sacred tradition was needed for this breakthrough. It was not until the second half of the twentieth century that the concept of Africa's traditional religion (or indigenous religion) began to gain currency. The cultural paradigm was part and parcel of the revolution.

Did Africans have a philosophy before the coming of the Western colonial penetration? We have raised this issue before. Again the oral tradition was central to the discovery that Africans had been a philosophical people all along — although they might not necessarily have known that they were engaged in philosophizing.

It is like a character in a play by the greatest French writer of dramatic comedy, Molière (1622–1672). The character discovers that he had been speaking "prose" all his life. The character did not know that others called his speech "prose." Similarly, an African did not necessarily know that others might call his solemn reflections and meditations "philosophy." The oral tradition has yielded new information about the profundity and complexity of traditional African thought.

It took a Westerner to have the first impact on the West — the Belgian Father Placide Tempels in his *Bantu Philosophy* (1949, 1959) turned out a truly seminal, if controversial, work.[2] It helped to put Africa on the philosophical agenda of the rest of the world. John Mbiti's *African Religions and Philosophy* (1969) established the inevitable connection between the religious and the philosophical.[3] Once again there was a heavy reliance on the oral tradition and on what I will later describe as the cultural paradigm.

The indigenous legacy of the study of Africa also included written versions along the Nile Valley. Certainly Ethiopia had a long tradition of both church history and royal history in Amharic, and in the classical Ethiopian language, Ge'ez.

The Islamized legacy of African studies in Africa is also extensive in written as well as oral form. The more purely oral Islamized tradition includes the richly informative and encapsulating poetry of the Somali people. In a sense, the Somali are among the most spontaneously poetic people in the world. Some of their poetry has captured details about their culture (anthropology), their past (history) and the interplay between their clans and their cattle (political economy).

African studies in Kiswahili are partly in the Islamized tradition, especially prior to the second half of the twentieth century. Swahili scholarship is both oral and written. As in the case of the Somali, some of the scholarship is captured in poetry, revealing some of the characteristics of ancient Swahili city-states like Pate and Kilwa. In Swahili scholarship, it is not always easy to tell where Islamic studies end and African studies begin. For example, much of Swahili poetry is didactic about exemplary human behavior, as in the case of the classical poem *Utenzi was Mwana Kukpona*. But exemplary Swahili behavior is both Islamic and African. In such poems we get a glimpse of the ideal social types in the Swahili anthropological paradigm.

Nor must we forget Swahili studies in the Arabic language. Just as present day Africans often write about their continent in European languages, earlier generations of Africans sometimes wrote about African affairs in Arabic. One striking example by an Mswahili is the Arabic manuscript by Shaykh Al-Amin Bin 'Ali Al-Mazrui, *The History of the Mazrui Dynasty of Mombasa.*[4] This document illustrates how difficult it is to determine where African studies end and Islamic studies begin. Long before this Arabic manuscript was translated into English by Reverend Ritchie, sponsored by the British Academy and published by Oxford University Press in 1995, it had been quoted extensively by the *Encyclopedia of Islam* in 1991. The *Encyclopedia* specifies that the Mazrui clan is one of the links between the Gulf States and Swahili civilization.[5] Such areas of African studies are a link not only between African and Islamic studies, but also between African and Arab scholarship. The overlapping categories in this case are Africa, Islam, and the Arab world.

Also highly Islamized is Hausa and Hausa-Fulani scholarship in western Africa, some of it once again in the Arabic language. But while Swahili city-states were both Islamized (religiously) and Arabized (genealogically), Hausa city-states were Islamized only religiously. Swahili rulers were Afro-Arab genealogically; Hausa-Fulani rulers were not Arab genealogically at all. The Hausa-Fulani were more purely "indigenous," if such a category makes sense in Africa. Hausa and Hausa-Fulani literature is about culture, religion, and the wider gamut of history. A great deal of Hausa poetry contains anthropological information about Hausa ideals, principles, and rules of conduct. Once again Africanity interacted with Islam.

THE WESTERNIZED LEGACY OF DENIAL

What about African studies and the third legacy of the Triple Heritage, the Westernized legacy? Clearly the earlier years of this phase were colonial in one sense or another. The colonial ethos affected which disciplines of African studies were viable, which perspectives were politically correct, and whether or not there were any indigenous authors at all. The Westernized legacy leaned heavily toward the written tradition in the first half of the twentieth century. It subsequently also became part of the new electronic media (radio, television, and audiotape). As the twentieth century was coming to a close the Westernized legacy of African studies was also venturing into cyberspace.

For two-thirds of the twentieth century (basically the colonial period), African studies was caught up in four great intellectual denials to which the African peoples were subjected at the time: the denial of history, the denial of science, the denial of poetry, and the denial of philosophy, including religious philosophy. These four great intellectual denials affected areas of research, nature of syllabi and curricula both in Africa and abroad, what the next generation of African scholars was trained for, and which academic disciplines were regarded as relevant from an African perspective.

The denial of history continues to be best illustrated in the notorious statement by Hugh Trevor-Roper, then Regius Professor of Modern History at Oxford University:

> Maybe in the future there will be African history, but at the moment there is none. . . . There is only the history of Europeans in Africa. The rest is darkness, and darkness is not a subject of history.[6]

Denying Africans the capacity for science is the second great denial. Researchers like Eric Morton have reminded us of David Hume's assertion that among people of colour are to be found "no ingenious manufactures . . . no arts, no sciences."[7] Could African studies therefore have anything to say to scientific studies?

Denying Africans the capacity for great poetry is the third great denial. This has been perpetrated especially from the American side of the Atlantic. It was no less a person than Thomas Jefferson, the American founding father, who had the following to say:

> Misery is often the parent of the most affecting touches in poetry. Among the blacks is there misery enough, God knows, but no poetry. Love is the peculiar oestrum of the poet. Their love [the love of blacks] is ardent, but it kindles the senses only, not the imagination. Religion, indeed, has a Phyllis Wheatley, but it could not produce a poet. The compositions published under her name are below the dignity of criticism.[8]

Thomas Jefferson, the author of the poetic phrase, "life, liberty, and the pursuit of happiness," had concluded that black people were incapable of writing great poetry, a myth that was dangerous to African literature as a whole.

Denying Africans a capacity for philosophy is the fourth great denial. But here comes a truly great paradox. Philosophy involves the use of reason and rationality. Among those who have accused the African people of being a-rational are great African poets. We use the term "a-rational" as distinct from "irrational," just as we use the word "amoral" as distinct from "immoral."

First we have Thomas Jefferson denying that Black people had a capacity for great poetry. Then comes a great Black poet like Leopold Sedar Senghor (former president of Senegal) who tells us that African epistemology begins not with "I think therefore I am" (which is a Cartesian formula) but with "I feel therefore I am." Leopold Senghor insisted that "emotion is black . . . reason is Greek." Was Senghor declaring that philosophy as a rational activity was alien to Africa? Was there such a thing as African philosophy?

Of course, there have also been Westerners who have denied that Africans have a capacity for philosophizing (historically those have included Thomas Jefferson, Calhoun, Hegel, and others). But what is distinctive about Negritudist poetry is that here is great African poetry which either denies Africa's capacity for philosophy (as Senghor's epistemology suggests) or denies Africa's capacity for science (as Aimé Césaire, the poet from Martinique, has affirmed in his poem which begins, "Hooray for those who never invented anything, Hooray for those who never discovered anything . . .).[9]

Negritudists have proved Jefferson wrong in his assertion that Blacks are incapable of great poetry. Césaire, the man who coined the word "negritude," is a great poet. The question that has arisen is whether such great poets have attempted to cast doubt on Africa's capacity for philosophizing and for science. African scholars have spent some time discussing such meta-philosophical issues as whether African philosophy is "African" or just "philosophy." But to most Africanist audiences in the world of African studies, at least, there can be no hesitation in reaching the conclusion that Africans are indeed capable of significant philosophical thought, from aesthetics to concepts of the human person, from democracy to the African personality, from the epistemology of "I feel therefore I am" to the metaphysics of the human condition.

THE CULTURAL PARADIGM

This brings us to the Cultural Paradigm in African studies, of which the oral tradition is a part. At its most ambitious, the cultural paradigm examines society from the perspective of the primacy of values, beliefs, symbols, modes of communication, and lifestyles. The whole issue of race is steeped in value, belief, and symbolism. Inevitably, therefore, African studies have reached out to the study of cultures and comparative civilization. The Cultural Paradigm in African studies has played a part in the following vital areas:

(a) In re-establishing that Africans are a historical people.

(b) In linking Africans to the culture of science.

(c) In re-establishing that Africans were a religious people before the coming of Christianity and Islam.

(d) In demonstrating that Africans have been a philosophical people all along.

(e) In linking African studies to mainstream theories which range from modernization to the end of history. (See our discussion on modernization theories, including discussions of Fukuyama and Huntington in Volume Two of this series.)

(f) In linking Africana studies to multicultural movements.

AFRICANA STUDIES AND MULTICULTURALISM

With regard to the last point, African studies has also been a major stimulus of the whole multicultural movement which has significantly shaken the educational world in the concluding years of the twentieth century. The crusade for "Afrocentrism" goes back long before the word itself was coined. It seems virtually certain that African-American demands for a "curriculum of inclusion" was one of the major stimuli of the whole multicultural movement in the United States and beyond. African studies was part of the package.

But before Afrocentricity stimulated multiculturalism there was the phenomenon of multiculturalism stimulating Afrocentricity. Is the whole philosophy of Afrocentricity the offspring of Edward Blyden's triple multiculturalism? (See our comparative analysis and discussion of the philosophies of Blyden and Kwame Nkrumah in Part III of the present volume). The focus is on the interplay between Western culture, Africanity and Islam. This is what we have already referred to as "Africa's Triple Heritage." This last term was coined by the present author.) Did African-American Afrocentricity in our times repay the debt by helping to stimulate a multicultural movement in the educational and academic worlds? Multiculturalism was once the cause of Afrocentricity; Afrocentricity has now become the cause of multiculturalism. African studies is one of the vehicles of them both.

Behind them all is a great rendezvous in the world of ideas and scholarship — a rendezvous between African studies and the cultural paradigm. It is a rendezvous which has touched intellectual debates as diverse as modernization theory and the clash of civilizations, personalities as ancient as Akhenaton and Ibn Battuta, statesmen as recent as Boutros Boutros-Ghali and Kofi Annan, and discoveries as deeply African as the oral tradition and the historicity of indigenous religion and thought in the Black experience. As the twentieth century comes to a close the African should have once again demonstrated through African studies that he or she is indeed a historical figure, a muse in both the oral and the written traditions, a scientific innovator, and a philosopher in action and thought. African studies have been the transmission belt for this African reassertion. The inner quest endures; the outer struggle continues.

NOTES

A version of this essay appeared as a chapter in *Encyclopedia of Africa: South of the Sahara*, ed. John Middleton (New York: Macmillan Library Reference USA, 1997), pp. xxxiii–xl.

1. Cited by Melville Herskovits. See his contribution to the collection, *Symposium on Africa* (Wellesley College, Massachusetts, 1960), p. 16.

2. Father R. Placide Tempels, *Bantu Philosophy* (English translation) (Paris: Présence Africaine, 1959).

3. John S. Mbiti, *African Religions and Philosophy* (London and Nairobi: Heinemann, 1969).

4. This has since been translated into English by J. McL. Ritchie (Oxford: Oxford University Press, on behalf of the British Academy, 1995).

5. *The Encyclopedia of Islam*, new edition, vol. 6 (Leiden: E. J. Brill, 1991), pp. 961–966.

6. Hugh Trevor-Roper, "The Rise of Christian Europe," *The Listener* (London: BBC Publications), November 28, 1963, p. 871.

7. David Hume, "Of National Characters," in *Philosophical Works of David Hume*, vol. 3 (Boston: Little, Brown Company, 1954), essay xxi, pp. 228–229. See also Eric Morton, "Race and Racism in the Works of David Hume."

8. Thomas Jefferson, *Notes on the State of Virginia* (Paris, 1784).

9. Aimé Césaire, *Return to My Native Land*, (Paris: Présence Africaine, 1939). English translation.

THREE

AFROCENTRICITY VERSUS MULTICULTURALISM
A DIALECTIC IN SEARCH OF A SYNTHESIS

There are people who know a great deal about Afrocentricity. Professor Maulana Karenga has been one of the cultural theorists in this area. Others are also experts on wider aspects of multiculturalism. There are those who regard Afrocentricity as an aspect of multiculturalism, and there are those who regard them as parallel themes, separate but equal. It is conceivable to regard them as in fact antithetical paradigms, paradigms which pull in different ways. This essay is concerned with discussing these different concepts.

Let us first identify elements important to the definition of the Afrocentric perspective. What are the elements leading towards the Afrocentric perspective? Firstly, Africa as being *subject* rather than *object*. Secondly, and related to it, is Africa as being *active* rather than *passive*. Thirdly, Africa as being *cause* rather than *effect*. Fourthly, Africa as being *center* rather than *periphery*. And finally, Africa as being *maker of history* rather than *incident in history*.

But what is the Africa we talk about in Afrocentricity? Sometimes the term used is *Africana*, meaning the Black world as a whole. I often prefer the term *Global Africa* as the sum total of firstly continental Africa; secondly the diaspora of enslavement, which was created by the dispersal caused by the horrors of enslavement; and thirdly, the diaspora of colonialism, the dispersal caused by the destabilization and long-term consequences and disruptions of the colonial era.

It is possible to regard Jesse Jackson as part of the diaspora of enslavement, and Ali Mazrui and his children as part of the diaspora of colonialism. Jamaicans in Britain are both part of the consequences of enslavement and part of the consequences of colonization. Global Africa becomes the sum total of that massive African presence on a world scale.

DEFINING AFROCENTRICITY AND MULTICULTURALISM

It is not enough simply to look at global Africa from a global perspective; Afrocentricity looks at the world from an African perspective. Afrocentricity is the study of the human condition from an African perspective. We shall return to that theme.

What are the defining elements in the multicultural perspective? A basic assumption is the parity of esteem of all cultures. It is almost as if there was a founding father, a kind of multicultural Jefferson, who has pronounced that all cultures are created equal and are endowed with certain inalienable rights, among them cultural life, cultural liberty, and the pursuit of cultural happiness.

Of course, not all cultures are factually equal any more than all human beings are factually equal, but they are morally equal just as all human beings are morally equal. If someone equates moral equality with factual equality it will soon be discovered that there is a problem, because people are not equal if you are testing them against the yardstick of empiricism. Similarly, cultures are not equal if you are testing them against the yardstick of pragmatism. But once you start from the moral position that all people are created equal, then the issue of whether this person is more intelligent than that one, this man is taller than that, this woman is more clever than that, all that ceases to be relevant. At some moral level all people become equal. Similarly, the multicultural perspective assumes that all cultures deserve parity of esteem. They are morally equal regardless of whether they are empirically equal.

In 1990–91 I served on the New York Syllabus Review Committee of the State of New York for High Schools. We spent about a year determining if the curriculum to which high school children of New York were exposed was excessively Eurocentric. The majority of us on the committee concluded after our deliberations that education in the state of New York was excessively Eurocentric. It was as if the whole system assumed that the pyramids were built by the Pharaohs instead of by the Egyptian people or the Egyptian peasants. This pyramid called the United States of America was not built just by the founding fathers, the pharaohs. It was also built by a lot of women, Black people, other minorities within the system, a lot of workers and peasants, a variety of people who have little recognition in the history books of the United States. The pyramid was not built just by Anglo-Americans. It was also built by varieties of nationalities, who have had scant salute in the annals of this particular society. There is also the pyramid called human civilization, which was not built by European pharaohs only, but included a lot of other people in its construction.

Our Syllabus Review report was called *One Nation, Many Peoples: A Declaration of Cultural Interdependence*. It was published, of course, by the State of New York's Education Department. It was inevitably controversial. No less controversial was my appendix to the report, which was called "Multiculturalism and Comparative Holocaust." American children needed to learn that genocide did not begin with the Nazis, but was perpetrated in the Americas by White men against Native Americans. Enslavement of Africans was also an experience of Holocaust proportions.

But what are the analytical differences between Afrocentricity and multiculturalism, apart from these elements which I have mentioned? Firstly, multiculturalism is a pluralistic method, seeking to represent diverse cultures: Latino (including Chicano, of course), Asian, African, Native American, women. Therefore multiculturalism is pluralistic in that sense. Afrocentricity is a dialectical method, seeking to negate the negation in an almost Hegelian sense, seeking to negate the negative portrayal of the most distorted history in the world, that of the African people.

While multiculturalism is a quest for diversity, Afrocentricity is an antithesis. It is an antithesis to the thesis of Eurocentrism. The antithesis is searching for a synthesis. The thesis ultimately was White history, the antithesis was Africana history. Is there a synthesis? The thesis is Eurocentrism, the antithesis is Afrocentricity. Is the synthesis multiculturalism?

Multiculturalism is also a rainbow coalition representing the colors of different global realities. Afrocentricity is a quest for a reconciliation of opposites, confronting Eurocentrism with its ultimate other — Africanity. It is confronting White focus with its ultimate other — Black focus. Politically, multiculturalism is a quest for the solidarity of the oppressed. It unites Blacks, Latinos, Native Americans, women, and other oppressed peoples. Politically, Afrocentricity is a declaration of racial independence; it seeks to promote global Africana, self-reliance. Urgent questions arise for those of us who are in Africana studies or who are ourselves Africans, in that global sense. Should we be inspired by Afrocentricity or should we respond to a quest for multiculturalism? Afrocentricity is predicated on the uniqueness of the African peoples. Multiculturalism is predicated on the universal cultural interdependence of all peoples. Afrocentricity emphasizes the impact of the African people on world civilization. Multiculturalism sees world civilization as a pooling of the cultural resources of many peoples. What Negritude is to the Black poet, Afrocentricity is to the Black scholar. They are a celebration of Africanity. Multiculturalism, on the other hand, is a chorus of diverse legacies. By definition, Afrocentricity is unipolar, a world with a center — Africa. Multiculturalism is multipolar, a universe of many centers. The question persists, where should I belong, where should Edmond Keller belong, where should Maulana Karenga belong, where should all those of us who are in Africana Studies belong?

A COST-BENEFIT ANALYSIS

There is a case to be made for Africana Studies to go in either direction, either to commit itself to unrelenting Afrocentricity, or to dedicate itself to uncompromising multiculturalism. First, the case for Afrocentricity. Africana Studies has been neglected for so long that only a thoroughgoing Afrocentric approach stands a chance of narrowing the gap. This is part of the reason why we should go the Afrocentric way, those of us who are in Africana Studies. This field has been neglected for so long that only an Afrocentric crusade stands a chance of producing results.

Secondly, there is so much prejudice against people of African descent that only an Afrocentric approach could change their image before the world. We are confronted with a massive wall of prejudice, and therefore a thoroughgoing Afrocentric approach becomes part of the necessary wherewithal for confronting that wall.

Thirdly, African contributions to world civilization have been so underestimated, or even denied, that only an Afrocentric crusade can hope to restore the balance. Fourthly, the African peoples may indeed be the Chosen People of history, a people of the day before yesterday and a people of the day after tomorrow. Afrocentrism is a paradigm shift which looks at human affairs as a response to the African condition. Afrocentricity becomes a perspective which moves Africa and people of African ancestry to the center stage of world history.

There are two types of Afrocentricity. Gloriana Afrocentricity emphasizes the great and proud accomplishments of people of African ancestry — Africa at its most complex. Africa on a grand scale. The castle builders, those who built the walls of Zimbabwe or the castles of Gondar, or the sunken churches of Lalibela. Some would argue, those who built the pyramids of Egypt. This is Gloriana Afrocentricity. There is also Proletariana Afrocentricity. This emphasizes the sweat of Africa's brow, the captured African as a co-builder of modern civilization. The enslaved as creator, the slave as innovator. Slave labor building or helping to build the Industrial Revolution in the Western world. Slave labor, for better or for worse, helping to fuel the capitalist transformation in the northern hemisphere. The colonized peoples, both as victims and as builders of the industrialized modern world. The resources of Africa, the minerals of Africa, extracted from beneath our feet, have been used for factories which have transformed the nature of the twentieth century. Without those minerals this century would have been vastly different.

Proletariana Afrocentricity is a story of victim as creator. In a way, even Negritude is a kind of Proletariana Afrocentricity, at least when it indulges in romantic primitivism, as expressed by Aimé Césaire: "Hooray for those who never invented anything. Hooray for those who never discovered anything. My Negritude is no tower and no cathedral. It delves into the deep red flesh of the soil." The primitivist version of Negritude celebrates Africa's simplicity rather than Africa's complexity. It salutes the African cattle herder, not the African castle builder. To that extent it is part of Proletariana Afrocentricity.

As for the case for multiculturalism, the argument would go this way. The problem is not merely the demeaning of African culture. It is the threatening hegemonic power of Western culture. Western cultural hegemony in the world cannot be challenged by Africana Studies alone. It must be tackled by an alliance of all other cultures threatened by Western hegemony — sometimes even by an alliance which includes dissident elements within Western culture itself.

The present world culture is Eurocentric, the next world culture is unlikely to be Afrocentric, even if that were desirable. The best solution is therefore a more culturally balanced world civilization. That is the burden of the next generation, to attempt to enlist the participation of other civilizations, not to provide an alternative hegemony, but to provide a new balance. Africana Studies should do joint projects with groups like Latin American Studies, Middle Eastern Studies, or studies of other parts of the Third World. Part of the mission is to reduce the global Eurocentric presence in scholarship, in research, and in education. The problem is not simply that African culture has been demeaned, that is true. African culture will continue to be demeaned, as long as Western culture is hegemonic, and Western culture is so triumphant in the very citadels of Africa. Only an alliance with other groups can even approximate a dent on this ever expansionist European giant and its extensions. If Africana is to go multicultural, it must go comparative internally. African Studies should include the study of global Africa. Even within Africana Studies we need to broaden out.

The history of Africa does not end on Africa's shores. In fact, African children in African schools in continental Africa are mistaught. "African history" is assumed to be the history of that piece of land which is bounded by those particular oceans. And yet one must ask, "When did those Africans exported as slaves cease to be part of African history? When they left Cape Coast in Ghana? When they were midway across the Atlantic? When they got to the Western Hemisphere? In the first hundred years? In the first two hundred years? What was the African cutoff point of those captives? When did they cease to be African? When did they walk out of African history?"

Those are questions which children in Africa itself ought to be encouraged to ask themselves. But this is not yet happening. On the contrary, current researchers are underplaying the slave trade in Africa itself. They are underplaying some of the links which could constitute the bridge with the externalized Black world. This shrinkage of the African consciousness needs to be arrested as a matter of urgency.

THE WORLD IS AFRICA WRIT LARGE

To return to Afrocentricity as a perspective on world studies: Afrocentricity is not just a method of looking at the history of Africa, but it is a method of looking at the history of the world. Afrocentricity moves the African experience to center stage. There is first the concern with the *evolutionary genesis*, the origins of our species. Because on present evidence our human species begins in the African continent, the entire human race becomes a massive global African diaspora. Every human being becomes a descendant of Africa. It is in that evolutionary sense that the rest of the world is a massive African diaspora.

Then there is the *cultural genesis*. If, from present evidence, our species began in Africa, then our basic institutions also began in Africa — human language, human family. Some who saw my television series probably remember my startling statement, *"We invented the family."* By that I meant precisely that if the species began in Africa, then Africans must have begun the kinship institutions which crystallized into the human family.

When I was filming the TV series *The Africans*, I wanted to do something about the First Supper. We went around looking for evidence of the First Supper. We were concerned not with the religious doctrine of Christianity of the Last Supper, but with the origins of socialized meals. When was the first time the satisfaction of a biological need was converted into a social routine called a meal? When did human beings begin to socialize on the basis of the satisfaction of biological needs?

We went to Tanzania to places where some of the earliest remains of our species were discovered. We were not looking for the remains of the first meal, but we did find places which did look like some of the earliest "dining tables." We took pictures and I did address the camera about these ideas, about African origins of some of these institutions. Television being what it is, the pictures were not strong enough for the story I wanted to tell. So in the end those particular pictures were part of the casualties in the film editing room. The story was too big for the pictures we managed to acquire. On the line was the issue of the First Supper, when human beings began to move from mere biological satisfactions to socialized institutions within our continent. On the line were the cultural origins of many of our other institutions, in the African continent.

Here then is the cultural genesis arising out of the evolutionary genesis.

Thirdly, there is the *civilizational genesis*, which is not exactly the same as the cultural genesis. Civilizationally, much of Africana Studies has focused especially on the role of ancient Egypt as a grand civilization which shaped not only other parts of Africa, but had a considerable impact on civilizations in the rest of the Mediterranean. Most recently discussion has emphasized its impact on ancient Greece. Martin Bernal's book *Black Athena* (1987) has generated a new examination of that debate. Bernal's approach to the subject is telling us that these distortions were not made by ancient Greeks. It was not the Greeks who did not acknowledge their debt to ancient Egyptians. It has been modern Europeans who have changed classical history. This massive macroplagiarism of lifting a whole civilization without footnotes was done not by the ancients but in the eighteenth and nineteenth centuries with revisionist European historians of the classics.

Bernal's thesis is that modern Europeans, entering a new era of racism and anti-Semitism, could not make themselves bear the thought that what they regarded as the pristine origins of their civilization should have had much to do with either Africans or such Semitic peoples as the Phoenicians. Modern Europeans therefore promptly understressed, if not obliterated, Egypt's contribution to Athens.

Martin Bernal is not, of course, a Pan-African Black nationalist. He is a White Irish Jew, a very different phenomenon from Edmond Keller, Maulana Karenga, and Ali Mazrui, who have their own Pan-African axe to grind. Bernal has since issued the second volume of *Black Athena*, a very detailed work with a lot of linguistic as well as archival evidence. A very impressive work. Bernal was previously a fellow at a Cambridge College in England, and he is currently based at Cornell University. His work has certainly strengthened Africa's civilizational genesis.

Fourthly, there is the *geographical centrality* of Africa. It is almost as if the Almighty in His infinite wisdom had cut Africa into two equal parts. Africa is certainly the only continent that is thus cut almost in half by the equator. Africa is also the only continent that is traversed by both the tropic of Cancer and the tropic of Capricorn. In many ways, therefore, Africa is also the most tropical of all continents by its centrality. The geographical centrality of Africa, therefore, is clear.

It is true that Europeans played games with the size of Africa, in its representation on the map, but there were certain things even European map-makers could not tamper with. Once they started drawing lines called latitudes and identified the equator, there was nothing they could do but reveal Africa as geographically the most central of all continents.

Fifthly, there is the *monotheistic genesis*, the debate as to whether monotheism began in Africa. There is disagreement among Africana scholars as to whether the Pharaoh Akhenaten was in fact the first thoroughgoing monotheist in history or not. His ruling years were 1379 to 1362 (B.C.) in Egypt. There is the related debate as to whether the Semites, who helped universalize monotheism, were originally African or not, because their distribution has since been on both sides of what is now the Red Sea. After all, the Red Sea itself was created by one massive earthquake which also created the Rift Valley. Indeed, was Moses an African? Was he an Egyptian? If he was indeed an Egyptian, did that therefore make him an African? All this is part of the monotheistic debate concerning the origins of Africa in that regard. It is in this sense that Afrocentricity has to be considered in many fundamental ways as a perspective on world history. The forces of world history often have their origins in Africa.

Great debates of Africa's global impact include the following questions: Was the ancient Egypt of the Pharaohs an African civilization? Was it a Black civilization? Cheik Anta Diop of Senegal led the way in answering this question, long before Martin Bernal. In fact Martin Bernal's first volume refers to Cheik Anta Diop on only one page. And yet this Senegalese man had been working on that theme for several decades before Martin Bernal. Ancient Egypt's Africanity is one of the great Afrocentric themes.

There has also been the debate about the Columbus Phenomenon. This has had two areas. One is the chronological debate, as to whether or not Christopher Columbus was really the first to cross the Atlantic. Had there been in fact others who crossed it before? And did those others include Africans? There are those huge discoveries in Mexico, of sculptured faces that bear so-called Negroid features. The stone heads weigh tons. Nobody disputes that they are about two thousand years old. They are pre-Christ, let alone pre-Columbus. There is no scientific disagreement about their age. The question is, Why do they look so African? People are arguing about the likeliest explanation as to why they look so African, but the most straightforward explanation would be that they look African because Mexico had been exposed to Africans before Christ, when those facial features were carved out.

There is also the moral debate about Columbus distinct from the chronological debate. Was Christopher Columbus the ultimate Black Man's Burden? Did he really inaugurate an era which devastated much of the African world, quite apart from the more devastating impact on Native Americans? Indeed, in some ways the Native American tragedy is also more irreversible. Civilizations were destroyed and genocide perpetrated. After Columbus, calamity!

AFRICA BETWEEN CAUSE AND EFFECT

Let us now return to contemporary Africa, and be sure we are looking at it from an African perspective — Africa as cause, rather than as effect. The same events in the twentieth century can be seen as cause or effect, depending upon the perspective. One of my favorite examples is looking at France and Algeria. A Eurocentric point of view would see the story mainly in the following terms. The French claimed Algeria as part of France, until Charles de Gaulle was returned to power in 1958. De Gaulle was soon convinced that it was an anachronistic crusade to try to keep Algeria as part of France. "Please let us have a sense of both history and geography. Algeria is Algerian. Let us be wise and make peace with the Brave." And then de Gaulle, the grand master of strategy, succeeded in handing over power to the Algerians in 1962. That version of the story recurs, I am sure, in many history books. De Gaulle is the hero of reconciliation. The version is taught to many Africans, and certainly to many Africans in Francophone Africa. It is Eurocentric in its emphasis on De Gaulle as the causal factor.

The real story is that Algerians fought for their freedom, and by doing so, changed not only their history, but the history of France. France was re-orientated fundamentally. Nor was the price paid by Algeria in this trans-Mediterranean equation negligible. The total number of people killed in all Africa's anti-colonial wars was about three million. A third of those were Algerians, killed between 1954 and 1962. Algeria was the costliest single anti-colonialist war in Africa's history. The French were utterly ruthless in wanting to keep Algeria French. As Algerians fought for their freedom and shook the foundations of the Fourth Republic of France, they did so much more fundamentally than the Vietnam War did when it shook the foundations of the American system. After all, the Vietnam War shook the foundations of American politics, but not those of the American constitution.

The Algerian War undermined the foundations of the French constitutional order itself. The French Fourth Republic finally quivered as it approached collapse. Indeed the French people hovered over a civil war. I was a student across the English Channel in England at the time. We were following the events hour by hour, trying to understand what was going on "across the border." Some British newspapers were carrying editorials in French for the first time in their history, appealing to the French people to step back from the abyss. They thought that only one man could save them; Charles de Gaulle came to the rescue. But who had created the situation where the old system was failing? It was Algerians fighting for their freedom. Charles de Gaulle insisted on a new Fifth Republic for France. "The Republic is dead; long live the Republic."

France became a little more stable then under the Fifth Republic. The European Community was led more effectively by France. France consolidated its leadership in important areas of Europe. France under de Gaulle consolidated its nuclear program. France opted out of the NATO military command while retaining political links with the North Atlantic Treaty Organization (NATO). France gave formal independence to Algeria in 1962 after giving formal independence to the bulk of its empire in 1960. And all these events happened because Algerians were fighting for their freedom, in the deserts and streets of Algeria, and releasing historic forces far from home.

While a Eurocentric point of view would glorify the role of de Gaulle in handing over independence, an Afrocentric view would say, "The history of France was changed by Africans fighting for their freedom, and not the other way around."

Then there is the history of Portugal and its own anti-colonial wars. Did Portugal just hand over independence to its colonies in the 1970s? We know how stubborn and lethargic Portugal had been for centuries. Portugal had resisted the Renaissance, it had ignored the Enlightenment in Europe, it had defied the Reformation, it had turned its back on the American and French revolutions, it had let the Industrial Revolution bypass it. And then the same Portugal which had been so resistant to every progressive movement in the history of Europe at last felt the pressure of Africans fighting for their freedom in Guinea Bissau, in Angola, in Mozambique. The same Portugal that had stood up against major historical forces in its own historical continent in Europe suddenly could not sustain its lethargy much longer.

In April 1974, the whole superstructure of lethargy, fascism, and conservatism collapsed. It was not a case of the Portuguese graciously handing over freedom to Angolans and Mozambicans. It was a case of Mozambicans, Angolans, and Guineans pushing Portugal into the twentieth century. They were helping to democratize Portugal precisely by forcing it to decolonize, compelling it towards new arenas of self-transformation.

An Afrocentric approach to modern history requires that we pause and say, "That's an *African* event." Be sure you do not overlook the impact of Africa upon Europe while being mesmerized by the influence of Europe upon Africa.

In any case, so much of knowledge has already been captured by the Eurocentric perspective. Europe named the world. Let us suppose that I have just travelled across the Atlantic, having just returned from Nigeria. Europe called that ocean the Atlantic, much as she named the Pacific. Nigeria is on the same longitude time as Britain. Nobody talks about Maiduguri Mean Time. We are guided by Greenwich Mean Time. Europe timed the world.

Europe named the continents as well as the oceans. Europe chose its own name, "Europe," and then chose names for the Americas, Australia, Antarctica, and even Asia and Africa. The name "Africa," originating from North Africa as a name for a sub-region, was applied to Africa as a whole by European map-makers and cartographers. Although the name "Africa" and the name "Asia" were not themselves of European origin, their application to respective continents as we know them today was part of European cultural supremacy.

Then Europe proceeded to name the universe — Mars, Venus, Saturn, Pluto — and named the tropics Cancer and Capricorn. And Europe positioned the world, as we have viewed it. We look at the map and Europe is at the top while Africa is below it. We do not know which observer in the cosmos decided that the world looked that way, placing Africa below Europe. There is no cosmological necessity for that way of looking at the world. It could have been the other way around, with Africa positioned above.

Such geographical perspectives are unlikely to change in the foreseeable future. We are unlikely to change the names of the planets, or the names of the oceans and continents, indeed even the name of Africa. Some names of African countries have changed, but not many. If the name was outrageously colonial (like the two Rhodesias), we have changed them. But Nigeria, probably named by Lady Lugard if the legend is correct, is unlikely to change its name. Kenya was named after one of its mountains, but the pronunciation was modified by English people. We modified the pronunciation. So the British used to pronounce it *Keenya*. After independence we have exercised our self-determination, and changed the pronunciation to *Kenya*.

On balance this is a world which was designed and shaped in most of its boundaries, many of its names, many of its directions, by outsiders. The naming of the universe has similarly been Eurocentric. In the face of this massive Western hegemony it becomes important for us to ask ourselves, "Can we fight Eurocentrism simply with Afrocentricity? Or should we join up with others?" Indeed, should we join up even with some Europeans, since not all Europeans are Eurocentric? In the United States the danger is narrower — it is Anglocentrism, rather than Eurocentrism. Let us enlist even Italian-Americans against Anglocentrism.

CONCLUSION

Asia might be the mother of all existing world religions that have spread across the nations. Europe may be the mother of all existing world secular ideologies. Africa is the mother of the human species itself. Can those three continents find ways of linking up? The most successful religion with Semitic origins is Christianity, because it has spread out the most. The most successful Semitic language is Arabic, because it has spread out the most. The most successful Semitic people are the Jews who have performed better than any other single group in recent history. The most ancient Semitic home may be Africa. Are there ways of linking up between Semitic civilizations and African civilizations? Can multiculturalism absorb Afrocentricity? Can Afrocentricity absorb multiculturalism?

I have been groping in that direction in relation to Africa, with my concept of *Africa's Triple Heritage*, which is an effort to link up multiculturalism with Afrocentricity, a marriage of perspectives. It takes more than one culture to create an Africa of today. It takes more than one civilization to give meaning to human reality.

> Every woman has two cultures
> Her own and her neighbor's.
> Every man has two races
> His own and the human race.
> Winds of the world give answer
> They are whimpering to and fro
> And who should know of Africa
> Who only Africa know?

NOTE

This essay was delivered as the James S. Coleman Annual Lecture at the University of California, Los Angeles, under the sponsorship of the James S. Coleman African Studies Center, May 5th, 1993. An earlier version of the lecture was delivered at the University of Wisconsin, Madison, in June 1992.

PART II

REDEFINING AFRICA

WHO ARE THE AFRICANS?

IDENTITY IN SEARCH OF UNITY

A fundamental question which we need to ask ourselves when it comes to the study of Africa is "What is the meaning of being African?" It was the poet-diplomat of Sierra Leone, Davidson Nicol, who once wrote:

> You are not a country, Africa,
> You are a concept,
> Fashioned in our minds, each to each,
> To hide our separate fears,
> To dream our separate dreams.

Africa is indeed more than a country — and less than one! More than fifty territorial entities with artificial boundaries call themselves "nations." All of them, except the Republic of South Africa and Namibia, have joined that international body called the Organization of African Unity (OAU). Yes, Africa is a concept, pregnant with the dreams of millions of people — from Lusaka to Lagos, from Marrakech to Maputo.

It is one of the great ironies of modern African history that it took European colonialism to inform Africans that they were indeed Africans. Europe's greatest service to the people of Africa was not Western civilization, which is under siege; or even Christianity, which is on the defensive. Europe's supreme gift was the gift of

African identity, bequeathed without grace or design — but a reality all the same.

The pioneer American Africanist, Melville Herskovitz, argued that Africa was a geographical fiction, probably because of the climatic, ethnic, and linguistic ranges evident on the continent. He referred to that old description of Africa by the Geographer Royal of France in 1656 — that Africa was "a peninsula so large that it comprises the third part, and this the most southerly, of our [European] continent." And a case can certainly be made for the thesis that North Africa is not only a western extension of the Arabian Peninsula and a northern extension of sub-Saharan Africa, but North Africa is also a southern extension of Europe.

But how then did Europe Africanize Africa? In what way is the sense of identity that Africans have as Africans an outgrowth of their historical interaction with Europeans? In fact, a number of interrelated processes were at work. First and foremost was the triumph of European cartography and mapmaking in the scientific and intellectual history of the world. If, figuratively speaking, Africa invented man in places like Olduvai Gorge, and the Semites discovered God in Jerusalem, Mount Sinai, and Mecca, Europe invented the world, at the Greenwich Meridian. Europeans and their descendants abroad named all the great continents of the world, all the great oceans, many of the great rivers and lakes, and most of the countries. Europe positioned the world so that we think of Europe as being above Africa rather than below the cosmos. Europe timed the world so that the Greenwich Meridian chimed the universal hour. What is more, it was Europeans who usually decided where one continent ended and another began. For Africa, Europeans decided that our continent ended at the Red Sea rather than at the Persian Gulf. Europeans may not have invented the name "Africa," but they did play a decisive role in applying it to the continental landmass that we recognize today.

The second process through which Europe Africanized Africa was that of racism in history. This was particularly marked in the treatment of the Black populations of the continent. The humiliation and degradation of the Black Africans across the centuries contributed to their mutual recognition of each other as "fellow Africans." An identity was born — and started its search for unity.

In Africa itself European racism convinced at least sub-Saharan Africans that one of the most relevant criteria of their Africanity was their skin colour. Until the coming of the Europeans into the sub-Saharan region, Blackness was taken relatively for granted. Fairer skinned Arabs sometimes penetrated the interior of Black Africa, but the Arabs were less segregationist than Europeans and were ready to intermarry with local populations. The primary differentiation between Arab and non-Arab was not skin color, but language and culture. It was Europeans who raised the barrier of pigmentation in Africa.

Related to racism were imperialism and colonization. These generated a sufficient sense of shared African identity for the movement of Pan-Africanism to be born. In the words of Julius K. Nyerere of Tanzania,

> Africans all over the continent, without a word being spoken either from one individual to another or from one African country to another, looked at the European, looked at one another, and knew that in relation to the European they were one.

Black consciousness south of the Sahara is an aspect of the African identity — but Black consciousness was itself born as a response to European racial arrogance.

But if blackness is such an important aspect of Africanity, how real is the Africanness of the Arabs north of the Sahara? In what sense, if any, is Africa truly one continent? Some people have recommended the establishment of a new African organization – exclusively for Black Africans. Ex-President Mobutu of Zaire [now Congo] — who once called Egyptians "brothers" — later called for Afro-Arab apartheid on a continental scale, a continent partitioned.

It is worth remembering that the cultural links between North Africa and Africa south of the Sahara are ancient. These links did *not* begin with the Arab conquest of North Africa in the seventh century of the Christian era. For example, Semitic languages are not limited to Arabic and Hebrew. Amharic, the dominant language of Ethiopia, is Semitic. This language is a custodian of one of Africa's oldest civilizations. Hausa, the most widespread language in West Africa, is partly Chadic and Semitic-related structurally, as well as being a borrower of a large vocabulary from Arabic. Swahili (or Kiswahili), the most widespread language in Eastern Africa, is not Semitic, but probably has borrowed as much from Arabic as the English language has from Latin and French. Then there is of course the role of Arabic, not only as the dominant tongue of Northern Africa, but also as the central language of Islamic worship both north and south of the Sahara, as well as world wide. In fact, at the global level, the most successful Semitic language is Arabic. Indeed, the majority of the world's Arabic speakers reside within the continent of Africa.

It remains to be seen whether Islam will surpass Christianity in number of adherents to become the most successful Semitic religion in Africa (as well as in the world). The rivalry between the two is joined. About half of the members of the Organization of African Unity (OAU) are also members of the Organization of the Islamic Conference (OIC). In the battle for the soul of North Africa, Islam has already won. From the seventh century A.D., North Africa was conquered from Christendom by the Arabs. Apart from the Coptic Church in Egypt, Christianity has almost disappeared from North Africa today.

South of the Sahara the rivalry between Christianity and Islam has gathered momentum. There are already more Muslims in Nigeria than there are Muslims in any Arab country, including Egypt. In all, the Black Muslim population of Africa is over one hundred million. Though uneven, Islam has spread all the way down to the Cape of Good Hope. Islam in the Republic of South Africa is some three hundred years old.

But of course the most powerful force in South Africa is not religion but race. The final act in the drama has started — the curtain has gone up for the finale of racial confrontation. From an African perspective, there is a silver lining to the cloud of Apartheid. Black South Africans, the most underprivileged Blacks of the twentieth century, may well become the most privileged Blacks of the twenty-first. The Black untouchables of yesterday in South Africa will become the Black Brahmins of tomorrow.

Now that the final curtain has come down on apartheid, Black South Africans will inherit their birthright — one of the richest parts of the globe. They will also inherit the largest technological base in Africa, created by African labor and White expertise. Thirdly, Black South Africans may eventually inherit the nuclear infrastructure which White South Africans had been developing. Indeed, South Africa under Black rule may well become the world's first Black nuclear power.

The slave trade had once reduced the African to the ultimate underdog. Will nuclear power elevate him back to equality? The nightmare of slavery awaits its final negation by the nightmare of nuclear power. A negation of the negation, in a true Hegelian dialectic. *Quo vadis*, Africa? Whither Pan-Africanism?

NOTE

Thoughts to mark the twenty-fifth anniversary of the Organization of African Unity (OAU), 1988.

FOUR

ON THE CONCEPT OF "WE ARE ALL AFRICANS"

B ernard Lewis once grappled with the question "What is a Turk?" and finally put forward, virtually as part of the definition, the "sentiment of Turkish identity" — simply thinking of oneself as a Turk.[1] Now the course of world history is being much affected by people who on occasion speak of themselves collectively as "Africans." How important to the definition of an African in politics is the quality of thinking of oneself as an African?

In many respects, as Melville Herskovits has maintained, Africa is a geographical fiction. "It is thought of as a separate entity and regarded as a unit to the degree that the map is invested with an authority imposed on it by the map makers."[2] The argument here is presumably that climatically the range in Africa is from arid deserts to tropical forests; ethnically, from the Khoisan to the Semites; linguistically from Amharic to Kidigo. What have all these in common apart from the tyranny of the map maker?

I

One possible answer is that they have a negative common element: they are alike one to another to the extent that they are collectively different from anything in the outside world. It is perhaps this question-begging assumption which makes President Nkrumah of Ghana insist that "Africa is not, and can never be an extension of Europe."[3] That argument was used against the notion that Algeria was part of France, and it continued to be used against Portuguese "integration" of Angola and Mozambique. In a televised New York debate with Jacques Soustelle when the future of "French" Algeria was still in question, Ghana's Ambassador Alex Quaison-Sackey employed the argument not merely as a variant formulation of the thesis that "Algeria had to be independent of France" but as a piece of evidence in support of that thesis.[4]

Did Quaison-Sackey and his President mean that no nation could — on account of some logical difficulty — overflow across continental boundaries? Was it to be inferred that, for instance, since the United Arab Republic was at the time an instance of "Africa" (represented by Egypt) overflowing into "Asiatic" Syria, Nkrumah's argument was an implicit prediction of the breakup of that union? And what of Bernard Lewis' Turkey — was it Asia overflowing into Europe or Europe spilling over into the Orient?

It seems more likely that Nkrumah's use of "can never" (in his "Africa . . . can never be an extension of Europe") is not one of incapacity but of moral rejection. Europe "can never" legitimately extend into Africa, however practical the extension might be empirically.

And yet the element of strict incapacity is not entirely absent from the Ghanaians' exposition of the thesis. It continued to be presented almost like a logical impossibility, the reasoning being something to the effect that if Algeria was part of Africa, and Africa was a separate continent from Europe, then Algeria could not be part of a part of Europe at the same time. The argument sounded persuasive, and continued to sound persuasive in regard to Portugal's "projections" into Africa. But, by itself as an argument, it sounds persuasive only if one accepts what Herskovits describes as "the preconceptions that arise from according continental designations a degree of reality they do not possess."[5]

Herskovits himself refers to the description of Africa by the Geographer Royal of France in 1656 as a "peninsula so large that it comprises a third part, and this the most southerly, of our continent."[6] And a case can certainly be made for the thesis that North Africa was in a sense an extension of Southern Europe for a long time — and if the connection with Europe was to an extent broken with the advent of Islam, it was only to turn North Africa into a western extension of the Arabian peninsula and the Fertile Crescent rather than a northern continuation of the area south of the Sahara.

And yet Nkrumah insists that not even "an accident of history" can "ever succeed in turning an inch of African soil into an extension of any other continent." To him it was self-evident, and "colonialism and imperialism cannot change this basic geographical fact."[7]

The reasoning implicit in this assertion seems to accord greater importance to "geographical facts" than to "accidents of history." Yet the choice of terms could surely be interchanged. To the Frenchman who opposed Nkrumah's thesis, the argument could just as well have been framed in the reverse semantic order: that no accident of geography could change the basic historical fact that Algeria had had a longer connection with Europe than with, say, the Congo or Tanganyika. Geographical facts are as much "accidents" as historical accidents are "facts." In the politics of Africanism, which aspects of which are really important?

The very term "Africanism" seems to imply that geography matters more, since "Africa" is a geographic designation. Nkrumah's stand can therefore he taken as further evidence for Max Beloff's argument in another context that "it is easier to understand the contiguities of geography than the continuities of history."[8]

And yet in regard to Africa the argument cannot rest there. History can be apprehended and felt without being "understood." Indeed, what makes geography important in politics is very often the history behind it. The whole span of historical development may not be relevant. The effect of a period of history is not always to be measured by the number of years it covers. Africa is certainly one instance where a few decades of history led to greater changes than the several centuries that preceded them. One of the changes that these decades have brought about is perhaps a new consciousness of "geographical contiguities" and a new response to them. And so, while acknowledging wide differences in culture, language, and ideas between various parts of Africa, Nkrumah could still insist that "the essential fact remains that we are all Africans, and have a common interest in the independence of Africa."[9] That they are "all Africans" may be no more than a recognition of a geographical fact: that they have "a common interest in the independence of Africa" is a "continuity" of history.

But is there an implied "therefore" between the two parts of Nkrumah's statement? At first glance it may seem plausible to suppose that if there is some kind of causal relationship between being Africans and being interested in African independence, the latter must follow from the former. This is true, but only partly. The other side of the argument is, paradoxically, that they are "all Africans" because of the common interest in independence; that until a craving for independence was born they were not "Africans" but Ibo, Kikuyu, Balunda, Egyptian, Somali, and Zulu. In other words, if Nkrumah's "We are all Africans" is an assertion of a self-conscious collectivity, then the collectivity is as much an effect as a cause of the self-consciousness.

Taking the argument a stage further, the craving for independence presupposes, of course, an absence of independence,[10] i.e., in this instance, the advent of the colonization of Africa. Are we then to conclude that it was colonization which made it possible for Nkrumah to say "We are all Africans"? And if so, what has happened to Nkrumah's repeated argument that the process of colonization had included "the policy of divide and rule"?

The two arguments are not impossible to reconcile. Certainly Julius Nyerere seemed to subscribe to both. In his furious letter to *The Times* (London) just before he resigned, he accused the paper's news reportage of trying to drive a wedge between "the Government and the people of Tanganyika on the one hand and the people of Kenya on the other." And, like a true nationalist, he wanted to "state quite categorically that the time for the policy of divide and rule has passed."[11] Yet Nyerere had been known to argue in a way which suggested that if the imperialists divided (as a policy) in order to rule, they also united (in effect) by the very act of ruling. At a symposium at Wellesley College almost two years earlier Nyerere had emphasized that "the sentiment of Africa," the sense of fellowship between Africans, was "something which came from outside." He said, "One need not go into the history of colonization of Africa, but that colonization had one significant result. A sentiment was created on the African continent — a sentiment of oneness."[12]

Carried to its logical conclusion this says that it took colonialism to inform Africans that they were Africans. I do not mean this merely in the sense that in colonial schools young Bakongo, Taita and Ewe suddenly learned that the rest of the world had a collective name for the inhabitants of the landmass of which their area formed a part — though this was certainly one medium by which Africans were informed by colonialism that they were Africans. A more important medium was the reaction against colonialism leading, as it did, to a new awareness of the "geographical contiguities" mentioned above, and the new responses that this called out. The result was felt even by the Arab North, so that a new type of Egyptian told his countrymen:

> . . . we cannot, in any way, stand aside, even if we wish to, from the sanguinary and dreadful struggle now raging in the heart of the continent between five million whites and two hundred million Africans. We cannot do so for one principal and clear reason: we ourselves are in Africa.[13]

Perhaps for the first time in that country's history a ruler of Egypt was taking a stand to awaken his countrymen to an implication of the "geographical fact" that they too were "in Africa." Almost as emphatically as his Ghanaian counterpart the Egyptian President was to commit himself to the policy of "We are all Africans."

But is the Egyptian an African in the same sense that Nkrumah is one? The answer must be a qualified "No." To the extent that they are both within a continent that underwent some form of colonial rule in recent history, and to the extent that this gives them a certain sense of fellow feeling, the Egyptian and Nkrumah are both "Africans." But while the Egyptian is an African only in the sense that Nehru is an Asian, Nkrumah is an African in a more significant meaning. To put it another way, Nasser is an Egyptian in a deeper sense historically than Nkrumah is a Ghanaian, but he is an African in a shallower sense emotionally than Nkrumah is an African. The continental feeling built up by colonialism was more emphatic in Africa south of the Sahara than it ever was either north of the Sahara or in Asia. The particularly marked artificiality of the sub-Saharan "nations," even when compared with those in Asia or North Africa, is certainly an important part of the explanation. The question then arises, from what is this importance derived?

One approach to the answer is to examine the individual side effects of this sub-Saharan artificiality. Among these were the collective labels that the colonial powers had to give to the multiplicity of tribes within each territory. The British administrator in India, for example, did not have to call Indians "Asians." When he did not call them Hindoos or Muslims, Gujerati or Punjabi, he lumped them together as "Indians." Such sentiment of oneness as this created was therefore limited to the Indian sub-continent instead of encompassing the entire Asian continent.[14] There was, to be sure, a degree of fellow feeling with other Asians. But this led to very little talk in Asia about a "United States of Asia," realistic or not. Nor was there the same degree of conviction behind any inchoate sense of belonging to the "same" race on a continental scale. As Lord Hailey observed, the spirit of Asianism had not "involved the emergence of a concept of pan-Asianism in the East."[15]

In sub-Saharan Africa, however, there was often no territorially exclusive term to designate the indigenous inhabitants in a given territory, at least not when these were being distinguished from the immigrant races. In India an exclusive club could have a sign "No Indians admitted." In Tanganyika or Kenya it would not have been racially specific to say "No Tanganyikans" or "No Kenyans" since these terms had little natural ethnic content.[16] The term "African" seems to have gained currency in some instances as a euphemism for the term "native." When the Legislative Council came into the multi-racial territories of East Africa, the seats for the races were allocated in continentalistic terms: "African" seats, "European" seats, and after the Indian partition, "Asian" seats.

Thus, to use Nyerere's rhetoric, "Africans, all over the continent, without a word being spoken either from one individual to another or from one African country to another, looked at the European, looked at one another, and knew that in relation to the European they were one."[17] In relation to another continent, this continent was one: this was the logic of the situation.

Nevertheless, he was putting it too strongly when he talked of Africans "all over the continent." For where the "nations" were not entirely artificial it was possible for the colonial powers to think of and describe the natives as "Somalis" and "Sudanese" without resorting to the all-encompassing "Africans." And to the extent that the narrower terms did not emphasize affinity with the rest of the continent, the "spirit of Africanism" of the Somalis or the Sudanese is not of the same depth as that of the "Tanganyikans." Indeed, this applies even to those natural nations within artificial ones, like the Buganda of Uganda. The point to remember is that where colonial boundaries approximate very closely to ethnic ones, and where there is a degree of homogeneity within the boundaries to give the concept of "nation" some substance over and above the mere existence of legal boundaries on the map, there is less of a pull toward identity with what Nyerere calls "Africans all over the continent." As Lord Hailey put it in connection with some such homogeneous, if especially small, territories, "Africanism is seen there mainly in terms of the maintenance of the national identity of the indigenous community concerned."[18]

It nonetheless holds that if, as Herskovits claims, Africa is "a geographical fiction," Tanganyika and Ghana are greater fictions. As an English settler in Africa wrote,

> The administration of some of these artificial divisions have made a practice of trying to foster a synthetic patriotism towards "Tanganyika" or the "Gold Coast." . . . These loyalties to a wholly artificial and unrealistic administrative boundary . . . tend to obscure and undermine the underlying sense of oneness across the continent which I have heard expressed in the constantly reiterated phrase "We Africans."[19]

But if the feeling of "We Tanganyikans" is beginning to undermine the feeling of "We Africans," for how long can we continue to think of the latter as less "synthetic" than the former? If Nigerians are developing a greater loyalty to "Nigeria" than to "Africa," for how long can it be maintained that they are less Nigerians than they are Africans? It is all very well, one might argue, for the sympathizers of African unity to lament that

> . . . the youthful generation of Africans . . . have seen in school colored maps of Africa . . . all the forty divisions clearly demarcated by thick black lines; and it is hard for them to remember that such concepts as "Nigeria" or "Tanganyika" are of very recent origin and are wholly artificial.[20]

But if a "youthful generation" finds it hard to remember that a fiction is a fiction, for how long can it remain so?

II

Here we come to the different levels of what has come to be known as "African nationalism." In 1944 a British Colonial Office Advisory Committee on Education in the colonies drew attention to the finding that travel and contact with other nationalities had given rise among Africans to a "dawning realization of themselves as Africans, even as 'nationals' of a territory like Northern Rhodesia, playing a part in world affairs."[21] It was, in other words, a consciousness not only of being "Africans" but also of being Africans from a particular territory. The term "African nationalism" very often fails to make this distinction. It is used to denote any form of nationalism *in* Africa and involving *Africans* — the nationalism that looks inward territorially, like that of Nigerians after independence; the nationalism that looks inward tribally, like that of the Kikuyu in the 1940s and 1950s; and the nationalism that looks outward continentally or regionally and envisions the submergence of the colonial units into a larger creation.

When, however, a distinction is made between these different meanings, the tendency is to think of the narrower territorial or tribal nationalisms as being in some sense "less nationalistic" than the wider continentalistic brand. The Nigerian who is for exclusively Nigerian interests thus becomes less of a "real Nationalist" than an Nkrumah or a Touré who seems prepared to sell his country's sovereignty for a vision of continental unity.[22]

Perhaps here the contrast with Europe is particularly striking. The rebellion against dynastic empires in Europe was, in a sense, a rebellion against large, multi-ethnic or multilingual states — a rebellion which could not easily be reconciled with pan-Europeanism. And even today that Englishman is nationalistic who is opposed to giving up the sovereignty of England for the sake of a united Europe. Why then is the particularist Nigerian less of a nationalist than the pan-African Nkrumah?

Both in Africa in its recent history and in Europe in the wake of "self-determination" after World War I, nationalism had denoted a commitment to what Nkrumah has described as "the application of . . . the right of a people to rule themselves."[23] This is just another way of expressing opposition to foreign rule in moral terms — and in an idiom that African nationalism inherited from European nationalisms. Where Africa parts company with Europe is on the crucial issue of what is a "foreigner."[24] In Europe the "foreign" ruler was generally himself a European. To have rebelled against him and then subscribed to the idea of "uniting" with him in a pan-European spirit was politically illogical.

In the case of the continental brand of African nationalism this difficulty does not arise since the "foreign" ruler is a ruler from outside the continent altogether. It is therefore quite consistently "nationalistic" to win independence for Ghana, set out to build it as a nation, create a sense of patriotism toward it, and at the same time declare an intention to submerge its "national" identity within a giant state on a continental or sub-continental scale. But even if this is conceded to be consistently nationalistic, what could make it a more justifiable definition of "the real nationalist" than the particularism of the Nigerian who refuses to give up his Nigerian "identity"?

One answer might be that the Nigerian is resigning himself to the arbitrary frontiers imposed by colonialism and therefore deserves to be regarded as less of a nationalist. This line of reasoning sometimes goes to the extent of implying that the creation of a "United States of Africa" would not be something entirely new but rather in effect a return to things as they were before the advent of divisive colonialism. The same Nyerere who said at Wellesley College that colonization gave birth to African fellowship told the Royal Commonwealth Society that it was *pre*-colonial African history which demanded that "African unity must have priority over all other associations"[25] — as if the colonial period had interrupted a fellowship that went far back before it.

The argument here had virtually become "We were all Africans until colonialism split us into Tanganyikans, Kenyans, and Nigerians." It is certainly true that they could not have been Nigerians and Tanganyikans before the advent of colonialism, since colonialism created Nigeria and Tanganyika. The logical jump is in the assertion that they must "therefore" have previously been just "Africans." Nor is it a simple case of the very word "African" being itself *non*-African in its inception, however true that may be. Rather, it is a case of the inhabitants of the continent having known other, often narrower group classifications than the "Tanganyikans" and "Nigerians" of post-colonial days.

And yet there is a persistent reluctance in the continentalistic type of African nationalism to acquiesce in the map drawn up at Berlin in 1884.[26] Indeed, the Berlin Conference which partitioned Africa served as the inspiration of the first All-Africa people's conference held in Accra in December 1958. One observer maintained at the time that the connection between the two conferences occurred to the Chairman of the Accra Conference, Mr. Tom Mboya.[27] Mboya's slogan "Europeans, scram out of Africa" was meant not only to echo the phrase "European scramble for Africa" but also to amount to a demand that Europeans should pull out now, so that Africans could set about putting Africa "back together again."

Anyone, then, who did not subscribe to this vision of putting Africa back together again was something short of a true African nationalist. There might be differences of opinion over how far into the future this aim was to be pushed, and over the form and pattern in which Africa was to be put together. But a considerable consensus had developed at least on the point that African unity is possible only when the European ruler has "scrammed out" of the continent as a whole. In the words of Sékou Touré, "the liberty of Africa is indivisible."[28]

This doctrine of indivisibility is persistent in the language of nationalism in Africa. In part it arises out of the same factors which led the colonial powers to apply the broad term "African" to indigenous inhabitants of different parts of the continent. In one sense the African nationalist has to think of Africa as "indivisible" because the rest of the world tends to think of it as such. At least outside Africanists' circles, it is frequent enough to hear an atrocity in the Congo being stretched in significance and deemed a reflection not merely on Congolese but also on African capacity for, say, self-discipline. In the face of such generalizations, actual or anticipated, a nationalist from Ghana may decide that if he cannot defend himself by pointing out that he is not Congolese, he might as well defend himself by defending the Congolese — by discovering exclusively "external" causes for the troubles of that country.

At this level then, the African image of their own indivisibility is a reflection of the image of Africa that the outside world has tended to hold — going back to the days when Africans were classified together as "all backward" or "all primitive," with little regard for the enormous variations of social and political development in different parts of the continent. It is significant that the reflection has become more real than the original before the mirror of time — and empty European generalizations like "They are all Africans" are becoming less empty as the Africans themselves, in fellowship, affirm that so they are indeed.

But the doctrine of African indivisibility has intellectual as well as psychological roots; and the New World has certainly played a part in this. It was, for example, from Abraham Lincoln, as well as

from John Stuart Mill, that Julius Nyerere says he learned of Western notions of institutionalized democracy.[29] And yet Nyerere himself was not educated in America. Clearer traces of American influence are to be discerned in those African nationalists who did spend
formative years in the United States — the most famous of these
being Azikiwe of Nigeria, Nkrumah of Ghana and Banda of Nyasaland. Pan-Africanism has then a root in the New World not only
because Afro-Americans like DuBois and Garvey launched it onto a
world stage but also because many even of the African fathers of
Pan-Africanism were themselves exposed to elements in American
political thought.

It is, of course, dangerous to single out specific ideas in African
thought and trace them to the New World. But one can at least haz-
ard an estimate and even point to certain American thinkers who
were especially influential. American writers today sometimes give
the impression of putting Thomas Jefferson first as a persistent
intellectual force in the world.[30] In doing so they are in danger of
projecting their own estimate of important American thinkers onto
the rest of the world. Actually, for every African who has heard of
Thomas Jefferson, probably several knew of Abraham Lincoln —
even if only as the liberator of Negro slaves in his country. Some
may well have acquainted themselves with the kind of arguments
Lincoln used in support of that liberation — especially, that the
Union could not "permanently endure half slave and half free."
This was, in fact, a classic formulation of the doctrine of the indivisibility of freedom; and it has been echoed down the generations
since. In 1899 the American Anti-Imperialist League was already
extending Lincoln's ideas to colonialism at large and asking America not to betray Lincoln by persisting in colonizing the Philip-
pines.[31] By 1947 an African leader, Nnamdi Azikiwe, was arguing in
West Virginia that "one half of the world cannot be democratic and
the other half undemocratic"[32] — and the conclusion to be drawn
was that the colonies must be liberated.

By 1962 America, which had dramatized that argument nation-
ally by a Civil War a century ago was being asked by an old defender
of white settlers in Africa, Mrs. Elspeth Huxley, to make it clear to
the now independent African governments that their countries
could not, "any more than others, contract out of the rule that freedom is indivisible."[33] In regard to the position of the white settlers
— of whose rights she had long been champion in opposition both

to Margery Perham[34] and to African aspirations — the colonial wheel had come just about full circle.

But if the Africans were now betraying the ideal of an indivisible freedom, what had their struggle been all about?

III

The question can be answered best by examining first what any nationalism is all about. Frederick Hertz once defined national consciousness as "the combined striving for unity, liberty, individuality and prestige."[35] Need these four aspirations be of equal weight? Must liberty, for example, be as important as, say, prestige to any people with a national consciousness? Can the precise combination of the different elements vary in importance not only within the "consciousness" of a single nationalist but also between one nationalist and another?

This opens up the relevance of the particular circumstances which give rise to national consciousness. If there have been occasions of what John Stuart Mill might describe as "collective humiliation,"[36] it would make a difference what form the humiliation took. Did it deal a blow just to a people's "prestige" — as by, say, beating them in a space race to the moon? Did it go further and actually deprive them of their "liberty"? Did it "divide" them in order to do so? On the answers to such questions would rest the aspirations of such a people within their national consciousness, and indeed their very aptitude for realizing them.

For example, one of the major differences between English-speaking and French-speaking Africans is that the latter have been the more culturally creative of the two. It has been pointed out often enough that Leopold Senghor of Senegal was a poet, Keita Fodéba of Guinea a producer of ballets, Bernard Dadié of the Ivory Coast a novelist and Cofi Gadeau a playwright, before they held office in their respective states. One reason advanced to explain this is that the Africans who were ruled by France were more exposed than their British counterparts to "collective humiliation" in the cultural field. Their creativeness was thus a response to the assimilationist assumption that African culture was inferior to that of France.[37]

And yet, curiously enough, far less talk of "our British heritage" is heard among English-speaking Africans than of "our French cultural background" among at least the Brazzaville group of former

French subjects. The latter's rebellion against French cultural arrogance has not really taken the form of a determined attempt to tear away from the French influence — in spite of Senghor's homage to *Négritude*. Theirs, in fact, is less a rebellion than the paradox of rebellious emulation. While Nkrumah and Nyerere would at least like to believe that such a thing as "African Socialism" is fundamentally indigenous, Senghor prefers to talk in the more rational but less nationalistic terms of a "socialism based on the seminal cultural values of both Africa and Europe."[38] This approach, even if more persuasive, surely constitutes a lesser degree of insistence on the distinctiveness of an African personality. Sékou Touré is in many ways unrepresentative of the French-speakers — and it was perhaps because of his stronger Africanism that at his meeting with Senghor in 1962 on the question of settling African differences he was informed once again of Senghor's belief that Africa should be "open to all the pollen of the earth and to all the fertilizing contributions of the various civilizations and continents."[39] The reason for Senghor's insistence is that to him the concept of "We are all Africans" is, if equated with what he calls "continentalism," a form of autarchy — and "like all autarchies it denies the interdependence of peoples. . . ."[40]

On such occasions Senghor comes dangerously near to joining those "cosmopolitans" whom Rousseau once accused of trying to "justify their love of their country by their love of the human race and make a boast of loving all the world in order to enjoy the privilege of loving no one."[41] Presumably it would then be the English-speaking Nkrumah with whom the nationalistic Rousseau would be in sympathy. In Rousseau's terms, Nkrumah at least justifies his love for Ghana by his love of the African rather than the human race. And even when he makes a boast of loving all the world, it is but to love a continent. "We are all Africans — and the rest of the world is not," is the essence of his outlook.

Yet it is possible to exaggerate the difference between these two African views. No one acquainted with the varied sides of Senghor's philosophy can doubt that he, too, has a deep emotional attachment to his own race. To say that he and Nkrumah differ only as to the means for achieving a common end would be not only platitudinous but also somewhat inaccurate, unless that end is given a broad name like "Africa's assertion of herself." The two African outlooks would still differ in their interpretations of what would constitute such an assertion.

Nevertheless, agreement even on broad objectives must be deemed significant for the future course of African history. It remains now to examine the impulse behind those objectives and the nature of the quest. What is the central aspiration in the national consciousness of the emerging African?

IV

The language of African nationalism in recent times has tended to suggest that the central aspiration was liberty, indivisible or not. Single word slogans like Uhuru, Kwacha and "Free-Dom" have emphasized this. So has the understandable conceptual framework which makes "anti-colonialism" a demand primarily for "liberation" — and proceeds from there to the precarious conclusion that the basic motivation behind African nationalism is a desire for "freedom." That African freedom is immensely important to the African nationalists is, of course, beyond doubt. But it is not to be hastily assumed that the average African really shares Lord Acton's conception of liberty, not as a means to a higher political end but as itself the highest political end. The average African does not rate liberty even in the sense of "independence" so high. Instead, there are higher political ends for which such liberty, as a means or prerequisite, is needed.

One alternative end which might suggest itself is equality. And it is certainly an end now obscured in all the chanting of "independence" in the remaining colonies and "freedom from neo-colonialism" in the countries already sovereign. Even in Kenya, which has only just emerged from being a "White Man's Country," the cry for equality has all but disappeared from the vocabulary of the African nationalist. The days when *Pan-Africa* could carry an article by a Kenya nationalist under the heading of "Kenya Today: Equality is Our Slogan"[42] seem to have really receded into history.

All the same it must be emphasized that nationalism in Africa is still more egalitarian than libertarian in its ultimate aspirations. This is not to underestimate the logical complications in any attempt to disentangle the concepts of equality and of liberty — complications that may be suggested by recalling that the first Declaration of Independence from British colonial rule opened with the premise that "all men are created equal." And yet disentangling the two concepts can surely be carried at least to the extent of suggesting that whereas the Americans proclaimed "equality" in pursuit of independence, the African nationalists have now sought independence in pursuit of equality. Indeed, the development of African nationalism is a progressive metamorphosis of what would be acceptable as an adequate expression of racial equality.

In that development can be traced a transition from the notion that "freedom is indivisible" to the notion that "equality is indivisible" — that until all Africans are regarded as the equals of Europeans, no African can be sure that he is accepted as an equal. To substitute Tom Mboya's phraseology, "as long as any part of Africa remains under European rule, we do not feel that Africans will be regarded in the right way."[43] What this means is that "the manumission of mother Africa from the foreign yoke"[44] is essential not only for its own sake but also for elevating the African in the eyes of the world — and in African eyes too. The underlying logic of this belief is that the slave needs his freedom to be the equal of free men, as well as to exercise it.

On closer analysis, however, the African quest combines the aspiration of equality with those two other nationalistic aspirations which Hertz described as "individuality and prestige." The obvious designation for the combination is "dignity" — a word even more imprecise than "equality." Perhaps it is useful to coin a term like "dignitarianism" for such a movement, and then give it some precision by definition. It can, for example, be defined to exclude the nationalism that takes its minimal or strictly "human" dignity for granted and only seeks to reunite, say, Germans with fellow Germans across an artificial border. African examples of such unification-minded nationalisms include the Bakongo, confident of themselves in relation to their neighbors, but seeking to unite with fellow Bakongo. Then there are the Ewe, still restive at division. In their cases "dignity" has been a vague incidental to the central aspiration of reunification — no matter how often it was used as a rallying slogan.

Sub-classifications are possible within the dignitarian forms of nationalism. There is the nationalism that seeks to protect its "dignity" from some impending danger, real or imaginary. Examples are the nationalism of the Afrikaaners of South Africa and, in a different context, that of the immigrant elite in Liberia and of the Amharic aristocracy in Ethiopia. These peoples have had no doubt about their own "dignity" as they have seen it. Their recent preoccupation, in varying degrees of intensity, has been with how to ensure its continuation. This, then, is protective dignitarianism.

The nationalism of re-unification, like that of the Arabs, or even of the Bakongo, can be dignitarian if unity is envisaged as a means of recovering some lost dignity in a glorious past. Here again it is a question of degree of emphasis rather than of the complete absence of this or that aspiration. As Thomas Hodgkin put it, "since Byron reminded the Greeks of Sappho and Marathon every nationalist myth has included this element of past greatness."[45] But Hodgkin goes on to note that although "no Western European seriously questioned the fact that there had been periods in the past when Arab and Indian civilizations, owing little to European stimulus, flowered . . . the case of the peoples of Africa is different."[46] For them it is not a simple case of recovering a dignity which every one concedes they once had. It may indeed be an attempt to recover their own respect for themselves, but it is also an endeavour to win for the first time the respect of others. Self-respect and respect by others, difficult to separate as they usually are, are in the Africans' case even more so. Theirs, then, is an assertive rather than strictly "restorative" dignitarianism — the kind that impelled Jomo Kenyatta early in 1962 to advise the Europeans of Kenya to learn for the first time to address the African as *Bwana*.

And when, out of similar convictions, Premier Obote, on the achievement of Uganda's independence, refused to extend his country's recognition either to South Africa or, in spite of the Commonwealth link, to the Federation of Rhodesia and Nyasaland, that old Lincolnian notion of an indivisible freedom had found its ultimate maturity in the concept that the dignity of man was indivisible.[47] On such a level, the African nationalist of whatever shade of Africanism, becomes Rousseau's "cosmopolitan" — rising from the emotion of "We are all Africans" to the aspiration of "We are all men."

The emotion is likely to persist for as long as the aspiration is no more than an aspiration. Nationalism feeds on ambition, and ambition feeds on "conflict" or competition with others. The ambition is the creation of a respected image of *Bwana* Mwafrika,[48] and the conflict is with the forces in the way. And so there will remain, even now that independence has been substantially achieved, an area of life within which Africans may continue to feel that they are, in Lumumba's phrase, "brothers in race, brothers in conflict."[49] To the question whether they are brothers because of "race" or because of the "conflict," it can only be said that the two merge together and become virtually indistinguishable.

NOTES

An earlier version of this essay appeared in *The American Political Science Review* 57, no. 1 (March 1963): 88–97.

1. *The Emergence of Modern Turkey* (Oxford University Press, 1961). See especially his Introduction: The Sources of Turkish Civilization, pp. 1–17.

2. Melville J. Herskovits, "Does 'Africa' Exist?" *Symposium on Africa* (hereafter referred to as *Symposium*), Wellesley College, Wellesley, Mass., 1960, p. 15.

3. Speech to the 15th Session of the United Nations General Assembly, 23 September 1960. Publication of the Permanent Mission of Ghana to the United Nations, p. 9.

4. See NBC Script of "The Nation's Future," December 3, 1960, NBC Television Debates.

5. *Symposium*, p. 16.

6. Ibid.

7. Speech to 15th Session of U.N. General Assembly, p. 9.

8. "The Prospects for Atlantic Union," *The Times* (London), February 2, 1962.

9. Preface, *I Speak of Freedom* (London: Heinemann, 1961), p. xiii.

10. A distinguished African philosopher argued at a meeting in Oxford that a state of independence was a state of nature — and one to be "gained" only because it had been lost, certainly not as something new.

11. *The Times* (London), January 19, 1962.

12. "Africa's Place in the World," *Symposium*, p. 149. For brief analysis of his argument see my article "Why Does an African Feel African?" *The Times* (London), February 17, 1962, reproduced in Canada in *The Globe and Mail*, February 22, 1962.

13. Gamal Abdul Nasser, *The Philosophy of the Revolution* (*Economica* English edition, Buffalo, 1959), p. 74. A discussion of the limits of Nasser's role in Africa occurs in my article in *African Affairs* (Journal of the Royal Institute of African Affairs, 1963) entitled "Africa and the Egyptian's Four Circles."

14. Indeed, that the Indians considered one another "fellow Indians" at all was, to a great extent, an outcome of their shared colonial experience too. But fellow *Asians* was much too sophisticated. As Iain Lang observed in a review in *The Sunday Times* (London, February 25, 1962) "If you were to tell a Punjabi peasant or a Malay fisherman that he was an Asian he would be most unlikely to know what you were talking about." Roy Sher-

wood (*Peace News*, London, March 1962) even moralises on the subject, saying: "A regrettable survival of colonialist thinking is the lumping together of all the non-white peoples of the Indian and Pacific Oceans under the comprehensive term 'Asians.'" The phenomenon is discussed in Michael Edwardes' *Asia in the Balance* (A Penguin Special), 1962. No less significant, however, was the phenomenon of "Asian" jubilation over the 1905 Japanese victory over Russia.

15. *An African Survey*, revised 1956 (Oxford University Press, 1957), p. 252.

16. Such clubs or hotels could, of course, carry either the double-negative sign of "No non-Europeans admitted" or the sign "Europeans only." But a country like South Africa would present complications since Japanese, though geographically "non-Europeans," were legally "white." Official South African terminology prefers to call their black citizens "Bantu," but Albert Luthuli, in his Nobel Prize lecture, asserted his own preference for the term "African." Kenya certainly needed also a proper name for the "blacks" more acceptable than "natives." Nor was the stratification in Kenya simply between "White" and "non-White." For example, three scales of pay used to prevail — "European," "Asian" and "African" — just as three types of lavatories, schools and the like were provided. Even further sub-divisions were observed in some instances, but these are less relevant to this discussion.

17. *Symposium*, p. 149.

18. *An African Survey*, p. 255. The small High Commission territories are indeed extreme examples of this, but this only puts them at one end of the scale.

19. Frank Johnson, "United States of Africa," *Pan-Africa*, vol. 1, no. 6 (June 1947). See esp. pp. 3–4. The journal included at the time among its "Associate and Contributing Editors" Kwame Nkrumah and Jomo Kenyatta.

20. Frank Johnson (reproduction of above article), *Voice of Africa*, vol. 1, no. 4 (Accra, April, 1961).

21. *Education in African Society*, Colonial No. 186, 1944, p. 55.

22. A strong, radically nationalist trend has existed within at least the younger generation of Nigerians. Following the 1962 Commonwealth Prime Ministers' Conference, speculation in Britain started as to why the Nigerian Government, with all its pragmatism, rejected out of hand a proposal for associate membership in the EEC. Walter Schwarz, speaking on the European Service of the British Broadcasting Corporation in October, 1962, suggested that "Nigeria's Government, always open to attack from its own youth for being too lukewarm about its nationalism, simply finds it politically impossible to lag behind Ghana on this issue." See also my article, "African Attitudes to the EEC," *International Affairs* (London, January,

1963). Visiting newsmen to Nigeria once discovered at a special meeting with young Nigerians at Nsukka that most of the youth were strongly in favor of Nkrumah's brand of militant African nationalism, without by any means necessarily coupling it with hero-worship for Nkrumah. One reference to this meeting appeared in the *New York Times*, March 3, 1962. Of course, the radicalism of youth is not peculiar to African countries; but young people are a stronger pressure group in the new states than in some of the older ones.

23. Speech to 15th Session of U.N. General Assembly.

24. See my article "Edmund Burke and Reflections on the Revolution in the Congo," *Comparative Studies in Society and History*, January, 1963.

25. *Commonwealth Journal* (London, Royal Commonwealth Society), vol. 4, no. 6 (November-December, 1961): 254.

26. There is some ambivalence about this. It is permissible, at least as an ideal, to unite two *complete* countries. But a change of frontiers that would, say, make Ghana bigger and Togo smaller, and still leave two countries independent, is unacceptable to most Africans. In such a case, most Africans would agree with the UN representative of the Ivory Coast who put forward the policy of accepting the territorial limits obtaining at the time of independence at least "in order to avoid internecine wars which might jeopardize the independence just acquired with such difficulty." (UN Document A/PV.1043, October 27, 1961). The Brazzaville group is clearly unenthusiastic about any radical or immediate unification measures; but this distinction between changing colonial frontiers by complete integration and changing them by partial annexation would be accepted by many of even the most radical Pan-Africanists.

27. Edwin S. Morisby, "Politics of African Unity: No Longer Tail to the Asian Dog?," *Manchester Guardian*, January 2, 1959.

28. "Africa's Destiny," *Africa Speaks*, ed. James Duffy and Robert A. Manners (Princeton, 1961), p. 35.

29. " . . . the idea of government as an institution began to take hold of some African 'agitators' such as myself, who had been reading Abraham Lincoln and John Stuart Mill . . . ." — Nyerere, "The African and Democracy," *Africa Speaks*, p. 33.

30. Saul K. Padover makes a somewhat different claim — that a great interest in Jefferson had emerged abroad after a long period of ignorance. See his "Jefferson Still Survives . . . ," *New York Times Magazine*, April 8, 1962, p. 28.

31. "We hold with Abraham Lincoln, that '. . . when the white man governs himself, that is self-government, but when he governs himself and also governs another man, that is more than self-government — that is despotism. . . . Those who deny freedom to others deserve it not for themselves, and under a just God cannot long retain it.'" — Platform of the

American Anti-Imperialist League, October 17, 1899, reprinted in *Great Issues in American History*, vol. 2, ed. Richard Hofstadter (New York, Vintage Books, 1961), p. 203.

32. Zik's speech to graduates of Storer College, Harpers Ferry, West Virginia, on the occasion of his receiving the honorary degree of Doctor of Literature, June 2, 1947. See *ZIK* (Cambridge University Press, 1961), p. 83.

33. "Africa Struggles with Democracy," *New York Times Magazine*, January 21, 1962, p. 10.

34. Elspeth Huxley's correspondence with Margery Perham was published as a book, *Race and Politics in Kenya* (London, Faber and Faber, 1944), with an introduction by Lord Lugard. Eighteen years later, when it was a question of white settlers' rights as against the British Government rather than of their rights as against the Africans, the two women were at last in agreement. "Having often disagreed over Kenya's affairs," they said in their joint letter to *The Times* (London, July 5, 1962) "we now find ourselves in harmony about one issue — the claims of the European farmers for compensation" — from the British Government.

35. *Nationality in History and Politics* (New York: Oxford University Press, 1944), pp. 12–13.

36. *Representative Government,* ed. R. B. McCallum (Oxford: Basil Blackwell, 1946), p. 291.

37. Thomas Hodgkin and Ruth Schachter, "French-Speaking West Africa in Transition," *International Conciliation*, no. 528 (May, 1960): 387.

38. "West Africa in Evolution," *Foreign Affairs*, vol. 39 (January, 1961): 244.

39. See *Africa 1962*, No. 15, July 27, 1962, p. 4.

40. "West Africa in Evolution," p. 243.

41. *Contrat Social* (1st version). See C. E. Vaughan, *The Political Writings of J. J. Rousseau*, vol. 1 (Cambridge, 1915), p. 453.

42. *Pan-Africa*, vol. 1, no. 6 (June, 1947): 7. *White Man's Country* is the title of a famous book by Elspeth Huxley about Lord Delamere's Kenya. At the time Mrs. Huxley was convinced that there was not even such a thing as an "African," and she was therefore something of a precursor of Herskovits. As late as 1950 she was being taken to task by an "African" in these terms: "On the evidence of the many varied ethnic groups which exist in Africa, she (Mrs. Huxley) asserted that there was no such thing as an African. This assertion was made during a radio debate with Leonard Woolf. One wonders why an entity that did not exist had to be debated." Dr. S. D. Cudjoe, *Aids to African Autonomy* (London, The College Press, 1950), p. 23.

43. Reported in *Mombasa Times* (Kenya), January 11, 1962.

44. The phrase is from Dr. Azikiwe's message to President Nkrumah

on the occasion of Ghana's fifth anniversary as an independent state. See *The Times* (London), March 7, 1962.

45. *Nationalism in Colonial Africa* (London: Frederick Muller, 1956), p. 172.

46. Ibid.

47. Obote's stand on the Federation of Rhodesia and Nyasaland was the more interesting because, while he refused to recognise the present Government of the Federation, he was nevertheless against the Federation's dissolution — a stand which put him almost in a class by himself among African nationalists.

48. This means more than "Mr. African"; it has deeper connotations of respect. On its own the Swahili word *Bwana* can be translated loosely as "Sir." On October 14, 1961, Jomo Kenyatta said, "Non-Africans who still want to be called 'Bwana' should pack up and go, but others who are prepared to live under our flag are invited to remain." On January 28, 1962, the price of being welcome in Kenya was raised a little higher. It was no longer enough that the immigrant should cease to expect "Bwana" for himself: "I want Europeans, Asians and Arabs to learn to call Africans 'Bwana.' Those who agree to do so are free to stay," said Kenyatta. *The Times* (London) aired a controversy — with distinguished Africanists taking part — on what Kenyatta really meant by his demand. *The Sunday Times* (London) carried a controversial article by Tom Stacey on June 3, 1962, on the subject. By that time Kenyatta himself had explained that he was demanding respect rather than servility from the Kenya European. The quest for this "respected image of Bwana Mwafrika" can conflict with "freedom" in some sense. See my article "Consent, Colonialism and Sovereignty," *Political Studies* 11, no. 1 (February, 1963).

49. In his address to his compatriots on the occasion of the Congo's independence. Like many another African nationalist, he would have addressed the rest of the continent in similar terms. A translation of the speech is reproduced under the title "The Independence of the Congo" in *Africa Speaks*. The phrase occurs on page 93.

FIVE

THE BONDAGE OF BOUNDARIES
TOWARDS REDEFINING AFRICA

Three immense post-colonial taboos have been violated in the Horn of Africa in the 1990s. First, the taboo against resurrecting a trusteeship system for a country already deemed independent. The taboo has been violated in the wake of American and, subsequently, the United Nations' temporary "tutelage" of the Somali people to help them back to a capacity for self-government. This is the taboo of recolonization.

The second violated taboo is secession from an existing African state in the post-colonial era — the independence of Eritrea with the full cooperation, if not enthusiastic blessing, of Ethiopia, of which it was once a crucial constituent province. The Eritrean flag was raised in May 1993 at a ceremony at which the President of Ethiopia was among the distinguished guests. This is the taboo of officially sanctioned "secession."

The third violated taboo is ethnic decentralization by a state which was previously unitary. Having lost Eritrea, the rest of Ethiopia is groping for a federal or confederal constitutional order within which "tribes" would have the kind of ethnic autonomy that African systems of government in the post-colonial era have persistently sought to deny them. This is the taboo of retribalization.

The question which arises is whether these three broken taboos constitute a sign for the future. Are we heading for an Africa that will more readily lend legitimacy to ethnic self-determination? Will we witness other validated "Eritreas" in the future? And will the very word "tribe" regain some of the legitimacy it lost when even the eight-volume *UNESCO General History of Africa* banned its use in all eight volumes covering the entire period of human evolution on the African continent?

Underlying these three broken taboos in post-colonial Africa is a wider question. How many of the state boundaries of present-day Africa will remain intact in a hundred or a hundred and fifty years? Until now it has been taken for granted that the last thing to be decolonized in post-colonial Africa will be the colonial boundaries of the new states. Civil wars have been fought, and at least two million lives have already been lost defending the colonial boundaries of countries such as Nigeria, Zaire, Sudan, and, in a special sense, Ethiopia.

Over the next century the boundaries of the majority of present-day African states will probably change in one of two main directions. One direction will be *ethnic self-determination*, which will create smaller states, comparable to the separation of Eritrea from Ethiopia. The other direction of changing boundaries will be that of *regional integration*, towards larger political communities and economic unions. The decision of the Economic Organization of West African States (ECOWAS) to intervene militarily in the Liberian civil war in the 1990s was a special case of *Pax Africana*.

In addition there is a third factor which may help modify boundaries in Africa — the return of colonialism in a new form. Let us address this third colonial dimension before we return to the more indigenous forces of ethnic self-determination and regional integration.

TOWARDS POSITIVE RECOLONIZATION?

In an official sense, the United Nations (UN) ceased to be a trusteeship power in Africa as recently as 1990 when Namibia became independent. Countries which had previously been trusteeships of the United Nations included Cameroon, Togo, and mainland Tanzania (the former Tanganyika). A new form of UN trusteeship was heralded in 1960 when things fell apart in the former Belgian Congo upon the withdrawal of the imperial power. Patrice Lumumba, Prime Minister of independent Congo, invited the world body to come and help him maintain law and order and save the territorial integrity of the Congo. In the global politics of the period, the United Nations' role was so minimal that while it did indeed save the territorial integrity of the Congo, it failed abysmally to save the life of the man who had invited the world body in the first place. UN troops watched as Patrice Lumumba was arrested publicly and humiliated by his enemies — and then taken away to an absolutely certain death in Katanga in 1961.

What the United Nations demonstrated in the Congo in the early 1960s is that the world body nevertheless could affect the fate of the boundaries of an African state. On that occasion, the United Nations intervened to oppose Katanga's secession from the Congo. The UN saved those boundaries despite opposition from the former colonial power, Belgium, and a few other European members of the North Atlantic Treaty Organization (NATO).

Outside Africa in the 1990s the United Nations has demonstrated that it can change the boundaries between states — awarding Kuwait in 1993 new oil wells previously owned by Iraq and depriving Iraq of its only seaport to the Gulf. Wittingly or not, the world body is creating new reasons for border clashes between Iraq and Kuwait for decades to come. The parts given to Kuwait are inhabited by Iraqis, without a single Kuwaiti civilian in sight for miles and miles.

In Somalia in the 1990s UN troops have so far ignored the self-proclaimed separatist Republic of Somaliland, which has declared its independence from the rest of Somalia. The UN is presumably treating separatist Somaliland the way it treated separatist Katanga in the 1960s, as an illegitimate upstart. So far, therefore, the world body is playing the role of safeguarding the colonial boundaries. That is not a neutral role. It is a role on the side of the territorial status quo.

However, considering the role that the United Nations has already played concerning the border between Iraq and Kuwait, there is no guarantee that the world body will continue to be on the side of the territorial status quo. If the problem of stability and anarchy in Somalia turns out to be insurmountable, the sanctity of Somalia's borders may one day be reexamined. Separatist Somaliland may yet survive to enjoy a legitimate UN seat, if not this time around, then after the next collapse of the Somali political patchwork.

Nor can a full-blooded trusteeship system entirely be ruled out in the course of the twenty-first century. External recolonization under the banner of humanitarianism is entirely conceivable. Countries like Somalia and Liberia, where central control has collapsed with great suffering for the people, may invite an inevitable intervention.

However, while the resurfacing of colonialism is indeed conceivable, the return of "the white man's burden" is far less likely. A future trusteeship system will be more genuinely international and less Western than it was under the old guise. Stable neighboring countries will be involved in looking after less stable ones. Administering powers for the trusteeship territories could come from Africa or Asia, as well as from the rest of the membership of the United Nations.

ETHIOPIA: AFRICA'S PIONEER?

The most interesting scenario of them all in the twenty-first or twenty-second century will come if and when Ethiopia is called upon to be the administering power for Somalia on behalf of the United Nations. This would assume the survival of Ethiopia and its development and transformation. This scenario would also assume the disappearance of the historic animosities between the Somali and the ruling elites of Ethiopia. If Ethiopians and Eritreans can forgive each other, why cannot the Ethiopians and the Somali?

Ethiopia was once a Black imperialist power, annexing neighboring communities. Does the future hold a more benign, and even more humane, imperial role for Ethiopia? Will Ethiopia continue its destiny as Africa's pioneering laboratory?

Throughout the European colonial period in the rest of Africa, Ethiopia served another unique role. It survived as the single oldest oasis of African sovereignty on the entire continent of Africa. By comparison with the age of Ethiopia, Liberia (created in the nineteenth century) was a mere sovereign upstart of recent invention. Will Ethiopia be nurturing other fragile sovereignties next door in the future?

In 1974 a momentous social revolution occurred in Ethiopia. The ancient Solomonic dynasty was overthrown. The last Emperor, Haile Selassie I, was deposed and later died or was killed. Ethiopia was once again Black Africa's pioneering laboratory. A revolutionary Marxist-Leninist state was proclaimed. Those in charge were not hardened members of a vanguard party, but radicalized soldiers of what had once been an Imperial Army loyal to His Imperial Majesty Haile Selassie I. Although the differences from what happened in Russia were immense, the Ethiopian Revolution of 1974 was closer to the Russian revolution of 1917 than anything else that had happened in Africa. Both revolutions overthrew ancient monarchical institutions; both revolutions confronted the opposition of a hostile external world; both of them had to confront hostile Orthodox Christian churches (the Ethiopian and the Russian national churches are both in the Orthodox tradition); both revolutions were followed by immense internal civil conflict; both revolutions were captured by extremely brutal dictators (Stalin and Mangistu Haile Maryam); and both revolutions finally ended with ethnic fragmentation in the body politic. The Soviet Union lost fourteen republics and the Russian federation was under internal ethnic pressure. Ethiopia finally lost Eritrea in 1993 and virtually adopted a constitution of ethnic confederation for the rest of the country. Do these changes constitute another pioneering role for Ethiopia?

We now pose the scenario of a new historic destiny in the future: Ethiopia as an administering power on behalf of the United Nations, to help nurture the sovereignties of its smaller neighbors, Somalia and Djibouti being the most likely to need that kind of help in the decades to come. The recolonization of the future will not be based on the "White man's burden" or "The Lion of Judah." It may be based on "The Shared Human Burden."

TOWARDS POSITIVE RETRIBALIZATION?

Meanwhile, Ethiopia has already played an additional pioneering role, for better or for worse. It has graciously accepted the inevitable and let one of its crucial provinces (Eritrea) become an independent country. Ethiopia is also pioneering by experimenting with ethnic federalism as its new constitutional order.

Until these concluding years of the twentieth century, independent Africa has, rhetorically, been in favor of regional integration. In practice it has failed to realize it. Colonially created economic unions like the East African Community were dismantled, piece by piece, by the succeeding post-colonial governments of Kenya, Tanzania and Uganda.

On the other hand, until these final years of the twentieth century, independent Africa has been *against* ethnic self-determination, and its struggle in this domain has, on the whole, been quite successful. The most spectacular secessionist bids included that of Biafra (resulting in the Nigerian civil war of 1967–1970), that of Southern Sudan (resulting in the first Sudanese civil war of 1955-1972), and that of Katanga (resulting in the Congolese upheavals of the early 1960s). All those secessionist bids were frustrated, partly as a result of considerable Pan-African consensus in favor of the territorial integrity of colonial boundaries.

To summarize, Africa's struggle *for* regional integration has until now been a relative failure. On the other hand, Africa's struggle *against* ethnic self-determination has until now been a substantial success. Both the failure of regional integration and the stifling of ethnic self-determination have until now helped preserve the inherited colonial boundaries. What is likely to change the fortunes of ethnic self-determination and make it more legitimate in Africa? What is likely to transform the chances for regional integration in Africa and make it more politically and economically viable?

TOPPLING THE SACRED COWS

Post-colonial Africa is being forced to go back to the drawing board about many of the sacred cows and taboos of the 1960s. *Tribe* has been a dirty word among African intellectuals. *Tribalism* has been a negative slogan in African politics. Do the credentials of the tribe need to be re-examined, the legitimacy of tribalism be reviewed?

The unitary state was one of Africa's sacred cows of the 1960s, and federalism was taboo almost everywhere outside Nigeria. The Congo (formerly Zaire) rejected federalism as a solution to its immense propensity for instability. Post-colonial Kenya renounced *majimbo* (regional decentralization) as a prescription for fragmentation. Uganda abolished the neo-federal status enjoyed by Buganda. Even the newly united Tanganyika and Zanzibar (constituting a new Tanzania) and the newly united British and Italian Somaliland (constituting the post-colonial Somalia) adopted what was basically a unitary system. Only Nigeria continued to adhere to the federal principle. Is that blind post-colonial enthusiasm for the unitary state all over the rest of Africa now demanding a careful review?

Distrust of pluralism was another widespread tendency of post-colonial African ideologies. It was this anti-pluralistic tendency which gave birth to so many one-party states in different parts of

Africa. The 1990s witnessed revulsion and rebellion against the one-party system in one African country after another. One beneficiary of this restoration of pluralism has been the democratic process, however fragile. The other beneficiary of the revival of pluralism has been ethnicity and politicized tribal identity. The question persists whether these dual processes of redemocratization and retribalization cancel each other out. If, under certain conditions, democracy and tribalism are indeed compatible in a plural society, then that is one more trend which may subsequently lead to ethnic self-determination. The relationship is tense.

Another sacred cow of the 1960s was *modernization and development.* Later on the word "modernization" was quietly dropped, but in reality the term "development" was defined to include the old "modernist" opposition to tradition. What was opposed as "traditional and non-modern" included "tribal" ways and customs, and indigenous techniques and technologies. The abject failure of almost all development techniques adopted so far, with all their cultural alienation and calculated distance from traditionality, is forcing African policy-makers to rethink and review the relevance of tradition for development and growth. Was the opposition between the modern and the traditional a little too neat, a little too simplistic, to serve as an effective guide for genuine development? As modernization theories have fallen into disrepute, and as traditional wisdom is beginning to regain respectability, ethnicity as the fountain of tradition must also have its credentials reassessed. Prospects for future ethnic self-determination are improving.

Not all state boundaries of post-colonial Africa will be changed in the next century as a result of ethnic self-determination. The other great modifier of boundaries will, as we indicated, be regional integration in the sense of the unification of two or more countries. The question now arises as to what would promote regional integration when previous African efforts at political amalgamation have been so unsuccessful. In other words, why should this succeed in the future when it has failed in the past?

TOWARDS ENLARGEMENT OF POLITICAL SCALE?

In Southern Africa one predisposing factor was the genuine end of apartheid in South Africa. The subregion is pre-eminently well placed for successful economic union in the first instance. The economies of the smaller countries are already so intricately linked with the economy of the Republic of South Africa that apartheid was the main stumbling block in the way of legitimizing extensive economic cooperation. SADEC, as a Southern African organization, was originally formed partly to reduce the other countries' dependence on South Africa. But in the post-colonial and post-apartheid era the subregional organization is bound to be led by the Republic of South Africa itself. Whether South Africa itself will subsequently federate or amalgamate with Lesotho, Swaziland, Botswana, and Namibia into an even larger country is certainly one of the possibilities of the twenty-first century.

Elsewhere in Africa regional integration may be fostered by the desperation of worsening economic realities. Kenya, Uganda, and Tanzania will almost certainly be compelled in the twenty-first century to revive the moribund East African Community, which they allowed to peter out in the mid-1970s when it had once been one of the most promising economic unions in the world. Also, in the course of the twenty-first century, those three countries will at last be forced to bring to fruition the East African Federation which their founding fathers (Jomo Kenyatta, Milton Obote and Julius K. Nyerere) talked about in the 1960s and which they never found the political will to create.

Another factor likely to help the cause of regional integration in Africa in the coming decades is the demonstration effect of successful political and economic unions abroad. In spite of the ambivalence of Great Britain and Denmark, Western Europe is on its way towards ever-deepening economic integration. Parts of the former Central and Eastern Europe will join the European community in the course of the twenty-first century. Before long the pooling of European sovereignties on political matters will also be inevitable. If Europe had been Africa's tutor on the nation-state in the twentieth century, Europe may well become Africa's tutor on how to transcend the nation-state and form larger unions in the twenty-first century.

Asia has had comparable lessons of pan-regionalism for Africa to examine, the most successful of which has been the Association of South East Asian Nations (ASEAN). And North America is well on its way towards realizing the mother of all free-trade areas, a mega-economic arena of cooperation which may cover the whole western hemisphere in the course of the twenty-first century. Africa's tiny pockets of economic isolationism will look increasingly anachronistic against the background of a world responsive to dynamic regionalist expansionism. Pan-Africanism as an ideology of wider union within Africa may gain more and more converts in the face of this external demonstration impact.

Another stimulus for regional integration in the coming decades will be the attitude of aid donors, perhaps with special reference to the role of the World Bank and its leadership function among Western donors. The World Bank has been moving towards favoring regional projects and supporting trends towards regional integration. The influence of Western investors may also favor larger markets — against the competition for Western investment from Eastern Europe, Russia, India, Vietnam, China and elsewhere. If Africa is to remain even remotely competitive for foreign investment, it has to put its house in order — and put an end to its excessive economic fragmentation.

Wider cultural integration in some parts of the continent will be yet another stimulus for regional integration in the course of the twenty-first century. In West Africa the situation is complex. Nigeria is a giant of nearly one hundred million people. The power of the Hausa language may in time lead to the integration of the Republic of Niger into Nigeria. The power of the Yoruba language may in time lead to the integration of the Republic of Benin into Nigeria. This assumes that Nigeria will in any case replace France as the dominant power in what is now "Francophone West Africa."

The real rival to Nigeria in post-colonial Africa in the first instance was never Ghana under Kwame Nkrumah, or Libya under Muammar Gaddafy, or distant South Africa. The real rival to post-colonial Nigeria has all along been France. By all measurements of size, resources, and population, in West Africa Nigeria should very rapidly have become what India is in South Asia or South Africa has been in Southern Africa: a hegemonic power. One of the factors that have marginalized Nigeria has been the massive French presence in West Africa, mainly in its own former colonies, but also in Nigeria itself.

In the twenty-first century France will be withdrawing from West Africa as she gets increasingly involved in the affairs of Eastern and Western Europe. France's West African sphere of influence will be filled by Nigeria, by far a more natural hegemonic power in West Africa. It will be under those circumstances that Nigeria's own boundaries are likely to expand to include the Republic of Niger (the Hausa link), the Republic of Benin (the Yoruba link) and conceivably Cameroon (part of which nearly became Nigerian in a referendum in 1959).

Zaire is another African giant whose role may be affected by wider cultural integration. Zaire is the largest French-speaking country in the world after France. In the course of the twenty-first century it will become the largest French-speaking country in the world in population. In mineral resources it is already the richest French-speaking country in the world. If Zaire attains stability, it will replace France in Africa in a sense different from the role of Nigeria in West Africa. Zaire may become the Francophone magnet for the whole of French-speaking Africa. After all, Zaire is perhaps the only country in Francophone Africa where European culture is, in the final analysis, subordinate to African spontaneity. Supported by Zaire's mineral resources, one can envisage vigorous Francophone cultural leadership emanating from Kinshasa in the twenty-first century.

Will Zaire's boundaries remain the same? There was a time when Angola would have been vulnerable to annexation by Zaire. But Angola's rival mineral wealth may help preserve its own separate identity. On the other hand, Congo (Brazzaville) may work out a federal relationship with Zaire in the course of the twenty-first century. It would help the transition if Zaire reverted to its own older name of Congo (Kinshasa). [It is now called the Democratic Republic of the Congo.] There are close cultural and historic ties between the two Congos. It is also conceivable that Zaire will work out a confederal relationship with Burundi and Rwanda. All three countries were once ruled by Belgium and have been deepening their relationship as a result of that experience.

Also relevant in the interplay between culture and regional integration is the role of the Swahili language in Eastern Africa. Kiswahili is already a national language in Tanzania and Kenya, and is widely spoken or understood in Uganda, Zaire, Rwanda, Burundi, Mozambique, and parts of Malawi. It is already the most successful indigenous language on the African continent. The question which arises is whether the spread of the language will make it easier to attempt wider regional integration. For example, will Kiswahili conquer enough of Mozambique and Malawi to link them both to Tanzania? And how would this relate to Tanzania's links with Kenya and Uganda?

The one cultural variable in Africa that has not translated into regional integration so far is religion. Africa has a triple heritage of religion — indigenous, Islamic and Christian. Of the three traditions, the one with the greatest power of solidarity is Islam. Indigenous African religions are tribal and therefore not Pan-African. Christianity in Africa does have the power to mobilize believers to political solidarity, but on the whole the most responsive to the trumpet call of solidarity is Islam. Yet, while Islam in Africa is responsive to global solidarity (e.g. identifying with Palestinians) and national solidarity (e.g. identifying with fellow Muslims in Nigeria), Islam is not a bond of Pan-African solidarity to any significant extent (e.g. Hausa Muslims in Nigeria identifying with Baganda Muslims in Uganda). Islam is not yet a great Pan-African bond.

Still, Africa is probably the first continent in the world to have an absolute Muslim majority. There are more Muslims in Nigeria than there are Muslims in any Arab country, including Egypt (the most populous Arab state). Islam in South Africa goes back three hundred years. In the continent as a whole (i.e., including Arab Africa) the Muslim population may now exceed 55%, though there are more Christian countries than there are Muslim countries. The larger African countries include Muslim populations, among them Nigeria, Egypt, Ethiopia, Zaire, Morocco, and others. In addition, while it is true that Islam at the moment is not a great Pan-African factor, the religion is spreading faster in the continent than either Christianity or atheistic ideologies. Islam's expansion has been aided by the end of colonialism, the decline of western cultural influence, the rise of Muslim petro-missionary activity, the racial tolerance of Islam as compared with the Euro-Christian racist record, and by Africa's search for alternative moral codes in the face of post-colonial normative anarchy.

IN THE SHADOW OF GLOBAL APARTHEID

Yet another stimulus for Pan-Africanism and regional integration in the twenty-first century will be the threat of global apartheid which has been unfolding since the end of the Cold War. The world may be getting polarized afresh, but this time racially once again. The phenomenon of a world with only one superpower has strengthened Europe while weakening regions like Africa. Paradoxically, France seems to have become more responsive to the United States' leadership since the Cold War ended, even though France and the rest of Europe (outside the former USSR) need the United States less now than they did in the face of the old Soviet menace.

Africa, on the other hand, is probably worse off than ever in most respects in this new world after the Cold War. With the loss of socialist allies in international organizations, Africa has become more marginalized. Resources available for solving Africa's problems are beginning to decline in the face of competing claims on the West and on international lending institutions — claims from the former members of the Warsaw Pact and, increasingly, from Vietnam. Other Asian friends of the old Soviet Union such as India are now returning to the West for aid and investment, partly in response to global changes which have turned more decisively in favor of market ideologies, if not market forces. In short, India is returning to the capitalist fold, and even China is courting Western investment. All these new rivals on the global market place are deepening Africa's marginalization, thus creating a Black Cinderella on the world stage.

The question which arises is whether the triumph of these blind market forces is polarizing the globe along racial lines more deeply than ever — with Black people almost everywhere at the bottom, and White people in control of global wealth, with Asian people in intermediate levels of stratification. Is this the global apartheid which is emerging — at its sharpest between White and Black? Is the racial divide structural (caused by historical and ecological factors)? Or is the global apartheid overt, caused by conscious racism? Are we witnessing humankind's temporary return to the world of the "White man's burden"? Somalia may be a precursor of things to come, a throwback to the words of Rudyard Kipling's poem.

WHITHER AFRICA?

The nation-state as a political entity is in danger of being superseded by wider loyalties of race and skin colour. The demons of racism have been unleashed in the Northern Hemisphere as well as in post-Cold War Europe, with devastating consequences for minorities in those countries. Pan-Caucasianism (solidarity of Whites) may once again be racializing the state.

On our return journey in this reverse evolution of overt and structural apartheid, one global protection for Africa may be larger economic and political unions. In the face of such global marginalization and a new international racial polarization, African states may be forced to re-examine the potential strengths of African unification, the potential dividends of regional integration. With nations, as with individuals, it may sometimes be appropriate to proclaim powerfully, "We must all hang together — or hang separately!" This realization may contribute towards a redefinition of the boundaries of African states in favor of larger entities in the course of the twenty-first century, but the most fundamental of all changes in the next century and a half will be the boundaries of Africa itself. Where does Africa end?

TOWARDS RE-DEFINING AFRICA

It is not often remembered that the decision as to where Africa ended was not made by Africans themselves but was reached by European cartographers. These mapmakers ignored the fact that the Arabian Peninsula was once part of Africa and was torn off from it by one colossal earthquake which also created the Rift Valley. The European mapmakers also ignored the fact that the cultural links between Africa and the other side of the Red Sea included the Africanness of Moses before he took the Hebrews across the Red Sea. Long before Islam, the links between the two sides of the Red Sea included the linguistic links by which Amharic and Tigrinya, two of the leading languages of Ethiopia, have remained Semitic languages in the same sense as Hebrew and Arabic.

Since then the bonds between the two sides of the Red Sea have been deepened by two interrelated processes: Islamization (the spread of the Islamic religion) and Arabization (the spread of the Arabic language). We know that North Africa has been transformed by both processes. It has become not only Muslim but also Arab. Northern Sudan has experienced both processes. Northern Nigeria, on the other hand, has experienced Islamization (religious assimilation) without Arabization (linguistic assimilation).

The only part of Africa where Arabization has been faster than Islamization has been in Southern Sudan. There the Arabic language has been spreading faster than the Islamic religion. The two processes may still struggle for attention in Southern Sudan even if the subregion succeeds in becoming a separate country. Certainly the pull of the Arabic language may remain compelling in this multilingual subregion even if the locals were to win territorial freedom.

It is certain that the Muslim part of Africa will be much larger a century from now than it is today. But what about Arab Africa? Will that also be larger? Will Southern Sudanese have become Arabized? Will Mauritania have become completely Arab? How Arab will Eritreans be a century from now? After all, Egyptians were not Arabs at all when Islam first arrived in an age of limited communication fourteen centuries ago.

If more of Africa is Arab a century and a half from now, will this lead to a redefinition of the Arab world? Or will the world at long last accept that the Arabian Peninsula is part of Africa? The African continent ends at the Persian Gulf, and not on the shores of the Red Sea. Bring out your atlases and start pencilling in the changes.

NOTE

A version of this article appeared in *The Economist* (London), commissioned for a special issue to mark the 150th anniversary of *The Economist* (September, 1993) vol. 328, no. 7828. Reproduced in *Boundary and Security Bulletin* [International Boundaries Research Unit] vol. 2, no. 1 (April 1994): 60–63.

SIX

TOWARDS ABOLISHING THE RED SEA AND RE-AFRICANIZING THE ARABIAN PENINSULA

Now that Eritrea has become independent of Ethiopia with the blessing of Addis Ababa, and with the approval of the Organization of African Unity (OAU), the whole issue of Africa's colonial borders has been re-opened afresh. The self-proclaimed Republic of Somaliland has also found new optimism that its separation from Somalia will be confirmed. And voices of separation, and even echoes of "Biafra," have begun to be heard in Nigeria in the wake of the latest political frustrations. How long can Africa's colonial borders survive?

What is not realized is that the toughest colonial border of them all is the border separating Africa from Asia. Is the Red Sea a rational dividing line between Africa and Asia? Or was the Red Sea itself yet another irrational colonial border imposed by Europe, ignoring the cultural continuities and historical links across the strip of water?

In the old days the European powers sometimes found it convenient to use a river as the frontier between two of their dependencies. In the colonial period the so-called Belgian Congo and the so-called French Congo were separated by the Congo River. The imperialists preferred the logic of a physical feature (a river) rather than the logic of cultural continuities (shared language and culture) across the river.

Similarly, in choosing a frontier between Africa and Asia, the imperial powers chose the Red Sea. Was that logic of a frontier of water justified? Even if a frontier of water was needed to separate Africa from Asia, was the Red Sea the right water? Was it more rational than the Persian Gulf?

The juxtaposition of the name of a continent (Africa) and the word sea (such as Red Sea) raises a definitional problem. Are we giving the oceans an excessive say in determining where one continent ends and another begins? Can there be continents without the sea to define them? Certainly Asia could conveniently have become two continents if only a crack had occurred somewhere east of India, and created a thin strip of water right across from the Bay of Bengal to the Arctic Ocean.

European mapmakers, desperate to distinguish the Orient from the Occident, had insisted on an imaginary line between Europe and Asia without the help of a strip of water. But that was as far as the mapmakers were prepared to go without a water boundary to help them. What lay to the east of Europe was a mass of undifferentiated Asia.

I am, of course, exaggerating the definitional tyranny of the sea in relation to the boundaries of continents. Africa was connected to Asia at the Isthmus of Suez before Ferdinand de Lesseps started chopping up nature and creating the Suez Canal. Most continents had some land connection to some other continent before man intervened. Nevertheless, apart from the divide between Europe and Asia, the sea has played a disproportionate role in dictating where one continent ends and another begins.

A central thesis of ours in this essay is that the Red Sea has no business defining the northeastern boundary of Africa — it has no right to divide Africa from Arabia.

Where then is Africa? What is Africa? How sensible are its boundaries? Islands can be very far from Africa and still be part of Africa, provided they are not too near another major landmass. But a peninsula can be arbitrarily dis-Africanized.

Madagascar is separated from the African continent by the five-hundred-mile-wide Mozambique Channel. Greater Yemen, on the other hand, is separated from Djibouti by only a stone's throw. Yet Madagascar is politically part of Africa, while Greater Yemen is not.[1]

Much of the post-colonial African scholarship has addressed itself to the artificiality of the boundaries of contemporary African states. But little attention has been paid to the artificiality of the boundaries of the African continent itself. Why should North Africa end on the Red Sea when Eastern Africa does not end on the Mozambique Channel? Why should Tananarive be an African capital when Aden is not?

There have been discussions in Africa as to whether the Sahara Desert is a chasm or a link. Continental Pan-Africanism asserts that the Sahara is a sea of communication rather than a chasm of separation. Yet there are some who would argue that North Africa is not "really Africa." Why? Because it is more like Arabia.

But in that case, why not push the boundary of North Africa further east to include Arabia? Why not refuse to recognize the Red Sea as a chasm, just as the Pan-Africanists have refused to concede such a role to the Sahara Desert? Why not assert that the African continent ends neither on the southern extremity of the Sahara nor on the western shore of the Red Sea? Should not Africa move northwards to the Mediterranean and north-eastwards to the Persian Gulf?

The most pernicious sea in Africa's history may well be the Red Sea. This thin line of ocean has been deemed to be more relevant for defining where Africa ends than all the evidence of geology, geography, history, and culture. The northeastern boundary of Africa has been defined by a strip of water in the face of massive ecological and cultural evidence to the contrary.[2]

The problem goes back three to five million years ago when three cracks emerged on the eastern side of Africa. As Colin McEvedy put it,

> One crack broke Arabia away, creating the Gulf of Aden and the Red Sea, and reducing the area of contact between Africa and Asia to the Isthmus of Suez.[3]

The "contact" at the Isthmus was definitional. It depended upon looking at the Red Sea as a divide. Three cracks had occurred on the African crust, yet only the one which had resulted in a sea was permitted to "dis-Africanize" what lay beyond the sea. The other two cracks resulted in "rift valleys," straight-sided trenches averaging thirty miles across. The eastern and western rifts left the African continent intact — but the emergence of a strip of water called the Red Sea has resulted in the geological secession of Arabia.

But what a geological crack had once put asunder, the forces of geography, history, and culture have been trying to bind together again ever since. Who are the Amhara of Ethiopia if not a people probably descended from South Arabians? What is Amharic but a Semitic language? What is a Semitic language if not a branch of the Afro-Asian family of languages? Was the Semitic parental language born in Africa and then crossed the Red Sea? Or was it from the Arabian Peninsula originally and then descended upon such people as the Amhara, Tigre, and Hausa in Africa? How much of a bridge between Arabia and Africa are the Somali? All these lingo-cultural questions have raised the issue of whether the geological secession of Arabia three to five million years ago has been in the process of being neutralized by *Afrabia,* the intimate cultural integration between Arabia, the Horn, and the rest of Africa.

In the linguistic field it is certainly no longer easy to determine where African indigenous languages end and Semitic trends begin. There was a time when both Hamites and Semites were regarded as basically alien to Africa. In due course Hamites were regarded as a fictitious category, and the people represented by the term (like the Tutsi) were accepted as indisputably African. What about the Semites? They have undoubtedly existed in world history. But are they "Africans" who crossed the Red Sea, like Moses on the run from the Pharaoh? Or are the Semites originally Arabians who penetrated Africa? These agonizing problems of identity would be partially solved overnight if the Arabian Peninsula was part and parcel of Africa, or if a new solidarity took roots. This is what the concept of Afrabia is all about.

The cultural effort to re-integrate Arabia with Africa (Afrabia) after the geological divide five million years previously reached a new phase with the birth and expansion of Islam. The Arab conquest of North Africa was a process of overcoming the divisiveness of the Red Sea. Twin processes were set in motion in North Africa: Islamization (a religious conversion to the creed of Muhammad) and Arabization (a linguistic assimilation into the language of the Arabs). In time the great majority of North Africans saw themselves as Arabs — no less than the inhabitants of the Arabian Peninsula.

In short, the Islamization and Arabization of North Africa were once again cultural countervailing forces trying to outweigh the geological separatism perpetrated by the birth of the Red Sea millennia earlier. North Africans have been cast in a dilemma. Are they as African as the people to the south of them? Are they as Arab as the people to the east of them? What has yet to be raised is the question of whether the Arabs east of the Red Sea are as African as are the Arabs north of the Sahara.

But if the Red Sea could be ignored in determining the north-eastern limits of Africa, why cannot the Mediterranean also be ignored as an outer northern limit? There was indeed a time when North Africa was in fact regarded as an extension of Europe. This goes back to the days of Carthage, of Hellenistic colonization, and later, of the Roman Empire. The concept of "Europe" was at best in the making at that time. In the words of historians R. R. Palmer and Joel Colton,

> There was really no Europe in ancient times. In the Roman Empire we may see a Mediterranean world, or even a West and an East in the Latin and Greek portions. But the West included parts of Africa as well as Europe. . . .[4]

Even as late as the seventeenth century the idea that the land-mass south of the Mediterranean was something distinct from the landmass north of it was a proposition still difficult to comprehend. The great American Africanist, Melville Herskovits, has pointed out how the Geographer Royal of France, writing in 1656, described Africa as "a peninsula so large that it comprises the third part, and this the most southerly, of our continent."[5]

The old proposition that North Africa was the southern part of Europe had its last desperate fling in the modern world in France's attempt to keep Algeria as part of France. The desperate myth that Algeria was the southern portion of France tore the French nation apart in the 1950s, created the crisis which brought Charles de Gaulle to power in 1958, and maintained tensions between the Right and the Left in France until Algeria's independence in 1962, with an additional aftermath of bitterness in the trail of Charles de Gaulle's career.

This effort to maintain Algeria as a southern extension of a European power took place at a time when in other respects North Africa had become a western extension of Arabia. From the seventh century onwards Arabization and Islamization had been transform-ing North Africa's identity. Because Africa's border was deemed to be the Red Sea, the Arabs became a "bicontinental" people, impossible to label as either "African" or "Asian." Indeed, by the twentieth century, the majority of the Arab people were located west of the Red Sea (i.e. in Africa "proper") although the majority of the Arab states were east of the Red Sea (deemed as Western Asia).

The Arabic language has many more speakers in the present African continent than in the Arabian Peninsula. Arabic has become the most important single language in the present African continent in terms of number of speakers. The case for regarding Arabia as part of Africa (Afrabia) is now much stronger than for regarding North Africa as part of Europe (Eurafrica). Islamization and Arabization have redefined the identity of North Africans more fundamentally than either Gallicization or Anglicization has done. In spite of the proximity of the Rock of Gibraltar to Africa, the Mediterranean is a more convincing line of demarcation between Africa and Europe than the Red Sea can claim to be as a divide between Africa and Asia.

All boundaries are artificial but some boundaries are more artificial than others. Afrabia has at least two millennia of linguistic and religious history. This makes it an older and more profound geocultural reality than Eurafrica.

CONCLUSION

We live in an age when a people's perception of themselves can be deeply influenced by the continent or region with which they associate themselves. Until the 1950s the official policy of the government of Emperor Haile Selassie was to emphasize that Ethiopia was part of the Middle East rather than part of Africa. Yet it was the Emperor himself who initiated the policy of re-Africanizing Ethiopia as the rest of Africa approached independence. Ethiopian self-perceptions have been becoming slowly Africanized ever since. Cultural similarities between Ethiopia and the rest of Black Africa are not any greater than cultural similarities between North Africa and the Arabian Peninsula. Nevertheless, a European decision to make Africa end at the Red Sea has decisively dis-Africanized the Arabian Peninsula, and made the natives there see themselves as West Asians rather than as North Africans.[6]

Before the parting of the Red Sea, there was the parting of Africa to create the Red Sea. Several million years ago the crust of Africa cracked and the Red Sea was born. As we indicated, this thin strip of water helped to seal the identity of whole generations of people living on both sides of it.

Yet cultural change has been struggling to heal the geological rift between Africa and Arabia. Did the Semites originate to the east or the west of the Red Sea? Are upper Ethiopians originally South Arabians? Has Islam rendered the Red Sea a culturally irrelevant boundary? Has the Arabic language made the boundary anachronistic? Is it time that the tyranny of the sea as a definer of identity was at least moderated if not overthrown?

In any case, the tyranny of the sea is in part a tyranny of European geographical prejudices. Just as European map makers could decree that on the map Europe was above Africa instead of below (an arbitrary decision in relation to the cosmos), those mapmakers could also dictate that Africa ended at the Red Sea instead of at the Persian Gulf. Is it not time that this dual tyranny of the sea and Eurocentric geography was forced to sink to the bottom?

The most difficult people to convince may well turn out to be the inhabitants of the Arabian Peninsula. They have grown to be proud of being "the Arabs of Asia" rather than "the Arabs of Africa." They are not eager to be members of the Organization of African Unity (OAU), however helpful such a move would be for the OAU's budgetary problems. Will they at least embrace the concept of Afrabia? If Emperor Haile Selassie could initiate the re-Africanization of Ethiopia, and Gamal Abdel Nasser could inaugurate the re-Africanization of Egypt, prospects for a reconsideration of the identity of the Arabian Peninsula may not be entirely bleak.

At the moment, the re-Africanization of the Arabian Peninsula is only an idea in the head of a scholar. It has yet to become a cause in the hearts of people. Yes, what a geological convulsion put asunder several million years ago, the long cultural convergence between Africanity and Arabism may indeed at long last put together again.

NOTES

An earlier version of this essay appeared in *Africa and the Sea*, ed. Jeffrey C. Stone, Proceedings of a Colloquium at the University of Aberdeen, March 1984 (Aberdeen: Aberdeen University, African Studies Group), pp. 98–104.

1. I first developed this idea in a Keynote Address to a conference on

"Africa and the Sea" sponsored by the University of Aberdeen and held at Aberdeen, Scotland, March 16–17, 1984.

2. The issue of whether the Red Sea is a legitimate boundary of Africa is also discussed in Mazrui, *The Africans: A Triple Heritage* (London: BBC Publications, and Boston: Little, Brown Press, 1986), Chapter 1.

3. C. McEvedy, *The Penguin Atlas of African History* (Harmondsworth, Middlesex: Penguin Books, 1980).

4. See R. R. Palmer in collaboration with Joel Colton, *A History of the Modern World*, 2nd ed. (New York: Knopf, 1962), p.13.

5. See Melville Herskovits' contribution to *Symposium on Africa*, Wellesley College (Wellesley College, Massachusetts, 1960), p. 16.

6. This issue also features in Ali A. Mazrui's television series, *The Africans: A Triple Heritage* (London: British Broadcasting Corporation, and Washington, D.C.: WETA, Public Broadcasting System, 1986), Programme No. 1: "The Nature of a Continent."

SEVEN

AFRABIA
AFRICA AND ARABS IN THE NEW WORLD ORDER

Let me begin this essay on African-Arab relations with two models of historic reconciliation involving other societies. The Anglo-American model traces the transition from hostility to fraternity in the relations between the people of Britain and those of the United States from the late eighteenth century to the First World War. Are there lessons to be learned which are relevant for relations between Arabs and Africans historically?

The second model of reconciliation traces the transition from enmity to friendship between the United States and Japan from 1941 into the 1990s. Are there other lessons to be learned in this Americo-Japanese model which are also pertinent for African-Arab relations in historical perspective? Let us look at these two models of reconciliation more closely.

It was of course in 1776 that the Americans started their rebellion against the British. It became the American war of independence. For at least a century the British were a people the Americans loved most to hate. This included one additional war between the Americans and the British in 1812.

Today, Great Britain is perhaps the United States' closest ally — perhaps closer than even Israel and Canada are to Washington. The wounds of 1776 and 1812 between the Americans and the British have more than just healed. A new and deeper sense of shared identity has been forged.

In 1941 Japan committed treachery and bombed Pearl Harbor without declaring war on the USA. President Franklin Roosevelt described it as "a day which will live in infamy." Americans had good reason to hate the Japanese.

In August 1945 the United States dropped atomic bombs on Hiroshima and Nagasaki. The Japanese became the first physical casualties of the nuclear age, massacred and, in many cases, maimed for generations. The Japanese had good reason to hate the Americans. And yet within less than a *single* generation the United States and Japan became great political allies, and monumental trading partners.

In 1964 a revolution occurred in Zanzibar against a government which was perceived as Arab-led and a monarchy which was perceived as Omani. Bitter bloodletting and venomous hatred occurred between Swahilized Arabs on one side and Arabized Waswahili on the other. Arabophobia in parts of East Africa reached new depths. Afrophobia in parts of the Arab world was also unmistakable.

In reality it took about a century for the Americans and the British to stop hating each other, and longer still for them to become close friends. In relations between Africans and Arabs will we also have to wait a century for the wounds of the past to heal? Is the relevant model that between the United States and Britain? Or is the relevant model that between Japan and the United States? Forgiveness between Americans and Japanese had been quick, but was it shallow? Forgiveness between Britain and the USA had been slow, but was it deep?

Forgiveness between Arabs and Africans may be somewhere between the US-British model (slow but deep) and the US-Japanese model (quick but shallow). African-Arab reconciliation may be less slow than the Anglo-American fraternity and significantly deeper than the American-Japanese reconciliation. Afro-Arab reconciliation involves not only memories of the Zanzibar revolution, but even more fundamentally, memories of Arab involvement in the slave trade in Africa. Can the pain of the past be forgotten?

Global trends in the New World Order are dictating *speed* in African-Arab reconciliation and integration. Historical continuities and geographical contiguities may lend greater *depth* to the future relationship between Africa and the Arab world. But conscious steps need to be taken in pursuit of any new forms of solidarity. Forgiving the past is one thing; forging a new future is a bigger imperative.

The ideological walls separating Indo-China from the rest of South-East Asia are beginning to fall. The ideological walls separating Eastern Europe from Western Europe have been coming down. The economic walls separating the United States, Mexico, and Canada are also coming down. Will the walls separating Africa and the Arab world also come down as part of the New World Order?

THE CONCEPT OF "AFRABIA"

The French once examined their special relationship with Africa — and came up with the concept of "Eurafrica" as a basis of special cooperation. We in turn should examine the even older special relationship between Africa and the Arab world — and call it *Afrabia*.

It is arguable that some of the walls separating Africans from Arabs are as artificial as the divisions which separated Slavs from Germans in Europe. There has been much discussion about the artificiality of the Sahara Desert as a divide between Arab Africa and Black Africa. Even more artificial is the Red Sea as a divide.

After all, the majority of the Arab people are now in the African continent. The bulk of Arab lands are located in Africa. There are more Muslims in Nigeria than there are Muslims in any Arab country, including Egypt. In other words, the Muslim population of Nigeria is larger than the Muslim population of Egypt. The African continent as a whole is in the process of becoming the first continent in the world with an absolute Muslim majority.

But Afrabia is not just a case of the spread of languages and the solidarity of religion. Whole new ethnic communities were created by this dynamic. The emergence of Cushitic groups like the Somali in the Horn of Africa are one case in point. Oman, Yemen, and Saudi Arabia were also instrumental in helping to give birth to whole new ethnic groups on the eastern seaboard of Africa. Swahili culture and the Swahili city-states captured a whole epoch in African history and legacy. Oman is central to the modern history of the Swahili heritage.

The brave peoples of Eritrea are also part of the bridge of Afrabia. Even the Berbers are a special case of Afrabia. The very name "Africa" probably originated in a Berber language, and was initially used to refer to what is now Tunisia. The continent got its name from what is now "Arab Africa." Is there a stronger argument for Afrabia?

Then there have been the migrations and movements of populations between Africa and Arabia across the centuries. There is evidence of Arab settlements on the East African coast and in the Horn of Africa well before the birth of the Prophet Muhammad. And the fact that the first great muezzin of Islam was Seyyidna Bilal, who was from the African continent, is evidence that there was an African presence in Mecca and Medina which was pre-Islamic. Bilal was there before he converted, a symbol of an older Arabian link with Africa. Afrabia is a pre-Hijjriyya phenomenon.

Islam itself is almost as old in Africa as it is in Arabia. Muslims sought religious asylum in Ethiopia during the Prophet Muhammad's early days when he and his followers were persecuted in Mecca. Archeological excavations in Eastern Africa have discovered remains of mosques which go back to the earliest decades of Islam. Islam as a factor in Afrabia does indeed go back some fourteen centuries!

There is the impact of language on Afrabia. The language with the largest number of individual speakers in the African continent is still Arabic. The most influential indigenous African languages are Swahili (Kiswahili) in East Africa and Hausa in West Africa, both of them profoundly influenced by both Arabic and Islam, a manifestation of Afrabia.

Linguistic links between Africa and Arabia are, in fact, much older than Islam. Everybody is aware that Arabic is a Semitic language, but not as many people realize that so is Amharic, the dominant indigenous language of Ethiopia. Indeed, historians are divided as to whether Semitic languages started in Africa before they crossed the Red Sea, or originated in the Arabian peninsula and later crossed over to Africa. The very uncertainties themselves are part of the reality of Afrabia. So now that we are examining the New World Order, should we not re-evaluate these old frontiers and re-define our identities?

AFRABIA AND THE NEW WORLD ORDER

In the New World Order, two processes are under way, each one seeking to redefine the nation-state. The *centrifugal* forces create fragmentation and separatism. The most dramatic examples have been the disintegration of the Soviet Union. The *centripetal* forces create bigger economic and political communities. The year 1992 was intended to witness the deeper economic integration of the European Community, probably followed by the admission of more member states before the end of the century.

In the Arab world the most serious cases of internal centrifugal fragmentation within countries are in Iraq, Lebanon, and the Sudan. Iraq faces central oppression and ethnic separatism. The Kurds and the Shiites are up in arms, sometimes literally. Lebanon has not yet healed its sectarian divisions. The Sudan is torn not only by the civil war in the South but also by new religious and political tensions in the North. Centrifugal fragmentation in Africa includes not only the Sudan but also ethnic separatism in Ethiopia, Liberia, Somalia, Senegal, and — with lesser intensity — even in Nigeria.

In addition to national centrifugal tendencies, there are wider regional forces of fragmentation in both Africa and the Arab world. The Gulf crisis of 1990–91 was one of the most divisive events in recent Arab history. One unthinkable scenario occurred in August 1990 when one Arab country completely swallowed up another — the brief conquest of Kuwait by Iraq. The other unthinkable occurred in 1991, when Arab bombs and Arab missiles bombed fellow Arab cities. The wounds of division have yet to heal in the Arab world.

Africa did not enter the 1990s as deeply divided at the regional level as the Arab world did. But Africa's economic situation in the 1990s has been particularly severe, and the political will to pursue African unity has been weakened even further. Moreover, two happy developments in Africa during 1990–1991 have had the unintended consequences of diluting Pan-African commitment. From almost every point of view, the end of apartheid is good news for Africa and the human race. But the struggle against apartheid for so long had been a great unifying force in Africa, at least as compelling as the struggle against Zionism has been in the Arab world. While Zionism is still powerful and defiant, apartheid has crumbled. Pan-Africanism may have to pay a price for its own success. The end of apartheid could deprive Pan-Africanism of a major unifying force.

The other happy trend in Africa in the 1990s has been the struggle for greater democracy — from Dar-as-Salaam to Dakar, from Lusaka to Lagos, from Algiers to Kinshasa. African rulers are being called upon to become more accountable. While the pro-democracy movement in Africa has been an exciting development, it has focused the minds of citizens on domestic issues in each country rather than on continental issues of unification. The regional effect of democratic activism has, on the whole, been centrifugal — at least in the short run.

But while Africa and the Arab world are for the time being each internally divided within itself in terms of contemporary politics, the two overlapping regions, already cross-culturally linked by the forces of history and geography, are also being linked by the forces of an emerging *global apartheid*. It is to this new feature of Afrabia that we must now turn.

AFRABIA AND GLOBAL APARTHEID

The emergence of global apartheid is one wider trend worth watching. The White world is closing ranks in spite of the disintegration of the Soviet Union and Yugoslavia. Pan-Europeanism is reaching new levels of solidarity from the Urals to the Pyrenees Mountains. In North America a new mega-economy is emerging, encompassing the United States, Canada, and possibly Mexico.

But when you look closely at this New World Order, two disturbing trends emerge. Arabs and Muslims are disproportionately the frontline military victims of the new order. Blacks are disproportionately the frontline economic victims of the emerging global apartheid.

The military victimization of Muslims includes

(a) Permitting nuclearization of Israel but attempting to veto nuclear power in the Muslim world.

(b) Subsidizing Israel's military capability.

(c) US bombing of Beirut under Reagan.

(d) US bombing of Tripoli, Bengazi and Libya under Reagan.

(e) Shooting down of Iranian civilian aircraft in the Gulf and killing all on board under Reagan.

(f) Bush's decision to save time rather than lives in the 1990–1991 Gulf crisis, leading to the death of hundreds of thousands of people.

(g) Potential second strike against Libya.

Two-thirds of the casualties of US military activity since the Vietnam war have been Muslims — amounting to upwards of half a million lives. The Muslim victims have been primarily Palestinians, Iraqis, Lebanese, Libyans, Iranians, and others.

If Muslims have been frontline military victims, Blacks have been frontline economic victims of the New World Order. The economic victimization of Blacks includes

(a) Continuing support for incompetent and corrupt African regimes.

(b) The terrors of economic structural adjustment under the IMF and World Bank in the Black world.

(c) The injustices of the wider world of commodity prices against fragile African economies.

(d) The huge Black underclass in the United States, adding AIDS and drugs to poverty, crime, and social maladjustment.

(e) The rise of racism in Europe, e.g., in France, Germany and Belgium.

(f) The US Supreme Court's move to the Right, hurting gains in civil rights and minority advances.

The New World Order runs the risk of creating a disproportionate number of more dead Muslims, while it also runs the risk of perpetuating a disproportionate number of more poor Blacks.

Afrabia is potentially part of the answer. Reconciliation between Arabs and Africans will continue to be needed. Let us hope that it will not be as slow as the reconciliation between Britain and the USA after their 1776 and 1812 confrontations. It is hoped that the Afro-Arab entente will also not be as shallow as the cordiality between Japan and the United States. Africans and Arabs need to learn the lessons of speed from Japan and the USA, and the lessons of fraternity from the older experience of Britain and the United States.

We have had Arab institutions designed to help Africa, like the Arab Bank for African Development. We have not had African institutions designed to help Arabs outside Africa. The innovations needed would break the mould of Arabs always as donors and Africans always as recipients of foreign help. Afrabian institutions would pool the resources of both relatively wealthy Arabs and relatively wealthy Africans and address those resources to the needs of the poor in both Africa and the Arab world. Afrabian institutions would be under the joint control of both Arabs and Africans. At least it would be conceivable for African money to help poor Arab countries like Yemen or even Jordan, just as Arab money has sometimes helped even relatively well-endowed African countries like Zaire [now Congo].

Now that South Africa has achieved majority rule, will such experimentation take place? Will the first foreign aid from Blacks to Arabs come from postapartheid South Africa? This is at least one plausible scenario. Now that South Africa is both liberated and stabilized, there will be a need for a new summit meeting of Arab and African heads of state and governments, to take genuine stock of "the New World Order." It is to be hoped that high on that agenda for an Afro-Arab summit will be the creation of new and innovative Afrabian mechanisms of cooperation. As the Afro-Arab past is forgotten, a new Afro-Arab future can thus be forged. It can only be a minimum defense against the dangers of global apartheid.

CONCLUSION

In the New World Order it is not only Europe that is experiencing the collapse of artificial walls of disunity. It is not just the United States, Mexico, and Canada that will create a mega-community. It is not just Southeast Asia that will learn to readmit Indo-China to the fold. Also momentous in its historical possibilities is the likely emergence of Afrabia, linking languages, religions and identities across both the Sahara Desert and the Red Sea in a historical fusion of Arabism and Africanity.

But will Afrabia be a case of rich Arabs in a union with poor Africans? Actually, there are rich countries in Africa, poor countries in the Arab world, and vice versa. Africa's mineral resources are more varied than those of the Arab world, but African countries like Zaire [Congo] have been more economically mismanaged than almost any country in the Arab world.

Afrabia of the future will include postapartheid South Africa, richer and more industrialized than almost any other society in either Africa or the Arab world. The Afrabia of the future may be led economically by the oil-rich and the mineral-rich economies, but in a new order where equity and fairness will count as much between societies as they have sometimes done within enlightened individual countries. Amen.

NOTE

An earlier version of this essay appeared in *Ufuhamu* (UCLA) 20, no. 3 (Fall 1992): 51–62.

PART III

THE TRIPLE HERITAGE

AFRICA'S TRIPLE HERITAGE

Two forces taught me about Africa's triple heritage — my own personal experience and the ideas of Kwame Nkrumah. Nkrumah's book, *Consciencism*, identified three elements in the African personality: indigenous, Islamic, and what he called "Euro-Christian" contributions. His theory of "Consciencism" was in fact a search for a synthesis of these three forces.

Partly because of Nkrumah's recognition of a tripartite conscience in Africa, his own approach to Pan-Africanism was trans-Saharan. Ghana's founder president refused to recognize the Sahara Desert as a divide between "Arab Africa" and "Black Africa." He hosted meetings which were truly *continental*. Although not a Muslim himself, Nkrumah recognized the cultural and Islamic continuities between North Africa and Africa south of the Sahara. But intellectually what Nkrumah had done for me was to confirm the lessons of an earlier teacher in my life — personal experience itself. I was born and brought up in Mombasa, one of the old Islamic city-states of East Africa. A historic landmark in the old town is Fort Jesus, from which the Mazrui family once ruled the city. Not far from the Fort is the old Supreme Court of Mombasa where Sheikh Al-Amin bin Ali Mazrui used to hear appeal cases under the Shari'a. He was Kenya's chief judge of appeal under Islamic law. Sheikh Al-Amin was my father. At the time of my birth and coming of age in Mombasa, Kenya was under British colonial rule. After the death of my father, I went on to study at Manchester and Oxford rather than at Al-Azhar (even though he would have preferred that I had studied at Al-Azhar) and that effectively widened my exposure to the Western branch of my own triple heritage. How much of a product of Africa's triple heritage am I? Am I a walking embodiment of that complex cultural mixture? Of course, it is not just my own identity that is affected by the Triple Heritage, but any identity in Africa as a whole. Who are the Africans? This heritage encompasses the full diversity of African identities and life-styles, including two commonly discussed and often romanticized types of African civilization: complex kingdoms and empires on one side and decentralized "tribes without rules" on the other.

If there is a diversity of differing physical features among African groups, are these groups "races"? If there is a diversity of cultural differences among African groups, are these groups "tribes"? Where does Arabness end and Africanness begin? Is North Africa a southern extension of Europe, a western extension of Arabia, or a northern extension of the rest of Africa? Have Africans been trapped into thinking of their continent as a "black continent" when in fact Africa is nearer to Asia as a *multicolored region* than to Europe as primarily a continent of the *White* races? What are the myths of origin of African peoples? I am fascinated by the different myths of origin that Africa has produced — from the myth of Kintu among the Baganda to the legend of Solomon and Sheba in Ethiopia. Along the Nile Valley I have witnessed and identified different racial and cultural types as Black Africanness merges with Arabness almost in the transition from cataract to cataract. There is a diversity of physical features as the Nile meanders along its way towards the Mediterranean. The Blue Nile traverses the territory of an ancient triple heritage — indigenous, Semitic and Greco-Roman legacies. The White Nile traverses the territory of the modern triple heritage — indigenous, Islamic, and Western legacies. The two triple heritages coalesce as the two Niles merge.

The BBC/PBS filming and travelling introduced me again to some powerful examples of the triple heritage in action: African pilgrims going to Mecca in Western jets, Nigerian Muslim Emirs holding court, Zanzibar teenagers at a disco in a sixteenth century fort. In Ethiopia I found old evidence of indigenous, Judeo-Christian, Greco-Roman, Islamic, as well as modern Western influences: Greek coins; obelisks and inscriptions; an orthodox Christian ceremony which dates back to the fourth century; settlements of Falasha Jews, some of whom believe they are one of the lost tribes of Israel — we filmed them before their exodus to Israel. Other illustrations of the triple heritage in everyday life have included traffic jams caused by Friday prayers and overflowing mosques, the triple heritage of dress culture in Kaduna or Lamu, motorcyclists in flowing African robes and wearing reflector sunglasses. Western technology co-exists with, militates against, and sometimes reinforces the Triple Heritage—Western amplifiers broadcast the Mauledi Festival in Lamu; the Kaduna satellite station holds midday prayers; Western gadgets on sale in Western markets; President Numeiry pours Western liquor into the River Nile; the laundry, bath, and car-wash in the same river in Mopti, Mali.

What about the triple heritage in politics? Shehu Shagari, a Muslim President of Africa's largest country, once instituted a US constitution, used a US advertising agency to help his reelection campaign, and submitted his Cabinet to an American-style Senatorial scrutiny. Today the triple heritage of sport includes Nigerian Muslim aristocrats in their polo tournaments, Westernized Africans playing lawn tennis or golf, enthusiastic islanders watching a bull fight in Pemba, and screaming and laughing fans at an African soccer match, wearing the full diversity of Africa's dress culture. There is even a triple heritage of time — the Gregorian calendar co-exists not only with the Eastern Orthodox Calendar in Ethiopia, but also with the Islamic Calendar and with indigenous methods of keeping time. The lunar year in Nigeria decides when is the Festival of Eid el-Fitr; the solar calendar decides when is Independence Day. In Kiswahili 700 hours (7 a.m.) is called *saa moja* (one o'clock) — the day begins at sunrise, not at midnight. Saturday is the first day of the week in Kiswahili *(Juma Mosi)*. Why?

Then there is the triple heritage of the gender question. Africa is one of the last bastions of matrilinealism in the world — descent through the mother rather than the father. Is the battle being lost, given that both Islam and Westernism are so uncompromisingly patrilineal? The Jews are matrilineal; the Arabs are patrilineal. The Semites introduced some of the earliest complications. On the issue of female identity, Westernism has been the most sexist. Before the advent of the West neither married Muslim women nor married indigenously traditional African women necessarily gave up their names and adopted their husbands' family names. The whole concept of "Mrs. so-and-so" or "Madame so-and-so" is primarily Western. African wives and Muslim wives had originally kept their own family names after marriage. Just as the male of the species is a "Mr." whether he is married or not, the female of the species in Africa was a kind of "Ms." before the formula was ever invented in the West.

Christianity and Islam more generally are Semitic religions with deep roots in Judaism. Considering the impact of ancient Egypt on the history of monotheism and the Mosaic legacy, are the new Semitic religions bringing a new God into Africa? Or is the old monotheistic God of Akhenaten, the Egyptian Pharaoh, returning to Africa in a new manifestation of one-ness? It can be said that Akhenaten was the first monotheist.

We have explored linkages between the ancient triple heritage (indigenous traditions, Semitic strands, and Greco-Roman influences) and the modern triple heritage (indigenous, Islamic, and wider Western cultural forces). The Semitic tradition insists on a dichotomy — one cannot be both a Christian and a Muslim. The indigenous African tradition encourages mixture — most African Muslims retain links with indigenous religious practices; so do most African Christians, both north and south of the Sahara.

In some ways Africa is a bewildering mosaic of cultures in a single continent. They used to call the United States a "melting pot" of different nationalities. On the whole, Africa is not a continent of immigrant peoples (though there are exceptions); it is more a continent of immigrant cultures. Africa stands a better chance than America of becoming a true "melting pot" of ideas, of traditions, but it takes time. I have presumed to carry Kwame Nkrumah's intellectual torch one stage further. He called Africa's three forces "Consciencism." I prefer to call the whole phenomenon "Africa's Triple Heritage." Next to Nkrumah, my other teacher has been my own life itself, my personal experience:

"Fool, said my Muse to me;
Look in thy heart — and write."

NOTE

A longer version of this essay appeared as "Africa's Triple Heritage and I," in *Africa Events* (London) 2, no. 7/8 (July/August, 1986): 34–38.

EIGHT

ISLAM AND AFROCENTRICITY
THE TRIPLE HERITAGE SCHOOL

Is Afrocentricity incompatible with Islam? Or can both be part of a wider concept which might be called *Africa's triple heritage* — synthesizing Africanity, Islam, and the influence of the West in Africa? The answer to these questions lies not only in Africa as a continent but in *Global Africa*, that is, in Africa and its varied worldwide Diaspora. This essay is also in part about the perception of these three civilizations — Africa, Islam, and the West — by three particular political writers: Edward Wilmot Blyden (1832–1912), Kwame Nkrumah (1909–1972), and the present author, Ali A. Mazrui (1933–).

In discussing Ali Mazrui I am both the observer and the observed, both the story and the story-teller. I have decided to focus on the story, and discuss Ali Mazrui in the third person. From now on Ali Mazrui becomes a "he" rather than an "I."

Edward Blyden came to the triple heritage from a Christian point of entry. Blyden's upbringing was indeed Protestant, but distant from both Africa and Islam. He was born in the West Indies and was later ordained a minister of the Presbyterian Church in Liberia. Kwame Nkrumah approached the triple heritage from a Christian upbringing and an African environment, having been born in 1909 in the colonial Gold Coast. He did consider training for the priesthood early in his career, but he later became a self-styled "non-denominational Christian." Edward W. Blyden was a candidate in the presidential election in Liberia in 1885 — and lost. Kwame Nkrumah did become Ghana's prime minister (1957–1958) and president (1958–1966). Both leaders developed ideas about an "African personality" which was responsive to Islam. Was this a marriage between Afrocentricity and Islamophilia? Ali A. Mazrui was the only one of the three authors who approached the triple heritage from an Islamic point of entry. Like Blyden and Nkrumah, Mazrui was originally intended to train for a religious vocation. But in Mazrui's case the religion was Islam rather than Christianity. His father was the Chief Kadhi (Chief Islamic Justice) of Kenya who had intended the young Ali to follow in the father's footsteps as an Islamic jurist. The father's death when Ali was only fourteen years old tilted the balance in Ali's triple heritage. Ali Mazrui ended up at Oxford University for his D.Phil. rather than at Al-Azhar University in Cairo.

I. WHAT IS ISLAMOPHILE AFROCENTRICITY?

In their own very different ways, each of these three thinkers combined Afrocentricity with a sympathetic response to Islam. Together they are part of a school of Afrocentricity which accepts Islam as an ally of Africanity, rather than a rival or a threat. Islamophile Afrocentricity in the African Diaspora has included people of African descent who have converted to Islam partly for reasons of racial dignity or Black nationalism. In the United States, such people during this century have included outstanding political leaders like Malcolm X (Al-Hajj Malik Al-Shabbazz) and Louis Farakkhan, and outstanding sporting figures like Muhammad Ali (formerly Cassius Clay). In South Africa in the 1990s Islam began to make inroads into the Black townships after centuries of being confined to the Malay, Indian and "Colored" sectors of the country's multi-ethnic population. The election in Malawi of Bakili Muluzi as the first Muslim president in southern Africa has been noted by south African Muslims with considerable religious pride. In such sectors of the population Islam is once again viewed as an ally of Afrocentricity rather than as a rival or a threat.

A nineteenth century black pioneer in Islamophile Afrocentricity was indeed Edward Blyden, the Diaspora African who returned home to Africa and became a precursor of such doctrines as Negritude, Pan-Africanism, and Afrocentricity. Born in St. Thomas, the Dutch Virgin Islands, in August 1832, Edward Wilmot Blyden encountered his worst racial experiences in the United States when he went to seek education there in 1850. Because of his race, he suffered a number of humiliations, including rejection by the Presbyterian Theological College on racial grounds. It was in December 1850 that Blyden migrated to Liberia and to a life which was to deepen his Afrocentricity, on one side, and to arouse his interest in Islam, on the other. And yet, by a strange twist of fate, his initial entry into Afrocentricity and Islam was through Christian missionary education. Just as later nationalists like Kwame Nkrumah, Julius K. Nyerere, and Robert Mugabe were products of missionary schools, so was Edward Blyden. In Liberia he registered at Alexander High School, a newly established Presbyterian institution. The head of the school was Reverend D. A. Wilson, a graduate of Princeton Theological Seminary. So profound was the impact of the school upon Blyden, and so rapid was his own intellectual progress that in 1858, at the age of only 26, Edward Blyden was ordained a Presbyterian minister and became the principal of Alexander High School.

Paradoxically, although Ali Mazrui as a Muslim believes that Islam is the right religion for himself, it was Blyden who came closer to saying that Islam was the right religion for Africa. Blyden was far more forthright than Mazrui in praising Islam as compared with either African traditional religion or Christian practices:

> Islam in Africa counts in its ranks the most energetic and enterprising tribes. It claims as its adherents the only people who have any form of civil polity or bond of social organization. . . . Its laws regulate the most powerful kingdoms — Futah, Masina, Hausa, Bornou, Waday, Darfur, Kordofan, Senaar . . . it commands respect among all Africans wherever it is known, even where the people have not submitted to the sway of the Qur'an.[1]

II. THE SYMBOLISM OF EGYPT: PHARAONIC AND ISLAMIC

Islamophilia and Afrocentricity are at their most ambivalent on the issue of Egypt. Much of Afrocentric literature at large reveres ancient Egypt not only as the genesis of grand civilizations but also as the ultimate triumph of Black creativity. Most Afrocentrists regard ancient Egypt as having been a Black civilization. Today's Egypt is Muslim, a product of the Arab conquest of the seventh cen-

tury. Islamophobe Afrocentrists regard the arrival of Islam as a
negation of its Africanity — although the Arab conquest had in fact
been preceded by the Greek, Roman, and Byzantine conquests of
Egypt. Islamophobe Afrocentrists view Arabized Egypt as a betrayal
of the Afrocentric glory of Pharaonic Egypt.

What about Islamophile Afrocentrists like Edward Blyden? Blyden simply separated his sympathy for Islam from his fascination
with ancient Egypt. Blyden quotes with approval an author of an
Arabic and English Dictionary who, under the Arabic word *kusur*
(palaces) noted the following:

> The ruins of Thebes, that ancient and celebrated town, deserve to
> be visited, as just those heaps of ruins, loved by the Nile, are all
> that remain of the opulent cities that gave luster to Ethiopia. It
> was there that a people, since forgotten, discovered the elements
> of science and art, at a time when all other men were barbarous,
> and when a race, now regarded as the refuse of society, explored
> among the phenomena of nature those civil and religious systems
> which have since held mankind in awe.[2]

While Edward Blyden discusses the Blackness of ancient Egypt
and the multi-colored Islamicity of modern Egypt without attempting to reconcile the two, Ali Mazrui opts for the solution that
ancient Egypt was "African but not necessarily Black." Mazrui
argues that it was a Eurocentric fallacy to insist that ancient Egyptians had to have been Black in order to have been African. After all,
nobody insists that the people of Madras in India (black population)
have to be the same colour as the people of Hunan in China (yellow
in colour) for them all to be Asians.[3] Blyden and Mazrui both discussed ancient and modern Egypt as theoretical issues but Kwame
Nkrumah brought them into his own home: he married an Egyptian Coptic woman, probably a Coptic descendant of ancient Egyptians. Nkrumah's marriage was widely interpreted as a matrimonial
re-affirmation of his trans-Saharan Pan-Africanism.[4] It was almost
like a dynastic marriage between Africa north and south of the
Sahara. Was this a case of Pan-Africanism without Afrocentricity?[5]

Blyden was born a Diaspora Black, but became a citizen of continental Africa. Mazrui was born in continental Africa but became a
resident of the Diaspora. Their lives prepared them for trans-
Atlantic Pan-African commitment. Blyden went to the extent of
preaching a "Back to Africa" imperative to Black Americans, in the

literal sense of encouraging them to migrate to Liberia: in 1862, Blyden was mandated by the government of Liberia to try to interest American Blacks to return to ancestral Africa. Mazrui's concept of "Back to Africa," which features in many of his works, was a *cultural* imperative — preaching the case for cultural re-Africanization both in Africa and in the Diaspora.

Kwame Nkrumah was an intermediate category. He was born in Africa, briefly took up residence in the Diaspora, and then returned to his continental homeland. He graduated from Lincoln University, Pennsylvania, with a B.A. in 1939 and a B.Theol. in 1942, and obtained further graduate qualifications from the University of Pennsylvania in 1942 and 1943. His years in the United States had a profound impact on his Pan-Africanism and the style of his Afrocentricity. In his autobiography he identified Marcus Garvey as one of the two deepest intellectual influences on his ideological development. Garvey was, of course, the "Back to Africa" Black nationalist from Jamaica who galvanized African-Americans into a race-conscious movement in the years between the two world wars. Both Nkrumah and Garvey were trans-Atlantic Pan-Africanists.[6] Where does Islam fit into this Pan-African equation? How does it affect trans-Atlantic Pan-Africanism?

III. AFROCENTRIC ISLAM AND ISLAMIC AFRICANITY

In December 1992, Mazrui spent about seven hours in the company of the heavyweight boxing champion, Muhammad Ali ("The Greatest"). They were both in Philadelphia helping to raise funds for Somalia. The sponsoring agency for the fund raising was an African-American Muslim organization, Masjidullah. This was clearly a case of trans-Atlantic Pan-Africanism. But although the main mission in Philadelphia was helping Somalia, Muhammad Ali in retirement days had one additional role on almost all public occasions. He was a devoted, if quiet, missionary for the Islamic faith. Fans who flocked to him for autographs were handed brochures and leaflets introducing them to the tenets of Islam. The brochures and leaflets were indeed autographed by Muhammad Ali himself, and were sometimes accompanied by a signed photograph of the boxer in the ring. One important target for Muhammad Ali's missionary activity was the penitentiary of the United States where many Black folk languished in either misery or rage — or both. Islam provided a potentially creative purposefulness to that rage. Islam is a civilization of utter sobriety (no alcohol, no drugs, no cheap indulgence). It is a religion which is aghast at the corrupt laxity and indiscipline of the rich, and not merely censorious of the lapses of the poor. Malcolm X was an angry, destitute man converted to Islam behind bars. Mike Tyson more recently was an angry boxing millionaire converted to Islam in a quest for answers. Was Afrocentricity in alliance with Islam?

By a poetic twist of destiny, Islam did first arrive in the Americas in chains nearly four centuries ago. It came with enslaved West African Muslims. Islam now provides the hope of liberation to some of the descendants of enslaved Africans in the Americas. Islam can become Afrocentric; Africanity can become Islamic. Among Diaspora Africans of the Western hemisphere generally there are, in fact, two spiritual routes towards re-Africanization. One route is through Pan-Islam, the transition chosen by Elijah Muhammad and Malcolm X (or Al-Hajj Malik Al-Shabbazz). The other is the route directly through Pan-Africanism, the transition chosen by Marcus Garvey and the Rastafari Movement. The Pan-Islamic route has been particularly striking in Black America, where conversions to the Muslim faith are still on the ascendant.[7] The direct Pan-African route has often been led by Caribbean Africans, either in the West Indies or in North America.

One question which arises is, Why has Islam made much more progress among North American Blacks than among Blacks in Blyden's beloved West Indies? A second question is, Why does African traditional religion (or beliefs rooted in sacred Africanity) appear to be more visible in the new Caribbean after Blyden than among Africans of North America? One major variable was the tendency of African Americans to equate Brown with Black. No sharp distinction was made in the Black American paradigm between brown Arabs and black Africans. Mazrui's own dual ancestry as Afro-Arab would feel at home in this paradigm. Indeed, until the second half of the twentieth century, almost all "Colored people" in North America, whether they came from Africa or Asia or elsewhere, were treated with comparable contempt. When someone like W. E. B. DuBois (born American, died Ghanaian) argued that it was not Blacks who were a "minority" but Whites, he had added up the teeming millions of Asians with the millions of Africans to give the Colored races a massive majority in the global population.

If the transition from brown Asian to black African was so smooth in the Black American paradigm, the transition from Africanity to Arabness continues to be even easier. Indeed, of all the religions associated with Asia, the one which is the most Afro-Asian is indeed Islam. The oldest surviving Islamic academies are actually located on the African continent, including Al-Azhar University in Cairo and Fez in Morocco. The Muslim academy of Timbuktoo in what is today Mali is remembered by many Pan-Africanists with pride. In Nigeria there are more Muslims than there are Muslims in any Arab country, including the largest Arab country in population, Egypt. In 1981, Nigerian Muslims comprised the largest contingent worldwide making the pilgrimage (Hajj) to Mecca and Medina. On the other hand, there are more Arabs in Africa as a whole than in Asia. Indeed, demographically, two thirds of the Arab world lies in the African continent. Given, then, the tendency of the Black American paradigm to draw no sharp distinction between being Black and being Colored, Islam's Africanness was not too diluted by its Arab origins. Again, this was congenial to Ali Mazrui in ancestral terms. Elijah Muhammad, Malcolm X, and Louis Farakkhan have sometimes equated Islamization with Africanization. North American Black Muslims have seen Mecca as a port of call on the way back to the African heritage, as well as a stage on the way back towards God.

Islam in the post-Blyden Caribbean has had moments of great drama. Perhaps the greatest was in Trinidad in 1990 when Muslim reformers held the whole Cabinet (including the Prime Minister) hostage for about a week.[8] Nevertheless, Islam in the Caribbean has been handicapped by two factors. First, race consciousness in the Caribbean does not as readily equate Black with Brown as it has done historically in the United States. The Caribbean historical experience was based on a racial hierarchy (different shades of stratification) rather than racial dichotomy (a polarized divide between White and Colored). Arabs in the Caribbean racial paradigm therefore belonged to a different pecking order from Africans. Indeed, Lebanese and Syrians were more likely to be counted as White rather than Black. Because of that, the Arab origins of Islam were sometimes seen as being in conflict with Islam's African credentials. Despite his Caribbean origins, Edward Blyden would have been confused by that. Moreover, the Caribbean has a highly visible East Indian population, a large proportion of whom are Muslims. When Mazrui gave a lecture in Georgetown, Guyana, in 1988 on the subject of "Islam in Africa," the overwhelming majority of his audience were not Afro-Guyanese (eager to learn more about Africa) but Indo-Guyanese (eager to learn more about Islam). In the Black population in Guyana and Trinidad, there is a tendency to see Islam neither as African nor as Arab, but as Indian. The result is a much slower pace of Islamic conversions among Caribbean Africans than among African-Americans. Most Caribbean Blacks are unlikely to see the Muslim holy city of Mecca as a spiritual port of call on the way back to the cultural womb of Africa. On the contrary, Mecca is more likely to be perceived by the majority as a stage of cultural refuelling on the way to the Indian sub-continent.

In contrast, indigenous African religiosity has often prospered better in the post-Blyden Caribbean than in Black America. Why? One reason is that cultural nationalism in Black America is rooted in *romantic gloriana* rather than *romantic primitivism*. "Gloriana" takes pride in the complex civilizations of ancient Africa; primitivism takes pride in the simplicity of rural African village life. While this idealization of simplicity can capture the Caribbean mind both before and after Blyden, it seldom inspires the imagination of the African-American. The dominant North American culture is based on the premise of "bigger, better, and more beautiful." African American rebellion against Anglo racism therefore seeks to prove that Africa has produced civilizations in the past which were "as big and beautiful" as anything constructed by the White man.

In this cultural atmosphere of gloriana, African indigenous religion appears capable of being mistaken for "primitivism." Indigenous African rituals appear rural and village-derived. While Yoruba religion does have an impressive following in parts of the United States, and its rituals are often rigorously observed, the general predisposition of the African-American paradigm of nationalism is afraid of appearing to be "primitive." The Islamic option is regarded by African-Americans as a worthier rival to the Christianity of the White man. Parts of the Qur'an seem to be an improvement upon the White man's Old Testament. The Islamic civilization once exercised dominion and power over European populations. Historically, Islamic culture refined what we now call "Arabic numerals," invented algebra, developed the zero, pushed forward the frontiers of science, designed and built legendary edifices from Al-Hambra in Spain to the Taj Mahal in India. Black America's paradigm of romantic gloriana is more comfortable with such a record of achievement than with the more subtle dignity of Yoruba, Igbo, or Kikuyu traditional religion.

There is a related difference to bear in mind. Cultural nationalism in Black America often looks once again to ancient Egypt for inspiration, perceiving Pharaonic Egypt as a Black civilization. Caribbean Black nationalism has shown a tendency to look to Ethiopia. The Egyptian route to Black cultural validation again emphasizes complexity and gloriana. On the other hand, the Ethiopian route to Black cultural validation can be biblical and austere. Thinkers like Nkrumah and Mazrui are caught in between Egyptophilia and Ethiophilia. The most influential Ethiopic movement in the African Diaspora has become the Rastafari movement, with its Jamaican roots. Named after Haile Selassie's older, titled designation — Ras (Prince) Tafari were the title and name of Haile Selassie I before his coronation as Emperor of Ethiopia — the Jamaican movement evolved into a distinctive way of life, often austere. Curiously enough, the movement's original deification of the Emperor of Ethiopia was more Egyptian than Abyssinian. The fusion of Emperor with God-head was almost pharaonic. The ancient Kings of Egypt built the pyramids as alternative abodes. The divine monarchs did not really die when they ceased to breath; they had merely moved to a new address. (To die was, in fact, to change one's address and modify one's life style.) In this sense the original theology of the Rastafari movement was a fusion of Egyptianism and pre-Biblical Ethiopianism. The resulting life style of the Rastas, on the other hand, has been closer to romantic simplicity than to romantic gloriana. In North America the Rasta style is still more likely to appeal to people of Caribbean origin than to long-standing African-Americans, with their grander paradigm of cultural pride.

Pan-Africanism and Pan-Islamism are still two alternative routes towards the African heritage. After all, Islam did first arrive in the Americas in chains, brought to the Western hemisphere by West African slaves. In reality the family under slavery was better able to preserve its African pride than to protect its Islamic identity. Slavery damaged both the legacy of African culture and the legacy of Islam among the imported Black captives. But for quite a while Islam in the Diaspora was destroyed more completely than was Africanity. But now Islamization and Africanization in North America are perceived as alternative spiritual routes to the cultural bosom of the ancestral continent. It remains to be seen whether the twenty first century will see a similar equilibrium in Blyden's Caribbean as the search continues for more authentic cultural and spiritual paradigms to sustain the Global Africa of tomorrow.[9]

IV. BETWEEN ARABISM AND AFROCENTRICITY

It was in his book *Consciencism* that Nkrumah most explicitly addressed the triple heritage of African culture, Islam, and what he called "Euro-Christianity." For Nkrumah the biggest challenge for African philosophy was how to synthesize these three very different traditions of thought. Nkrumah's concept of consciencism was the nearest approximation to my concept of "the Triple Heritage" — a search for an African synthesis of three distinct civilizations.[10]

Nkrumah groped for a principle of compassionate ecumenicalism:

> With true independence regained . . . a new harmony needs to be forged, a harmony that will allow the combined presence of traditional Africa, Islamic Africa and Euro-Christian Africa, so that this presence is in tune with the original humanist principles underlying African society. Our society is not the old society, but a new society enlarged by Islamic and Euro-Christian influences.

He urged a new synthesis of these legacies to produce what he called "Philosophical Consciencism":

> The theoretical basis for an ideology whose aim shall be to contain the African experience of Islamic and Euro-Christian presence as well as the experience of traditional African society, and, by gestation, employ them for the harmonious growth and development of that society.[11]

Nkrumah embodied both African and Western civilizations, but his closest African allies outside Ghana were often Muslims. When the Casablanca group of radical African leaders was formed in 1961, Kwame Nkrumah was the only non-Muslim among them. The others were the Heads of State of Egypt, Guinea, Mali, Morocco, and the Algerian Government-in-Exile at the time. The Casablanca group was only disbanded after the Organization of African Unity (OAU) was formed in May 1963. When Nkrumah attempted to form a West African union, his partners were Guinea (Conakry) and

Mali, both Muslim countries. None of Ghana's Christian neighbors in West Africa were interested in Nkrumah's Pan-African gestures. After Nkrumah was overthrown in a military coup in February 1966, he turned for refuge to his old comrade-in-arms, Ahmed Sékou Touré of Guinea. Sékou Touré's regime was secular, but he lived to be a chairman of the worldwide Organization of the Islamic Conference (OIC). Nkrumah spent the last years of his life among Muslims in Guinea. As for the nature of his Pan-Africanism, it was not only trans-Atlantic but also trans-Saharan. Nkrumah regarded the Arabs of Africa as fellow Africans, and was outraged by French nuclear tests in the Algerian part of the Sahara in the late 1950s and early 1960s. He condemned the tests as an affront against the whole of Africa. If Ali Mazrui was the living embodiment of the triple heritage personally, Kwame Nkrumah practiced his "philosophical consciencism" in his foreign policy and in many other aspects of his life.

Let us conclude with the role of Arabic in Global Africa and how it has touched the lives of our three thinkers. Edward Blyden's interest in Islam was aroused partly because he was concerned about religion and partly because Blyden was a linguist and philologist who became curious about the Arabic language. He spent three months in Egypt, Lebanon, and Syria in 1866, partly in order to improve his command of Arabic. At that time Blyden was already professor of classics at Liberia College and wanted to introduce classical Arabic into his department there. By 1992 African-American Muslims were claiming Blyden for Islam. Was Blyden secretly converted to the divine message transmitted by the Prophet Muhammad? Was Blyden's Muslim name Abd-ul-Karim? His Islamophilia combined with his reputation as a kind of nineteenth-century Bilal had earned him not only the admiration of Blacks but also the admiration of Muslims in the Diaspora. In 1992 Dr. Khalid Abdullah Tariq Al-Mansour, an African-American Muslim, issued a special edition of Blyden's book, *Christianity, Islam and the Negro Race*, which virtually claimed Blyden for Black Islam.[12]

If Blyden was the nineteenth-century Bilal, who was the original Bilal in any case? Let us allow Blyden to tell us about Bilal:

> The eloquent Azan, or "Call to Prayer" which to this day summons at the same hours millions of the human race to their devotions, was first uttered by a Negro, Bilal by name, whom

Mohammed, in obedience to a dream, appointed the first Muezzin or Crier. And it has been remarked that even Alexander the Great is in Asia an unknown personage by the side of this honored Negro.[13]

Bilal, probably of Ethiopian origin, was the eloquent voice of prayer to fellow Muslims during the Prophet Muhammad's own lifetime. Blyden became a sympathetic, eloquent voice in favor of Islam addressing non-Muslims in the nineteenth century. Blyden did not call Muslim believers to prayer but rather he called believers of all religions to the imperative of tolerance. Blyden was a different kind of Bilal.

As for the Arabic language, all Muslims in global Africa have to learn at least parts of the Qur'an for prayer. To that extent Edward Blyden was blazing a trail for Diaspora Africans — the impressive effort of self-taught Arabic. Mazrui's relationship to the Arabic language is paradoxical. So is Nkrumah's. Mazrui is an African whose ancestry includes native speakers of Arabic. Nkrumah is an African whose descendants include native speakers of Arabic. In Africa as a whole the Arabic language has stimulated either the birth or the enrichment of African languages. Languages like Swahili, Hausa, Somali, and Wolof would have been almost inconceivable without Arabo-Islamic stimulation. In the African Diaspora it is less languages than concepts and names which have been stimulated by Arabic and related languages. Concepts like *ujamaa* (familyhood), *uhuru* (freedom), *imani* (faith) are a few of the cardinal points of Global African solidarity stimulated by the Arabic language. Then there are so many Muslim names in the United States which are regarded as Afrocentric. They include Karim Abdul Jabbar but also such names as Shahid, Jamal, Amina and others which are adopted by African-Americans regardless of religion.

V. CONCLUSION

Although Ali Mazrui was the one to coin the term "Africa's triple heritage," in reality he was standing on the shoulders of giants. His precursors have included historical figures as diverse as Edward W. Blyden on one side, and Kwame Nkrumah on the other. Believers in Africa's triple heritage regard Islam as an ally of Africanity rather than as a rival or threat. They accept Islamophilia as being compatible with Afrocentricity. The Western legacy, on other hand, tends to be underplayed and sometimes denounced as a threat to the other two. Although Nkrumah did speak of the need to synthesize the three legacies, he did describe Westernization in Africa as "the infiltration of the Christian tradition and the culture of Western Europe into Africa, using colonialism and neo-colonialism as its primary vehicles."[14]

Under whatever name, is the theory of Africa's triple heritage already a school of thought? It is certainly not restricted to the three thinkers addressed in this essay. Like-minded thinkers are scattered in different parts of Global Africa. Enthusiasts in this school include the Gambian scholar and thinker, Sulayman Nyang:

> In my view, the African encounter with the Abrahamic tradition has been very inspiring and spiritually elevating. The message of Abraham, as echoed and preached by the Old Testament prophets, Christ and Muhammad, is still reverberating in the African spiritual firmaments. The ringing of church bells and the booming voices of latter-day Bilals summoning fellow believers to prayer, make it crystal clear to all observers that Africa has finally joined the growing commonwealth of believers in the Abrahamic tradition.[15]

Sulayman Nyang is closer to Edward Blyden in those views than to either Kwame Nkrumah or Ali Mazrui. Yet all four are part of an energetic but controversial school of thought which identifies a triad of cultural vibrations in the heartbeat of Africa.

NOTES

An earlier version of this essay appeared as a chapter in John C. Hawley, ed., *The Postcolonial Crescent* (New York: Peter Lang Publishing, Inc., 1998), pp. 169–184.

1. "Islam and the African Race," *Fraser's Magazine*, November 1875. See *Christianity, Islam and the African [sic] Race*, new edition with an introduction by Khalid A. T. Al-Mansour (San Francisco: First African Arabian Press, 1992), p. 26.

2. Ibid., p.130.

3. Ali A. Mazrui, *The Africans: A Triple Heritage* (London: BBC Publications, and Boston: Little, Brown, 1986), pp. 23–40. See also Mazrui's obituary of Cheik Anta Diop, *Africa Events* (London), 1986.

4. See, for example, W. Scott Thompson, *Ghana's Foreign Policy, 1957–1966: Diplomacy, Ideology and the New State* (Princeton, NJ: Princeton University Press, 1969), p.49.

5. Pan-Africanism is indeed one more issue which binds Blyden, Nkrumah, and Mazrui into a shared vision, but with important differences. In Mazrui's *Africa's International Relations* (London: Heinemann, and Boulder, CO: Westview Press, 1977), he identified five distinct levels of Pan-Africanism: *sub-Saharan* (the unity of Black people south of the Sahara), *trans-Saharan* (the unity of the African continent as a whole, both north and south of the Sahara), *trans-Atlantic* (the unity of Africa and its own Diaspora across the Atlantic), *west hemispheric* (the unity of the people of African ancestry in the Western hemisphere) and *global* (the unity of all Africans and Black people world-wide).

6. See Nkrumah, *Ghana: The Autobiography of Kwame Nkrumah* (New York: International Publishers, 1957). Nkrumah's other great intellectual influence was V. I. Lenin.

7. Of course people turn to religion for a variety of complex reasons, many of those reasons being deeply psychological and moral. The decision to switch from one religious tradition to another often has even deeper and more complicated causes. In this short essay we will not even try to do justice to the phenomenon of conversion as a human experience. We are limiting ourselves in this essay to the relationship between race and religion, with particular reference to the interplay between Islam, Africanity, and Black consciousness.

8. These were Afro-Caribbean Muslims led by the charismatic Abu Bakr, under a movement called *Jamaat al-Muslimeen*. The siege gave Afro-Caribbean Islam global visibility.

9. Consult Steven Barboza, *American Jihad: Islam after Malcolm X* (New York and London: Doubleday, 1993).

10. Ali A. Mazrui, *The Africans: A Triple Heritage* (London: BBC Publications, and Boston: Little, Brown, 1986).

11. Kwame Nkrumah, *Consciencism: Philosophy and Ideology for Decolonization* (London: Heinemann, 1964), pp. 68–70.

12. See Edward W. Blyden, *Christianity, Islam and the African [sic] Race* with an introduction by Khalid A.T. Al-Mansour (San Francisco: First African Arabian Press, 1992).

13. Ibid., p. 37.

14. Nkrumah, *Consciencism*, pp. 68–69.

15. The "Abrahamic religions" are Judaism, Christianity, and Islam. See Sulayman Nyang, *Islam, Christianity and African Identity* (Brattleboro, VT: Amana, 1984), p. 9.

NINE

THE SPLIT SOUL
OF A CONTINENT

T hree civilizations have helped to shape contemporary Africa: Africa's own rich inheritance, Islamic culture, and the impact of Western traditions and lifestyles. The interplay of these three civilizations is the essence of the continent's triple heritage. Even before Islam came to Africa there was an older triple heritage in the continent — an interplay between African culture, Semitic culture, and the legacy of Greece and Rome. This ancient triple heritage is best illustrated in Ethiopia, where Christianity has flourished since the fourth century, where the impact of Judaism is captured in local versions of the legend of Solomon and Sheba, and where the Greco-Roman legacy is manifest in both social traditions and brick and mortar.

This ancient triple heritage evolved when the Semitic element (which was once both Hebraic and Arabian) narrowed to become mainly Islamic. On the other hand, the Greco-Roman legacy expanded to become the impact of modern Western civilization as a whole on African life and culture. But what is the African strand in these legacies? How much of an indigenous civilization did Africa have before the arrival of Islam and the West? One African school of interpretation emphasizes that Africa had indeed produced great kings, grand empires, and elaborate technological skills before the aliens colonized her. The evidence is from the remains of Great

Zimbabwe and the bronze culture of West Africa. Indeed, ancient Egypt was itself an African miracle and, in part, a "Negro" civilization.

Because this perspective prefers to emphasize the glorious moments in Africa's history and the grand civilizations it produced, we may call it the perspective of *romantic gloriana*. In contrast to this approach, there is the perspective of *romantic primitivism*. Here the idea is not to emphasize past grandeur, but to validate simplicity and give respectability to non-technical traditions. This historical perspective takes pride in precisely those traditions that European arrogance would seem to despise. In the words of Martinique's poet, Aimé Césaire, who invented the word *négritude*, "Hooray" to

> Those who have invented neither powder nor compass
> Those who have tamed neither gas nor electricity
> Those who have explored neither the seas nor the skies
> My negritude is neither a tower nor a cathedral;
> It plunges into the deep red flesh of the soil.
> Hooray for joy,
> Hooray for love,
> Hooray for the pain of incarnate tears.[1]

As Jean Paul Sartre once pointed out, this African reveling in not having invented either powder or the compass, this proud claim of non-technicalness, is a reversal of the usual cultural situation. "That which might appear to be a deficiency becomes a positive source of richness."[2]

Now let us juxtapose these two African perspectives. *Romantic gloriana* looks to the pyramids as a validation of Africa's dignity, takes pride in the ruins of ancient Zimbabwe, and turns to the ancient empires of Ghana, Mali, and Malawi for official names of modern republics. *Romantic primitivism*, on the other hand, seeks solace in stateless societies, finds dignity in village life, and discerns full cultural validity in the traditions and belief of rural folk. What both types of African society have shared is nearness to nature. For centuries the continent has had abundant animal life and vegetation, and the indigenous religions have fused God, man, and nature. Islam and Western Christianity have challenged this fusion. Only man alone is supposed to have been created in the image of God, contrary to indigenous African beliefs in which the image of God takes many forms. Among God's creatures only man alone is, according to Islam and Western Christianity, close to sacredness, in possession of a soul, and destined for spiritual immortality. This is contrary to indigenous African religions that allow other creatures to share in sacredness and sometimes endow mountains and springs which a holiness of their own.

The coming of Islam and especially of Westernism has disrupted the African's ancient relationship with nature. The impact of the West has been particularly harmful. Capitalism and the cash economy have resulted in the rape or prostitution of Africa's environment, often by Africans themselves. Under the impact of the profit motive which came with the West, the African no longer holds nature in awe — he holds it in avarice and greed. Traditionally, Christianity has neither sacred nor profane animals. Islamic doctrine includes profane animals (especially the pig and the dog) but no sacred ones. Indigenous African religions have always had room for both sacred and profane fellow creatures. By taking the animal kingdom outside the realm of moral worth, the Western impact on Africa has reduced animals to their economic worth.

But in the final analysis, Africa's triple heritage is a social complexity rather than merely an ecological doctrine. The triple heritage is about man's relationship not only with nature, not only with God, but also with man himself. Fundamentally, it is also about man's relationship with woman. Has Africa's triple heritage complicated the role of women in society or has it improved prospects for the female of the species? Islam gives women more economic rights (e.g., the right to inherit land) than they enjoy under indigenous "tribal" laws. On the other hand, Islam gives women narrower economic roles (e.g., cultivating the land or marketing the produce) than women pursue under indigenous traditions. There is a conflict here between formal rights (better protected by Islam) and practical roles (discouraged by Islam).

A similar dilemma can be detected in the West's impact on Africa. Uneducated or non-Westernized African women in the countryside are often at the core of agricultural production — tilling the land and sometimes marketing the produce. But with Western education women move from the productive sector to the service sector. They learn a European language and other verbal and literary skills, only to leave the soil in preference to the office. Western education turns African women into clerks and secretaries instead of cultivators. This is a case of functional marginalization. It may be true that the West's impact upon Africa may have raised the legal status of women, but it has narrowed the economic function of women. Women's rights are better protected in the post-colonial era, but the role of women is less fundamental to the society than it was before. In short, the African woman is confronted with expanding rights and a shrinking role in the post-colonial state.

But African problems are not merely between men and women. There are also problems between men and men in the political arena and economic domain. Africa's triple heritage is at the center not only of the conflict between indigenous and imported cultures but between tradition and modernity. The triple heritage has also affected the other basic conflict within the African condition — the tensions between city and countryside, between soldiers and politicians, between the elite and the masses, between ethnic groups and social classes, between the religious and the secular, between a longing for autonomy and the shackles of dependency.

Given the dilemmas of the African predicament, there are searches for new ways of understanding its problems and a quest for a new science to solve them. Western economists have in the past focused on theories of economic growth and economic development. In the case of postcolonial Africa, should we be looking for a theory of economic decay? Western aid donors have increasingly turned their consciences to those African countries that have always been poverty stricken or the least developed, and may always remain seriously deprived. But a country like Ghana was once well endowed and has since declined. Is it more deserving or less? Is Ghana's worsening underdevelopment and relentless decay a warning signal for Africa as a whole?

The problem of societal decay can be measured by diminishing productivity, declining stability, and the erosion of public morality. Dependency theories do not really explain decay. Taiwan and Singapore may be very dependent, but unlike Ghana, Uganda, and Zaire [now the Congo], they are booming rather than decaying. So why is Africa faced with the danger of decay? We may already have theories of economic "take-off." We now need a theory of crash-prevention. It is arguable that a country like Ghana had already "taken off" economically when it became politically independent in 1957. Why is the craft of state now losing altitude so dangerously? How can Ghana start ascending again? How much of a lesson to the rest of Africa is the whole story of countries like Ghana, Uganda, and the Congo [the former Zaire]? And what has the triple heritage got to do with these dilemmas between development and decay, between a capacity for self-help and a weakness for dependency? The soul of Africa is presently split three ways and is in search of its own inner peace. The split soul of a continent is what the triple heritage is all about.

ENVIRONMENT: IN TOUCH WITH NATURE

Because Africa is the most tropical of all continents (split almost in half by the equator), Africa's history and culture are preeminently products of Africa's geography and of the African genius for adaptation under harsh conditions. For centuries the African's most immediate neighbors were the animals with whom he shared the continent. Africa's location has brought in more human neighbors (Arabs and Europeans) but sometimes at the expense of older animal neighbors in the African environment. Africa's climate is a mixed blessing — generating a wide range of natural phenomena, from jungle to desert, from abundant life to deadly diseases. Post-colonial Africa is witnessing expanding human population, diminishing numbers of wild beasts, and a continuing struggle between man and the elements.

RELIGION: NEW GODS

Christianity had two entries in Africa. Its first influence emerged through Egypt and Ethiopia early in the Christian Era (as part of the ancient triple heritage of African, Semitic, and Greco-Roman influences). Its second arrival was through European colonialism (as part of the modern triple heritage of Africanism, Islam, and Westernization). This new European religious thrust found older gods in the continent. Indigenous religions were still alive and strong. Islam arrived in Africa during the seventh century.

TECHNOLOGY: NEW TOOLS

Today, different historical stages of technology co-exist at the same time within Africa — the "tribal" spear co-exists with the modern missile, the ironsmith with the steel mill, the talking drum with satellite broadcasting, witchcraft with nuclear physics, herbal medicine with advanced surgery. Both Islam and Westernism helped to introduce new tools of production (cultivation and man-ufacture), of construction (building both states and bridges), of communication (vehicles and verbs), of rehabilitation (different forms of medicine), and of destruction (from the Arab sword to the Western machine gun). This is quite apart from the rich heritage of skills independently evolved in Africa over the centuries.

The West has been better at transferring its tools of destruction than its tools of production. Post-colonial Africa is becoming mili-tarily more sophisticated but industrially less effective. The reli-gious strands of the Semitic and Western legacies have been partic-ularly successful in transmitting the tools of construction — from the churches and synagogues of Ethiopia to the mosques of the Sahel. Islamic tools of communication range from the role of lan-guages like Arabic, Hausa, and Kiswahili to the historic functions of dhows (boats) in East Africa and camels across the Sahara.

TENSION: NEW CONFLICTS

In many African societies guns came with the trans-Atlantic slave trade. Africa has in fact experienced a triple heritage of slavery — indigenous, Islamic, and Western-oriented. Indigenous slavery was the least commercialized and basically the most humane. With regard to Islamic slavery, why do we not hear of Black Arab rebel-lions and riots the way we hear of Black American riots? A major reason is that over the centuries Islamic culture and lineage have permitted both cultural assimilation and interracial marriages. If the father is Arab and free, then the child is Arab and free—even if the mother is an African slave. The trans-Atlantic slave trade was most race-conscious, the largest in scale, and the most resistant to assim-ilation. But at least the West generated its own abolitionist move-ment — while simultaneously generating new empire-builders. England, the leading abolitionist power in the nineteenth century, was simultaneously the leading imperialist power. Additional con-flicts afflicted Africa: imperial wars of conquest, primary African resistance, Africa's involvement in other people's wars (World Wars I and II, and the French War in Vietnam), and modern liberation wars against colonial rule and White minority regimes.

Postcolonial Africa has also experienced conflicts arising from artificial colonial borders (e.g., the Biafran War and the Somali/Ethiopian conflicts), from limited resources (e.g., rice riots in Liberia and water riots in Ibadan), from entrenched conservative institutions (e.g., the Ethiopian revolution), from new fragile institutions (e.g., the series of military coups all over Africa), from sectarian differences (e.g., the Sudanese civil war) and from emerging class differences (e.g., labor unrest).

The new triple heritage has given Africa the warrior tradition from indigenous culture, the *jihad* tradition from Islam, and the guerrilla tradition from revolutionary radicalism. This is quite apart from the tradition of the colonial army which sometimes inherited the post-colonial state. Was Idi Amin a Kakwa warrior or a modern soldier? The warrior tradition is sometimes disguised behind a modern uniform. Is Colonel Gaddafi an Islamic *mujahid* or a modern soldier? The *jihad* tradition is sometimes embodied in a modern revolutionary. Is Kenneth Kaunda a passive resister at heart? The Christian and the Gandhian sometimes merge against a background of tension and death.

STABILITY: UNEASY LIES THE HEAD

All societies have political systems, but not all political systems are states. Traditional Africa consisted of both states and stateless societies. The states were often in the tradition of *romantic gloriana*. The states in Africa (as everywhere) attained stability through instruments of coercion. The stateless societies attained stability through traditions of consensus. Both Islam and Westernism are state-building civilizations. Africa's stateless heritage has been endangered first by Islam and its state-building *jihads* and later by Westernism and its obsession with boundaries and standing armies. Africa's stateless societies ("tribes without rulers") are an endangered species, doomed to extinction. But meanwhile, "tribes" which were stateless in precolonial times (like the Langi of Uganda or even the Ewe of Ghana) have sometimes captured the post-colonial state. But what is the fate of the post-colonial state? It is subject to two negative pulls: the pull of tyranny (entailing centralized violence) and the pull of anarchy (involving decentralized violence). A major reason for the dialectic between tyranny and anarchy is the fragility of the institutions inherited from the colonial era. Politically, Africa is caught between two or more traditions. There is a culture gap between the new institutions from the West and the ancient cultures of Africa and Islam. The elder tradition gave special legitimacy to

Jomo Kenyatta's rule. The sage tradition has been manifested in *Mwalimu* (Teacher) Julius Nyerere and in Léopold Senghor. The Islamic sage tradition (the *mullah*) is perpetuated among the *marabouts* and *maallems* of Africa. The monarchical tendency in Africa has made President Houphouët-Boigny of the Ivory Coast construct his own Ivorian Palace of Versailles.

In southern Africa the interplay between tyranny and anarchy is partly an interplay between Whites and Blacks. White tyrannies are racially monopolistic, socially discriminatory, and sexually exclusive. All over Africa the political arena is male-dominated. The question has arisen whether androgynization of politics would help to moderate the scale of violence which has characterized the contradictory tendencies of anarchy and tyranny. Other political gaps which Africa has to narrow are the gaps between Whites and Blacks, the gaps between soldiers and politicians, between ethnicity and nationhood, between rich and poor, between the indigenous and the foreign elements of political culture and between the religious and the secular.

The search for solutions has included the experimental one-party state; the search for new ideologies, the use of a national language for national integration, the search for better leadership, and the use of external troops for internal stability (like the use of Cuban troops in Angola and Ethiopia and French troops in Chad and the Central African Republic). As they say, the struggle continues — and uneasy still lies the head that wears an African crown.

CULTURE: THE RESTLESS SOUL

Another element of the triple heritage is seen from the perspective of searching for a cultural synthesis. Africa's values are in conflict. The struggle continues for a new morality. Maybe Africa should not be trying to resolve the conflict between the ethic of monogamy and the ethic of polygamy. It should recognize both monogamy and polygamy — provided all parties consent under oath. Perhaps polyandry should also be admissible — provided all parties consent under oath. Perhaps issues like tribal nepotism and corruption are more serious morally than the number of wives or husbands that a single citizen may have. Africa is already debating issues like integrated legal codes, indigenized ideologies, the role of art in religion, and other dimensions of cultural synthesis.

GLOBAL AFRICA: THE BATTLE OF IDEAS

The West intended Africa to be a passive factor on the world scene — more acted upon than acting. Africa has frustrated that goal by the grand transformation of a people from objects in the designs of others into an active force in global history. Africans as a people are scattered around the world. One out of every five people of African ancestry lives outside the parent continent. The Jews called their dispersal around the world "the Diaspora." Africa has two Diasporas: the one created by the slave trade (especially Blacks in the Americas) and the one created by the disruptions of colonialism (including Africans in Europe).

The Diaspora of slavery in America attempted to dis-Africanize the imported sons and daughters of the "Black" continent. American history addressed the following commands to the Afro-American:

Forget your ancestry, remember what you look like,
Forget who you are, remember your skin color,
Forget you are African, remember you are Black.

In the second half of the twentieth century, Afro-Americans have been faced by three theoretical options:

• being partially re-Africanized in culture and allegiance.
• being more fully Americanized and integrated into mainstream USA.
• being separate as "Blacks," distinct from both Africa and White America.

From Africa's point of view the best solution would be if Afro-Americans were re-Africanized enough to care about what happens to Africa and Americanized enough to influence US policy towards Africa. Renewed interest in their ancestry — travel to Africa and contact with Africans — is the beginning of re-Africanization. As long as Afro-Americans are in the ghettos of America, their domestic influence on US policy will be thin. But if the temple of privilege is pulled down, work could start on the shrine of equality. The civil rights movement initiated the process. But by definition that was a struggle for rights. The second phase is a struggle for power. At the moment it is taking the form of running for elections and trying to penetrate the citadels of authority. One American city after another has elected a Black mayor. And when Jesse Jackson made a bid for the presidential nomination of the Democratic party, the unthinkable at last became mentionable — a Black effort to reach the very pinnacle of American power.

But while the Diaspora of slavery in America is experiencing less and less racism, the Diaspora of colonialism in Europe is confronting more and more discrimination. North Africans in France are vulnerable — a dozen racial murders a year! French racism is partly cultural rather than based on color. There seems to be less hostility towards Black Africans in France than towards lighter-skinned North Africans. The fact that Arabs are perceived more clearly as "Muslims" than are Senegalese may be part of the explanation. The French are more culturally prejudiced than the British, but have less color prejudice than either the British or the White Americans. To some extent a culture war is taking place in France between French civilization and Islam. The conflict includes moral tensions — Islamic prudishness versus French sexual libertarianism. Will France become more prudish as Muslims become more influential in French society? Or will Islam in France succumb to the temptations of French indulgence? For better or worse, the latter is more likely than the former. Islam is less likely to change French culture than Africa to change French politics. By fighting for their independence Algerians changed the course of European history as a whole. The stresses of the Algerian war tore down the French Fourth Republic and brought Charles de Gaulle back to power, resulting in a more stable constitution in France (the Fifth Republic) and helping to transform both the North Atlantic Treaty Organization (NATO) and the European Economic Community (EEC) under the influence of Gaullist designs. In a sense, both Algerian nationalism and Algerian Islam played a part in the struggle which put so much stress and strain on the French Fourth Republic.

A wider role of Islam in Africa's relations with the West lies in the economic domain — with special reference to the place of Arab and African oil in the world economy. The Organization of Petroleum Exporting Countries (OPEC) is primarily Muslim in composition, and the Muslim world continues to have the largest reserves of oil in the world. Libyan leader Gaddafi regarded oil as a historic opportunity for present-day Muslims to ensure an influential role for Islam in world affairs. But over the years Gaddafi's nationalism has become partially secular. He does share the late President Nasser's ambition of leading the three worlds of Islam, the Arabs, and the Africans. But at his most ambitious Gaddafi added a fourth and more comprehensive constituency — the tricontinental world of Africa, Asia and Latin America. The universe of exploited societies was to be represented by Libya in North-South confrontations, in Gaddafi's view.

The West has often supported or subsidized dissident movements within the Third World, like Reagan's support for UNITA in Angola and the contras in Nicaragua. Gaddafi has argued that if it is all right for the West to destabilize the Third World, it must be all right for the Third World to destabilize the West. Why are Reagan's dollars for Nicaraguan rebels morally different from Gaddafi's dollars for the Irish Republican Army, especially when the British government works hand in glove with the American in global strategy? The double standards are glaring. The same Reagan who said he would have no truck with killers of children let loose his planes (with British cooperation) to kill both adults and children in Tripoli and Benghazi. Were the American cluster bombs dropped on Benghazi designed to protect the innocent? Gaddafi himself has a lot to answer for morally. He has indeed sometimes supported terrorism. But there is one way in which he has served in world affairs — exposing the West's double standards. His behavior says to the West, "Do not do unto others what you would not want them to do unto you." The lesson has not been learned yet, but the struggle continues. As for his use of economic resources for global political purposes, that may be a lesson addressed to fellow Africans and other Third World societies. While Western investors "make a killing" in stock exchanges, African producers are often too passive. African governments are only just beginning to challenge the passive role that Western capitalism had intended for them. A country like the Congo (former Zaire) can hold some Western mineral stock exchanges for ransom — but her wealth promotes the development of other countries abroad and leaves her own economy pitifully stagnant. It is time for her to be a real and influential actor in global economic affairs.

There are two additional forms of power that Africa has dreamed about as instruments of global participation: the power of traditional sorcery and the power of modern science. What relevance has "voodoo" for international affairs? The answer lies in the story of the city of Berlin — as a symbol of the partition of Africa in the nineteenth century and a symbol of division in the twentieth.

From this city European statesmen worked the rules of the scramble for and eventual fragmentation of Africa. Did Africa's ancestors proclaim a curse upon Europe?

> Your racism will follow your own shadows and one day give birth to a monster of racism in your own midst. Your imperialism will one day haunt your own children — and give birth to a monster of aggression in your own midst. And as you divided us, tribe by tribe, clan by clan, so shall you one day be divided, nation against nation, ruler against ruler.

The curse of Africa's ancestors may have befallen Europe's descendants. And the wall of Berlin bore tragic testimony to the role of nemesis in modern history, the possible relevance of "voodoo" in global statecraft. But sorcery need not be an alternative to science; it can be its reinforcement. And the most secret of all sciences by Western rules is nuclear technology. Should Africa break the conspiracy of nuclear silence and acquire nuclear know-how itself? The West is saying, "Nuclear weapons are not suitable for Africans and children under sixteen." Can Africa afford to be so marginalized? Africa's first nuclear capacity will probably be inherited from White South Africa now that the Blacks have taken over. It may be part of the inheritance of Blacks in South Africa. Black South Africans were the Untouchables of the twentieth century in Africa. They will become the Brahmins of the twenty-first. In fact, two sets of Blacks will be the vanguard of the Black world in the twenty-first century—Black Americans, by then more powerful in their own society, and Black South Africans, heirs to both mineral wealth and industrial pre-eminence in Africa. The shift from passive Africans to active ones will have reached a new plateau of leverage and influence.

But in the final analysis, the battle of ideas must continue — Africa not just a learner, but also a teacher; not just an imitator of others, but a model in her own right. The most important of all lessons, when all is said and done, is a transition from a traditional belief that "my tribe is the world" to a new globalist vision: "the world is my tribe — the human race, my family."

NOTES

A version of this essay appeared in *Michigan Alumnus* (September/October 1986): 23–30.

1. Aimé Césaire, *Return to My Native Land* (Paris: Présence Africaine, 1939).

2. S. W. Allen's translation of Jean Paul Sartre's introduction to African poetry, *Black Orpheus* (Paris: Présence Africaine, 1963), pp. 41–43.

TEN

THE TRIPLE HERITAGE OF THE STATE IN AFRICA

The state was not a universal category in precolonial Africa. From a political point of view the African continent was a miracle of diversity ranging from empires to stateless societies, from elaborate thrones to hunting bands, from complex civilizations to rustic village communities. In this essay we address ourselves especially to the emergence of the state in Africa, relating that phenomenon to the triple political and cultural heritage of the African continent — the indigenous, the Islamic, and the Western.

Let us first explore some of the main attributes associated with the state. The first is the centralization of authority. When Louis XIV said "L'État, c'est moi," he was formulating this doctrine of centralism at its most extreme, when it actually focused on a single individual at the pinnacle of authority. In reality, the centralism can be relative rather than absolute. After all, although the United States of America uses the term "states" in the plural, the country as a whole is a nation-state within the tradition of the Treaty of Westphalia of 1648. The federal government of the country becomes both the focus and the mechanism of centralized authority.

Related to such centralization is Max Weber's principle of "the monopoly of the legitimate use of physical force." Weber regarded this principle as virtually the definition of the state. From our point of view we may accept the twin principles of centralized authority and centralized power as the defining characteristics of the state.

What should be borne in mind are additional accompanying characteristics usually associated with the state but not necessarily of definitional import. One of these accompanying characteristics of the state concerns a fiscal system of some sort. This could be a case of collecting tribute from integral units of the state, or an evolving system of taxation still in the making. A relatively centralized system of revenue collection has come to be associated with institutions of this kind. Also basic as an accompanying characteristic of the state in history has been a centrally supervised judicial system. The judicial system may in fact be internally pluralistic, accommodating different religious or customary courts, but the centralization is partly a case of overall jurisdiction, with the state sometimes modifying customary law to conform to certain central principles. The state would in any case keep an eye on the system which selects those who interpret religious or customary law and those who implement it.

In Africa's experience state formation has been linked to the broader triple heritage of Africa's history and culture — a heritage which encompasses indigenous, Islamic, and Western traditions. Some states in Africa were products primarily of purely indigenous forces, some were products of interaction between indigenous and Islamic elements, and others were outgrowths of a basic interaction between indigenous and Western ideas. There have been occasions when the heritage has indeed been a fusion of all three, indicating a historical meeting point involving Africa, Islam, and the West. However, in this essay our approach will be particularly comparative, focusing more on at least two traditions at a time, rather than on pure models of the state. After all, Africa has indeed been a melting pot of political cultures, a laboratory of diverse experiments in political formations.

AFRICAN POLITIES AND ISLAMIC STATES

Africa's interaction with Islam antedates European colonization of Africa by at least a millennium. In the seventh century Islam conquered Egypt and started the process of penetrating North Africa. Islam then spread down the Nile Valley as well as into northwest Africa. The politics of those societies responded to the impact of Islam, and some of those societies began to evolve institutions which reflected this basic interaction between Islam and indigenous responses. Especially important in state-formation is the precise balance between trade and warfare, between economic aspects and military dimensions. The history of Islam itself from the days of Muhammad is partly an equation involving exchange of goods and balance of arms. The Prophet Muhammad was himself a trader in his earlier years before he became a warrior in the name of Allah.

Islam has divided the world conceptually between *Dar el Harb*, the abode of war, and *Dar el Islam*, the abode of Islam. Within the world of Islam political co-operation and economic trade would be facilitated. Between the world of Islam and the world of war, lines of difference and strategies of protection would be evolved. Islam's penetration of the African continent continued this dialectic between the economic and the military. When Islam became an empire, Egypt for a while became the pivot of an international Muslim economic system. There was a time when the merchant class of Egypt became what has been described as a group so influential that it "increasingly shaped the policies of the Muslim states, developed commercial law and custom, and gave the civilization of Islam its strong emphasis on the bourgeois virtues of saving and sobriety, avoidance of waste or ostentation, and respect for scholarship."[1]

Then the spread of Islam into West Africa accompanied another economic process. The trans-Saharan trade produced missionaries in the market places. The Muslim shopkeeper was at times the equivalent of the clergyman. Islam was spreading as an additional commodity accompanying the grand paradigm of trade. Out of this began to emerge special kingdoms and emirates in West Africa, instances of new state-formation. There is a Hobbesian concept in Islamic statecraft — encouraging obedience to those who exercise authority, provided they do no violence to the principles that Muhammad advocated and God willed. This side of Islam is concerned with submissive fatalism.

But Islam is also a product of defensive fanaticism. While submissive fatalism might encourage acceptance and peaceful conformity, defensive fanaticism could generate rebellion. Again it went all the way back to the life history of the Prophet Muhammad. Against the political establishment of Arabia in his own day, Muhammad decided that his duty was to resist or go into exile. Under pressure he decided to flee into exile. The Islamic calendar to the present day is a commemoration of exile since it begins neither with the birth of Muhammad nor with his death, nor indeed with the moment when he felt that God had favored him with the revelation. On the contrary, the Islamic calendar goes back to the *hijra*, the moment when Muhammad decided to flee from persecution and seek refuge in another city, Medina.

When Islam came to West Africa it certainly displayed the same dialectic between submissive fatalism and defensive resistance. Islam was mobilized to resist European imperialism. Indeed, a substantial portion of Western Africa's primary resistance to European colonization was Muslim-inspired:

> Militant Islam presented the greatest challenge and mobilized the sternest resistance to the European occupation of Africa in the nineteenth century. Muslim polities, with their written languages, their heritage of state-making, and the cohesive force of a universal religion preaching the brotherhood of all believers, could generally organize resistance on a wider scale than political units whose extent was limited by the tide of common ancestry. Muslims also had a strong incentive to oppose the advance of Christian power.[2]

When European pressures were getting too strong for the leadership of the Sokoto caliphate in nineteenth-century Nigeria, the leadership thought of the *hijra* — "obligatory flight from the infidels." Sultan Attahiru Ahmadu led a hijra after the conquest of Sokoto, going eastwards. As a historian has put it, "The British finally overtook him at Burmi and killed him. However, many of his followers continued to the Sudan where their descendants still live today under the chieftaincy of his grandson, Mohammadu Dan Mai Wurno."[3] In Sudan, Muhammad Ahmed el-Mahdi revealed his own potentialities in the realm of defensive fanaticism. He was the precursor of Sudanese nationalism, rallying religion behind nationalistic causes, marrying piety to patriotism.

But Islam also had, in its other face, the face of submissive fatalism, a readiness to accept the inevitable. The same Islam that had fought so hard against European colonization later seemed to be ready to accept the inevitable hegemony of the West. Subsequently Islam profoundly influenced the colonial policy of at least one major imperial power, Great Britain. My own thesis is that the British policy of indirect rule was born out of a marriage of Islam, on one side, and the Anglo-Irish philosopher Edmund Burke, on the other. In a sense the legacy of Edmund Burke is what British political culture is all about. As a rule of political prudence Burke advised, "Neither entirely nor at once depart from antiquity." If a society does aspire to change direction, it will be a mistake to do it either totally or in one sudden move. Political prudence, according to Burke, requires political sensitivity to history. As he put it, "People will not look forward to posterity who never look backward to their ancestors."4 British political culture is a reflection in part of this broad political philosophy. The British are reluctant to turn their back on antiquity either entirely or at once. So they maintain ancient institutions and modernize them as they go along, and they are slower to modify traditional habits than many of their peers. This same Burkean gradualism in British domestic political culture came to influence British colonial policy. Indirect rule was based on a Burkean principle of gradualism. Many colonial policy makers felt convinced that you could not persuade Africans to look forward to posterity unless you respected their tendency to look backward to their ancestors.

But British indirect rule assumed a presence of defined institutions in African societies, rooted in the history of those societies. And yet many African societies were relatively decentralized without the state-like institutions of authority that the British would have preferred to use for purposes of government. Where was indirect rule to find its paradigmatic formulation? Lord Lugard, the architect of Britain's policy of indirect rule, found those institutions in the emirates of Northern Nigeria. As Lord Hailey came to put it in his classic *An African Survey*,

> It was in Northern Nigeria that this procedure of using Native Authorities was given a systematic form by Lord Lugard during the years which followed the declaration of the Protectorate in 1900. The area which was brought under British protection was the scene of the most effectively organized system of indigenous rule to be found south of the Sahara. Most of the old-established Hausa Kingdoms had embraced the Islamic faith, and under its influence there had by the early sixteenth century developed a well-organized fiscal system, a definite code of land-tenure, a regular scheme of local rule through appointed District Heads, and a trained judiciary administering the tenets of the Muhammadan law.5

The Fulani, who gained the ascendancy in the greater part of the Hausa country, used and helped to develop further this organized system of administration. And then Lugard and the British came. From this appraisal of the Hausa-Fulani institutions the British then evolved an elaborate system of native authorities in Nigeria, utilizing existing structures for indirect British control. Northern Nigeria especially afforded the British classical local instruments for indirect imperial rule. The old institutions of Hausa-Fulani states became part of the new institutions of the colonial state.

On the one hand, this appeared to be a healthy strategy of transition. African societies were not being disrupted precipitately, ignoring their habits and lifestyles. African societies were being ruled through institutions which they had come to understand across generations, but which were subject to gradual change. On the other hand, indirect rule in Nigeria aggravated the problems of creating a modern nation-state after independence. The different groups in the country maintained their separate ethnic identities by being ruled in part through their own native institutions. Northern Nigeria became particularly distinctive in its fusion of Islam and Africanity. The missionaries were kept out of that part of Nigeria and missionary education — which had helped to Westernize the South fairly rapidly — was relatively inaccessible to large parts of Northern Nigeria. Different sections of the population perceived each other as strangers, sometimes as aliens, increasingly as rivals, and ominously as potential enemies. As it happens, the stage was being set for the events which ultimately led first to the military coup in Nigeria in January 1966, then to the slaughter of the Ibo in Northern Nigeria in the same year, and then ultimately to the outbreak of a civil war from 1967 to 1970. The preservation of precolonial state institutions, especially in Northern Nigeria, had made the consolidation of postcolonial national institutions more difficult.

Clearly the British had been more respectful of African institutions through their policy of indirect rule than the French had been through their policy of assimilation. After all, the French policy of assimilation denied validity to indigenous structures and values, asserting a supremacy and uniqueness of French culture, and proclaiming a mission to Gallicize those over whom France exercised hegemony. The British policy of indirect rule, in contrast, allowed for cultural relativism among societies and was based on an assumption of cultural diversity in the universe. Hence British reluctance to tamper with local native institutions where they could be recognized by them, and British eagerness to use those institutions instead of inventing new ones. But there was a heavy political cost in places like Nigeria. Pre-colonial statehood militated against post-colonial statehood. The survival of the emirates of Northern Nigeria and the Kabakaship in Buganda, legacies of precolonial statehood, came to militate against the construction of one Nigeria or one Uganda after independence.

The sultanate of Zanzibar in East Africa presented distinctive problems of its own without altering the basic tension between the precolonial and postcolonial African state. From the days before European colonial rule Zanzibar had been a racially and ethnically plural society. By the end of the eighteenth century the ascendancy of the Arabs was already clear. It was consolidated by the rise of Seyyid Said bin Sultan. Sultan Barghash later provided the transitional rule from pre-European Arab ascendancy to the Arab oligarchy under European overlordship. Once again the British, having recognized monarchical institutions in Zanzibar reminiscent of their own in England, proceeded to give some kind of validity to those monarchical institutions and use them as a basis of indirect rule. In one sense the Arabs of Zanzibar were the equivalent of the Hausa-Fulani of Northern Nigeria. In both cases the maintenance of their particular political institutions from precolonial days augured ill for the transition to postcolonial nationhood. In the case of Zanzibar, the tensions between the privileged ethnic group and the others could not be mitigated by a shared rivalry of all of them against still other groups elsewhere. After all, the tensions between the Hausa-Fulani and others in Northern Nigeria were helped by the fact that all northerners had a sense of defensiveness against southerners. Zanzibar was too small a society to have those built-in safeguards of cross-cutting alignments. The result was the disastrous revolution of January 1964, barely a month after the British had departed. Those very Arab institutions of statehood which the British had so affectionately protected became the Achilles' heel of the new nation as it struggled to modern statehood after independence.

AFRICAN POLITIES AND THE WESTERNIZED STATE

But why were precolonial state-formations so difficult to reconcile with the demands of postcolonial statehood? Why did indirect rule in Nigeria, by preserving greater recognition of traditional institutions of statecraft, make the business of building the modern Nigerian nation-state tougher? Why was respect for the Kabakaship in Buganda a disservice to the task of state-formation in Uganda? Here it is worth bearing in mind another triple heritage — the heritage of the city-state, the empire-state, and the nation-state. To some extent Zanzibar was a city-state, though it gradually established enough hegemony in parts of what is today coastal Kenya and coastal Tanzania to be on the verge of becoming a proper empire-state. In the case of Zanzibar the empire in the making was a dynastic empire, with an Arab sultanate at the top.

In the history of Europe the city-state antedated the empire-state. In African history it is more difficult to disentangle the origins of the city as against the empire. Some of the emirates in West Africa were at once city-states and part of a wider empire at the same time. Subsequently the names of some of the greatest African empires were used after independence as names of the new nation-states. The empire-states of Ghana and Mali had bequeathed their historical names to modern states. The most durable of all Africa's empire-states turned out to be Ethiopia. Its last Emperor was Haile Selassie, an incarnation of precolonial statehood bound to confront sooner or later his moment of truth with postcolonial statehood. There is a basic conflict within the demands of a dynastic ancient empire and the responsibilities of a modern nation-state. Ethiopia had had a severe famine which was underpublicized, seemingly because a famine of such magnitude was considered by the royal household as an embarrassment to the Empire. When the Ethiopian Revolution began in February 1974, it has been suggested that a major contributor to the revolution was precisely the famine and the long delay by the Imperial Order in responding to it. By that time, it appeared that the dynastic empire-state would no longer be permitted to masquerade as a modern nation-state. The soldiers of Ethiopia, for a while cheered by the students and peasants of Ethiopia, solved the dilemmas by abolishing the ancient imperial statehood and replacing it with a modern ideology dedicated in the long run to the principle of the "withering away of the state" itself.

We might therefore conclude that one of the difficulties in the transition from a precolonial to a postcolonial state is precisely the normative and moral gap between the two. The values are fundamentally changed, the responsibilities redefined, the perspectives newly focused, the policies demanding reformulation. An important disruptive factor was the evolution of the principle of equality. In Africa this principle was by far better realized among the so-called stateless societies than among either city-states or empire-states. Many indigenous societies along the Nile Valley, or societies like the Tiv of Nigeria and the Masai of Kenya and Tanzania, have relatively loose structures of control and substantial egalitarianism. In contrast, societies like those of Buganda, Northern Nigeria, Ashanti, and other dynastic empires of West Africa, were hierarchical and basically unequal.

The new nation-state provided a basic contradiction. On the one hand, it championed almost as much equality as the so-called "primitive" and stateless societies which did not have kings or identifiable rulers. On the other hand, the new nation-state explicitly expected identifiable rulers, and asserted what Max Weber called the state's "monopoly of the legitimate use of physical force." The new postcolonial state was supposed to be as egalitarian as the Masai and the Tiv, and as centralized as the Baganda, the Ashanti, and the Hausa-Fulani. The new nation-state was supposed to be morally as egalitarian as the stateless societies of Africa, but politically as structured as the nation-states of Europe. This basic tension between moral equality from acephalous societies in Africa and political hierarchy from monarchical societies in Africa has been one of the central divisive elements in the postcolonial experience. In places like Rwanda and Burundi this dialectic pitched hierarchical Tutsi against egalitarian Hutu; in Nigeria it pitched deferential Hausa against individualistic Ibo; in Uganda it pitched monarchical Baganda against neo-republican Nilotes.

Another area of tension between the precolonial and the postcolonial African states concerned the differences in attitude towards territoriality. Most African societies have a high degree of land reverence. On the other hand, the principle of the modern nation-state includes a high sensitivity to territoriality. The mystique of land reverence in traditional Africa has had to seek a modus vivendi with the principle of territoriality of the modern state. The mystique of land reverence in Africa is partly a compact between the living, the dead, and the unborn. Where the ancestors are buried, there the soul of the clan resides, and there the prospects of the health of the next generation should be sought. Land was quite fundamental to both stateless African societies and to empires and city-states.

On the other hand, territory grew increasingly important in Europe, becoming almost sacrosanct in the legacy of the Treaty of Westphalia of 1648. Political communities under the new doctrine of the nation-state became increasingly definable in terms of boundaries, between one nation-state and another. Sovereignty was subject to territoriality; power was land-bound. But while the precolonial African state indulged in this land worship in relation to both agriculture and the burial of ancestors, the postcolonial state indulged in the worship of territory in relation to power and sovereignty rather than cultivation and ancestry. The dichotomy between the land worship of old and territorial worship in postcolonial states has not yet been resolved. All we know is that the last legacy of the colonial order to be decolonized is likely to be the territorial boundary between one African country and another. That colonial boundary currently helps define one African political entity as opposed to another. Each is jealous of its own inherited boundaries. Kenya defies Somalia; Ethiopia defies Somalia; Niger defies Nigeria; Morocco defies Mauritania; and most postcolonial African states defy any territorial changes. The ghosts of ancestors and land worship have been overshadowed by the imperative of sovereignty and territorial possessiveness.

CONCLUSION

We have attempted to demonstrate in this essay that there are two levels of a triple heritage of state formation in the history of Africa from precolonial times to independence. At one level the triple heritage consists of the indigenous heritage, the Afro-Islamic heritage, and the Western heritage of state formation. The purely indigenous takes us to Buganda before the European impact, and then explores the implications and repercussions of British colonization of that part of the world. The Afro-Islamic dramatizes the impressive diversity of Nigeria and illustrates the interaction between an Afro-Islamic heritage on the one hand, and an indigenous heritage in the south of the country on the other hand, and the repercussions of the stimulation which European contact inaugurated. But the Afro-Christian component in the history of state formation in Africa did not always include European stimulus. The striking exception to the intrusion of European Christianity is in fact Ethiopia, which has been Christian for a longer period than many parts of Europe, going back to the fourth century A.D. The rise of the Ethiopian state was quite indistinguishable from the rise of Christianity in Ethiopia just as the nature of statehood in Nigeria, especially in the North, was often indistinguishable from the nature of Islam in Nigeria. But there was the subsequent impact of the system of Westphalia of 1648, consummated after the Thirty Years War in Europe, and clearly an aftermath of the conclusion of religious wars in Europe and the emergence of the nation-states in the global system.

We have also attempted to demonstrate another level of the triple heritage — the heritage involving the city-state, the empire-state, and the new modern nation-state. Places like Kano and Zanzibar were partly settings for the city-state. But Songhay, Ghana, Mali, the Hausa-Fulani Empire, Ashanti, and possibly Zimbabwe were manifestations of the second tradition of empire-states. The third structure of statehood was the nation-state, very much a product of European history and very much a legacy of the Treaty of Westphalia of 1648.

This essay has attempted to point out a basic discontinuity between the precolonial African state and the postcolonial state. In the transition the British especially attempted to provide a *rite de passage*, a ceremony of transition from precolonial to postcolonial statehood. This ceremony of transition was the British policy of indirect rule, which attempted to use native institutions of government as instrumentalities for colonial control and as intermediate stages before full African incorporation into the global state system. But in the ultimate analysis the transition from precolonial to postcolonial statehood was bedeviled by two crises: the crisis of normative egalitarianism and the crisis of territoriality. The crisis of normative egalitarianism arose because African city- and empire-states were, on the one hand, less egalitarian than African stateless societies, and, on the other hand, less egalitarian also than the evolving European nation-states. The kingdom of Buganda was less egalitarian than England; the religious Marabouts of Senegal were less egalitarian than at least the legacy of France after 1789. As for Dahomey (now the Republic of Benin), it was in some ways more sexist than Europe and in other ways decidedly less sexist. The rise of the Amazons, female soldiers in combat, indicated an impressive ambivalence about a sexist division of labor between male warriors and female domestics.

But it was not merely the normative and moral cleavage which distinguished precolonial statehood from postcolonial manifestations. It was also the nature of responsiveness to land. Precolonial statehood had a kind of mystical deference to land, an obsession with the aesthetics and religiosity of the soil. The grand compact between ancestors, the living, and the unborn found an area of fulfillment in the religiosity of the land. The land was where crops were cultivated so that the living could continue to live and the future infants could be sustained. But the land was also a graveyard, a place where the ancestors were indeed laid to rest, a place where the last incarnation found repose before a new incarnation received stimulus.

The second major cleavage between the precolonial and the postcolonial is not land but morality. This is a conflict of values and principles, a tension between preferences. The precolonial state was basically inegalitarian, tracing its roots to hierarchy, privilege, and power. Indeed the precolonial state sometimes began as a city-state and then expanded enough to become an empire-state. One of the great ironies of the European era in Africa is that the era colonized the African imperial state and, by so doing, disimperialized it. Thus Buganda under British rule was indeed colonized, but after a while Buganda's capacity to imperialize the rest of Eastern Africa was blunted. British colonization of African empires reduced the imperial capacities of those empires. This was repeated elsewhere in the continent. British colonization of the Hausa-Fulani helped to disimperialize the capacities of those groups to exert hegemony over others. British colonization of Zanzibar helped to disimperialize Zanzibar's expanding hegemony over parts of Tanzania and Kenya.

After independence, in any case, some of the most acute tensions of African societies were tensions between legacies of egalitarianism and legacies of hierarchy. Legacies of egalitarianism had dual ancestry — the ancestry of the values of African stateless societies and the ancestry of the values of European liberalism and European socialism. The legacies of African hierarchy could be traced, on the one hand, to the impact of the city-states and the empire-states in precolonial Africa, and, on the other hand, to the legacy of the inequalities of European imperialism and European capitalism. Perhaps the state system, whatever its origins, ought to give way to a more humane and more equitable global system. But while the state system persists, it is important to bear in mind that its African manifestation is indeed tripartite in two fundamental senses. It covers the basic interaction among indigenous cultures, Islam, and Westernism. That basic interaction also includes the accompanying tripartite communication between the city-state, the empire-state, and the nation-state in the agonizing tensions of Africa's political experience.

NOTES

A version of this essay appeared in *The State in Global Perspective*, ed. Ali Kazancigil (Aldershot, UK: Gower, 1986), pp. 107–118.

1. Basil Davidson, *The African Genius* (Boston: Little & Brown, 1969), pp. 211–212.

2. A. S. Kanya-Forstner, "Mali-Tukulor," in *West African Resistance*, ed. Michael Crowder (New York: Africana Publishing Corporation, 1971), p. 53.

3. See Michael Crowder's introduction, ibid., p. 15.

4. E. Burke, *Reflections on the Revolution in France (1790), Works*, vol. 4 (London: World Classics, 1907), p. 109.

5. Lord Hailey, *An African Survey*, rev. ed. (London: Oxford University Press, 1957), pp. 453–454.

PART IV

MODERNITY AND DEVELOPMENT

ELEVEN

AFRICA ENTRAPPED
BETWEEN THE PROTESTANT ETHIC AND THE LEGACY OF WESTPHALIA

The West's cruelest joke at the expense of Africa is the construction of two contradictory prison houses — one incorrigibly and rigidly *national* and the other irresistibly *transnational.* One is the prison house of the sovereign state, a fortress of political and military sovereignty. The other is the prison house of capitalism, compulsively transnational and constantly mocking the very principle of national sovereignty. The politico-military prison of the nation-state is now the basis of the global system as a whole, it is hard to believe it was almost purely European a little more than a century and a half ago.

Also globalized this century is capitalism. Even the most fanatically socialist of contemporary societies are ensnared by the tentacles of international trade; the profit motive haunts socialist commodities, and the hard currencies of international exchange are the currencies of leading capitalist powers. Third World countries have discovered that going socialist in their domestic arrangements is not necessarily an adequate exit visa out of the global capitalist system. Many Third World socialist regimes soon discover that they are as heavily dependent on international capitalism as ever — in spite of adopting socialist or neo-socialist policies in their own countries. The regimes continue to struggle to compete in the market-place with their coffee, cocoa, or copper, desperate for "foreign exchange" defined in terms of dollars, pounds sterling, Deutsche marks, or Japanese yen. The bars of the capitalist prison are omnipresent. How, then, has Western civilization succeeded in creating these two incredibly resilient prison houses for Africa, the fortress of the sovereign state and the all-embracing market-place of capitalism?

In a previous article (Chapter 10 of the present volume) we demonstrated that the triple heritage of state formation in African history takes on two forms. At one level there is a triple heritage consisting of the indigenous, Afro-Islamic, and the Western heritages of state formation. The purely indigenous heritage is exemplified by Buganda before the European impact. The impressive diversity of Nigeria illustrates the interaction between an Afro-Islamic heritage on one side, and indigenous heritage on another side of the country, and the repercussions of the stimulation which European contact inaugurated.

We have also attempted to demonstrate another level of the triple heritage — the heritage involving the city-state, the empire-state, and the new, modern nation-state. Places like Kano and Zanzibar were, in part, settings for the city-state. Songhay, Ghana, Mali, the Hausa-Fulani Empire, and Ashanti were manifestations of the second tradition of empire-states. The third structure of statehood was the sovereign state, very much a product of European history and very much a legacy of the Treaty of Westphalia of 1648.

We have seen that there is a basic discontinuity between the precolonial African state and the postcolonial state.[1] In the transition, the British, especially, attempted to provide a *rite de passage*, a ceremony of transition from precolonial to postcolonial statehood. This ceremony of transition was the British policy of indirect rule, which attempted to use native institutions of government as instruments for colonial control and as intermediate stages before full African incorporation into the global state system.

Still, in the ultimate analysis, and as we have discussed in detail in another essay, the transition from precolonial statehood to postcolonial statehood was bedeviled by two crises – the crisis of normative egalitarianism and the crisis of territoriality. (See Chapter 10 in the present volume, "The Triple Heritage of the State in Africa"). It must be recognized, however, that it was not merely the normative and moral cleavages that distinguished precolonial statehood from postcolonial manifestations. It was also the nature of responsiveness to land. (See "The Triple Heritage of the State in Africa.")

While the precolonial African state indulged in land worship in relation to both agriculture and the burial of ancestors, the post-colonial state indulged in the worship of territory in relation to power and sovereignty, rather than cultivation and ancestry. The dichotomy between these different forms of land worship has yet to be resolved. In fact, the last legacy of the colonial order to be decol-onized is likely to be the territorial boundaries demarcating one African country from another — inherited boundaries which are jealously guarded. The imperative of sovereignty and territorial possessiveness is at the root of many of the ongoing conflicts on the African continent.

The Second World War was an important divide in this aspect of Africa's history. There is widespread consensus that the war con-tributed towards Africa's political liberation. It helped Africa's quest for modern statehood. But what about economically? Did the war tighten the shackles of dependency or loosen them? Did it lay the foundations of economic self-reliance or prepare the way for greater external capitalist control of African economies?

The war facilitated Africa's political transition to modern state-hood partly by undermining Europe's capacity to hold on to empires. Britain was exhausted and also impoverished by the time the war ended. France had been humiliated by Germany. Related to this exhaustion and impoverishment of Western Europe following its own fratricidal war was the destruction of the myth of European invincibility in the eyes of the colonized peoples. Suddenly some-body noticed in Bombay that the Emperor's clothes of modern tech-nology were not clothes at all — the British Raj was naked! And when the Indians started pointing fingers and exposing the naked-ness of their Emperor, other subject peoples elsewhere heard it too. That is one reason why the precedent set by India in challenging British rule became an important inspiration to many African nationalists.

The second effect of the war was to broaden the general social and political horizons not only of ex-servicemen who had served in the war, but also of many Africans who had remained behind. The idea of listening to the radio for overseas news concerning the war gathered momentum during the war. For millions of Africans all over the continent the Second World War was an important inter-nationalizing experience. By the end of it many Africans were ready to agitate for freedom and independence.

The Second World War was also politically liberating for Africa because at the end of it the pinnacle of world power was no longer in Western Europe but had divided itself between Washington and Moscow. Both of these two superpowers had a tradition of anti-imperialism in at least some sense, though both superpowers were also guilty of other forms of imperialism. What is clear is that the rise of the Soviet Union and the pre-eminence of the United States after the Second World War created two pressures on European powers to make concessions to African nationalists struggling for independence. The West's fear of the Soviet Union sometimes retarded the process of liberation for a time, but in the end it also facilitated the process, convincing Westerners that it was a good idea to give independence to moderate Africans while there was still time and so avert the threat of radicalizing Africans still further and driving them into the hands of the Soviet Union.

Although the Second World War was indeed politically liberating for Africans in the sense we have mentioned, the same war was an important stage in the incorporation of Africa into the capitalist world system. Partly in pursuit of war needs, African agriculture was modified to produce urgently needed supplies of food for Europe at war. In some parts of Africa there was a major depression when the wartime demand for African-produced goods declined, but the structure of African agriculture had by then already entered a new phase of export bias. The trend towards slanting African agriculture in this direction continued unabated, but on balance the principle of developing African agriculture to serve European needs was quite well entrenched. The war had helped to consolidate it.

Another way in which the war created the foundations of further economic dependency lay in the manner in which it helped to transform colonial policy from the morality of maintaining law and order in Africa *(Pax Britannica)* to a new imperial morality of increasing development in the colonies and pursuing the welfare of the colonized peoples. Britain established the Colonial Development and Welfare Fund as part of the machinery of this new imperial vision. It was not enough to stop Africans fighting each other. It was not enough to control cattle raids between different communities and tribes. It was not enough making an example of political agitators in order to maintain the mystique of Pax Britannica. It was not enough to use the slogan of law and order. Imperial power was a kind of trust, a mandate to serve the subject peoples.

The vision itself, of course, was much older than the Second World War. It was even explicit in Rudyard Kipling's notorious poem "The White Man's Burden," first published in *The Times* on February 4, 1899:

Take up the White Man's burden —
Send forth the best ye breed —
Go bind your sons to exile
To serve your captive's need.
To wait in heavy harness,
On flattered fold and wild —
Your new caught, sullen peoples,
Half-devil and half-child.

Take up the White Man's burden —
The savage wars of peace —
Fill full the mouth of Famine
And bid the sickness cease;

Take up the White Man's burden —
No tawdry rule of kings,
But toil of serf and sweeper —
The tale of common things.
The ports ye shall not enter,
The roads ye shall not tread,
Go make them with your living,
And mark them with your dead.

The developmental imperative of service was certainly very explicit in this poem, but on balance it was not in fact until the Second World War that development as a major imperative of colonial policy became a genuine exertion. New projects for rural development were more systematically implemented, and new trends in educational policy were soon discernible. Virtually all the major universities in Black Africa were established after the Second World War, many of them soon after the war in response to the new developmental imperative in colonial policy.

Yet these thrusts of development were themselves a further stimulation toward Africa's incorporation into Western capitalism, without a great deal of concern for how this integration might affect the Africans themselves. The Colonial Development and Welfare Fund contributed, in its own way, towards deepening both Africa's economic dependency on the West and Africa's cultural imitation of the West. Important biases in the direction of development included, firstly, the export bias we have just mentioned. Cash crops for export were given priority as against food for local people. One-quarter to one-third of the total cultivated area in some of the more fertile colonies was devoted to the production of such export commodities as cocoa in Ghana, coffee in Uganda, groundnuts [peanuts] in Senegal and The Gambia, pyrethrum in Tanganyika, and tea in Kenya.

Another distortion that occurred in the development process was the urban bias. Much of the economic change which occurred internally subordinated the needs of the countryside to the needs of the towns. One consequence was the volume of migration from rural areas to urban centers. The crisis of habitability continued to beset the lot of country folk. Young men struggled for a while, then downed their tools and hit the high road towards the uncertain fortunes of the capital city.

A third bias within each country was the subregional distortion. Some parts of the country were just much more developed than others. This burden of uneven development had its own stresses and strains. By being more developed than its neighbors, the Buganda subregion of Uganda, for example, acquired not only extra leverage, but also the passionate jealousies and distrust of other parts of the country. With less than one-fifth of the population of Uganda, Buganda held sway and exercised undue leverage over the political and economic destiny of the country as a whole. In spite of help from the Baganda, Uganda is now very difficult to govern. But it is equally as difficult to govern without Baganda help. The chronic instability of Uganda is partly the result of ethnic confrontations and partly the outcome of uneven development among the different subregions and groups in the country.

The fourth distortion in the history of development in Africa occurred in parts of the continent settled and, at least for a while, controlled by White settlers. In 1938, out of a total of £1,222 million capital invested in Africa, no less than £555 million was invested in South Africa from outside. A further £102 million was invested in Rhodesia. These countries, under White settler control, acquired in addition considerable economic muscle in their own parts of the continent, with leverage over their neighbors. Rhodesia exercised economic influence over Zambia, Malawi, Botswana, and

Mozambique. Kenya, while still a colonial territory, exercised considerable economic influence on the neighboring countries of Tanganyika, Uganda, and Zanzibar. South Africa itself is now basically a giant in the southern African subcontinent with considerable potential for buying friends or neutralizing enemies.

The fifth bias in Africa's development takes us back to capitalism. For in this case we are indeed dealing with the capitalist bias in Africa's recent economic history. The capitalist bias can itself be broken down into five distinct biases:

1. absorption into international structures of trade and capital flows,
2. belief in the efficacy of market forces,
3. faith in the profit motive and private enterprise,
4. distrust of state initiatives in the economy, and
5. optimism about the developmental value of foreign investments.

It is partly the nature of these five biases in the history of the economic changes in the continent that has condemned the continent to the paradox of retardation — a continent well endowed in mineral wealth and agricultural potential which is at the same time a continent of countries which the United Nations has calculated to be the poorest in the world. Until the 1970s, the terms "poor countries" and "underdeveloped countries" were virtually interchangeable. Clearly, countries like South Yemen [People's Democratic Republic of Yemen (Aden), which in 1990 joined with North Yemen, Arab Republic of Yemen (Sana) to form the Republic of Yemen] or Tanzania were both poor and underdeveloped. But the emergence of oil power has shattered this easy equation. Virtually all Third World countries are still technically underdeveloped, but only some of them are now poor.

In the 1980s it was no longer possible to think of Saudi Arabia as a "poor" country. On the contrary, it is now one of the best-endowed countries in the world in oil wealth and dollar reserves, but it is also one of the least developed nations today. What is true of Saudi Arabia as a country is true potentially of Africa as a continent. In terms of resources, Africa is one of the best-endowed regions of the world, but it is still the least developed of the inhabited continents. This is the pathology of technical backwardness. A related paradox is that the richest inhabitants of Africa are non-Africans. The poorest in per capita terms are indigenous Africans themselves. Of course, there are rich Blacks as well as rich Whites in the continent, but again, we find that there are more White millionaires per head of the White population of the continent than there are Black millionaires in relation to numbers of Blacks. This is the pathology of maldistribution.

The third interrelated paradox is that while the continent as a whole is, as indicated, rich in resources, it is so fragmented that it includes the majority of the poorest nations of the world. The paradox here is of a rich continent which contains many poverty-stricken societies. This is the pathology of a fragmented economy. Estimates of Africa's resources are on the whole tentative. Not enough prospecting for resources under the ground has taken place, but it is already fair to say that, outside of the [formerly] Communist regions of the globe, Africa has 96 per cent of the world's diamonds, 60 per cent of its gold, 42 per cent of its cobalt, 34 per cent of its bauxite, and 28 per cent of its uranium. Africa's iron reserves are probably twice those of the United States, and its reserves of chrome are the most important by far outside the former Soviet Union. In the 1970s the United States imported 98 per cent of its manganese from abroad, nearly half of which was from Africa.

The West's interest in Africa's oil has also increased significantly, partly in proportion to the political uncertainties surrounding the Middle Eastern suppliers. Had Nigeria joined the Arab oil embargo of the United States in 1973, the consequences for America would have been severe. In 1974 — the year following the embargo — the United States' balance of payments deficit with Nigeria was already three billion. It rose to five billion two years later. For the time being America's dependence on Nigerian oil continues to be critical.

Then there is Africa's agricultural potential. The Republic of Sudan, Africa's largest country in square miles, may indeed develop into a major bread basket for parts of Africa and the Middle East by the end of the twentieth century. More effective irrigation would facilitate full exploitation of the impressive fertility of this part of the continent. Then there are Africa's water resources, including some of the greatest rivers of the world. Potentialities for building dams and generating hydro-electric power have only just begun to be exploited. Solar energy for domestic and public purposes is still in its infancy, but it should be remembered that Africa is the most exposed of all continents to the sun. The Equator cuts Africa right in the middle. Africa is the only continent crossed by both the Tropic of Cancer and the Tropic of Capricorn. Tapping solar energy in Africa, once the technique becomes sophisticated, could be an additional impressive source of power and energy. With regard to uranium, Africa's resources may be significantly greater than presently estimated. One country that became a uranium-producing state fairly recently is Niger, formerly a French colony.

Against this background of mineral, agricultural, and other resources in Africa there is also the disconcerting fact that Africa has some of the least-developed countries in the world. The overwhelming majority of the countries that the United Nations regards as the "poorest" in the world are in fact in Africa. They range from Upper Volta [now Burkina Faso] to Rwanda and Burundi, and from Somalia to Tanzania. The continent itself seems to be well-endowed with resources, but a disproportionate number of people in the population of the continent are undernourished and underprivileged. A situation where a continent is well endowed but the people are poor is a situation of anomalous underdevelopment. A substantial part of the explanation lies in the nature of Africa's economic interaction with the Western world across time. And a major stage in that interaction was the Second World War and its distorting consequences.

Has the attainment of formal African sovereign statehood changed any of this? Links between African countries and the former colonial powers, as well as links between African economies and international capitalism, have sometimes been abruptly severed in certain cases. Those African countries that have attempted to do so precipitately have sometimes found themselves in the agonies of serious economic hemorrhages.

The links may sometimes be with a country other than the former colonial power as such. This is particularly true of Mozambique with its own historical connections with the Republic of South Africa. Mozambique hires out thousands of workers to the Republic of South Africa in exchange for gold and related contributions to Mozambique's foreign exchange reserves. Other economic links between Maputo and Pretoria, which were temporarily severed on attainment of Mozambique's independence, may in fact be restored in the years ahead. The possibility of encouraging South African investment in Mozambique, and certainly the probability of increasing trade with South Africa, is all part of the picture of historical continuities in Mozambique's predicament.

Then there is the problem that African countries encounter when they assume that to go socialist domestically is a way of disengaging from the international capitalist system. Many soon discover that they are as heavily dependent on international capitalism as ever — in spite of adopting socialist or neo-socialist policies in their own countries.

One reason is simply the fact that global capitalism is much more obstinate and resilient than its critics assume. Even the largest of the Communist countries — the Soviet Union [which is no longer officially Communist] and the People's Republic of China — are sensing a growing dependency on the world market, which in turn is dominated by capitalism and its methods. International trade is substantially born out of the rules of capitalist interaction. The major currencies of world exchange are currencies of capitalist powers. The major centers of the technology of production are disproportionately capitalist. The nerves of the world economy are at the same time nerves of world capitalism. Small countries in Africa that decide to go socialist domestically may find that they are still prisoners of the international monetary system, of the international market for copper and cocoa, of the international rules of credit, and the international fluctuations of supply and demand. For example, going socialist in Nkrumah's Ghana or Nyerere's Tanzania was not an exit visa from world capitalism. Because African economies are particularly fragile, this global background of capitalism makes even domestic socialism shaky. That is one major reason why there has not been a single really successful socialist experiment in Africa — not even the equivalent of the success story of either Kenya or the Ivory Coast as capitalist models.

A related difficulty that confronts socialism in Africa is the prior distinction between dependent capitalism and indigenous capitalism. This is a matter of degree rather than a sharp dichotomy. Dependent capitalism is the kind in which, even locally within a society like the Ivory Coast, there is a disproportionate role for foreign capital, personnel, and expertise. Thus the French role in the Ivory Coast economically is much greater than seems necessary to most impartial observers. Therefore, capitalism in the Ivory Coast is more dependent than capitalism in, say, Nigeria.

Kenya lies somewhere in between. Radical African analysts of the Kenyan economy tended to draw no distinction between it and the model of the Ivory Coast. But there has been a growing realization that the local entrepreneurial class in Kenya is more assertive, aggressive, and autonomous than its equivalent in the Ivory Coast. From the point of view of prospects for socialism, the question has arisen as to which one is the surer road to radicalization.

A British political economist, Colin Leys, wrote an influential book about "neocolonialism" in Kenya some years ago.[2] The main thrust of the book at the time was that Kenyan capitalism was of the "çomprador" variety. Less than three or four years later Leys was busy re-examining his original thesis, and was coming to the conclusion that capitalism in Kenya was less dependent and more autonomous than he had at first assumed.

One classical debate among Africanist Marxists is whether endogenous capitalism of the Kenyan variety, or of the Nigerian model, is a more effective prelude to socialism than dependent capitalism of the Ivorian variety. Western history would seem to teach us that when capitalism reaches a certain level of maturity it becomes difficult to dislodge. Marxists have been expecting socialist revolution in places like Great Britain since the nineteenth century — but Marxists are still waiting.

On the other hand, situations where capitalism has only just begun and is still very dependent have turned out historically to be precisely the appropriate breeding grounds for effective radicalism. The history of countries as diverse as the [former] Soviet Union and North Korea, Cuba and South Yemen [now joined with North Yemen since 1990 to form the Republic of Yemen], would seem to imply that dependent capitalism is a surer way towards socialism than indigenized and more deeply entrenched capitalism.

Still, history is one thing and doctrine is another. Marxist theory in its classical formulation did assume that a bourgeois stage of development was a necessary and inevitable pre-condition for a socialist revolution. As Engels put it,

> A bourgeoisie is . . . as necessary a pre-condition of the socialist revolution as the proletariat itself. A person who says that this revolution can be carried out easier in a country which has no proletariat or bourgeoisie proves by his statement that he has still to learn the ABCs of socialism.[3]

By this argument, Kenya must surely be closer to socialism than Tanzania is, since Kenya has more of a bourgeoisie and more of a proletariat than Tanzania has evolved so far. Similarly, the Republic of South Africa is closer to a genuine socialist revolution than Mozambique is — since South Africa is at a higher state of capitalist development and has evolved a much bigger African proletariat class proportionately as well as absolutely than Mozambique can claim to have done.

Although framed differently, such debates have been known to shake the political climate of such ideologically active campuses as the University of Dar es Salaam. Are there autonomous processes of class formation taking place in Africa, or are these mere reflections of the wider forces of imperialism? What should be clear is that Africa is unable to break out of the frontiers of international capitalism — whether or not an African regime decides to go socialist.

We have seen that the triple heritage of the state operates on two levels in Africa. However, in spite of this heritage, Africa has still fallen prey to two contradictory Western legacies. One of the most elaborate traps that the West has set for Africa has proven to be the state system, in which each nation state is a fortress of political and military sovereignty (i.e., the heritage of Westphalia). The other trap is the bequest of the "Protestant" ethic, a capitalism that is compulsively transnational and constantly mocks the principle of sovereignty.

In this essay we have tried to demonstrate the economic side of Africa's predicament — the consequences of capitalist penetration, especially from the Second World War onwards. This has been Africa's economic prison house. The state system of Westphalia is excessively national and "sovereign." Capitalism, on the other hand, is compulsively transnational and increasingly corporate. Africa has been entrapped between the territoriality of statehood and the supra-territoriality of capitalism.

Most African economies have already been deeply integrated into a world economy dominated by the West. African countries which go socialist domestically find that they are still integrated in the world capitalist system. The rules of that system are overwhelmingly derived from principles evolved in the history of capitalism. In international trade, countries seek to maximize their returns and to acquire profit. The rules of business and exchange at the international level, the banking system which underpins those exchanges, the actual currencies used in money markets and in meeting balance of payments, are all products of the capitalist experience. Countries like Vietnam, Angola, and even Cuba discover soon enough that their best economic salvation is to gain international legitimacy by Western standards. [Vietnam has made great strides in this direction, though Cuba is still failing in gaining that legitimacy.] It is part of the ambition of these countries to begin receiving Western benefaction, to have easy access to Western markets for their goods, and to be admitted to Western currency markets as well.

What all this once again means is that Third World countries can make their internal domestic arrangements socialist while remaining deeply integrated in the international capitalist system at the same time. It has also been argued that a country like Tanzania is today more dependent on the world capitalist system than it was before it inaugurated its neo-socialist experiment under the Arusha Declaration in 1967.

Independent Africa has already discovered that the last thing it is willing to decolonize are the colonial boundaries of its postcolonial statehood, but it has yet to discover that the last thing it can conceivably socialize are its obstinate links with world capitalism.

NOTES

An earlier version of this essay appeared as a chapter in *The Expansion of International Society*, ed. Hedley Bull and Adam Watson (Oxford: Clarendon Press, 1984), pp. 289–308.

1. See Chapter 10 of the present volume.

2. Colin Leys, *Underdevelopment in Kenya: The Political Economy of Neo-Colonialism, 1964–1971* (London: Heinemann, 1975).

3. F. Engels, "Russia and the Social Revolution," *Volksstaat* (Leipzig, April 21, 1875).

TWELVE

AFRICA
GENDER ROLES IN TRANSITION

In the beginning was man and woman. Their first child was human culture itself.

A loose translation of the Swahili proverb

In many traditional African cultures there has been a belief that God made woman the custodian of *fire, water,* and *earth.* God Himself took charge of the fourth element of the universe — the omnipresent *air.*

Custody of fire entailed responsibility for making energy available. The greatest source of energy in rural Africa is firewood, and thus the African woman incurred a disproportionate responsibility for finding and carrying huge bundles of firewood, though quite often it was men who chopped down the big trees initially. Custody of water involved a liquid which was a symbol of both survival and cleanliness. The African woman became responsible for ensuring that this critical substance was available for the family. She trekked long distances to fetch water. But where a well needed to be dug, it was often the man who did the digging. The custody of earth has been part of a doctrine of *dual fertility.* Woman ensures the *survival* of this generation by maintaining a central role in cultivation — and preserving the fertility of the *soil.* Woman ensures the *arrival* of the next generation in her role as mother — the fertility of the womb. Dual fertility becomes an aspect of the triple custodial role of

African womanhood, though always in partnership with the African man.[1]

What has happened to this doctrine of triple custody in the period since the colonial days? Different elements of the colonial experience affected the roles of men and women in Africa in different ways.

Among the factors that increased the woman's role on the land was wage labor for the men. Faced with an African population reluctant to work for low wages for somebody else, colonial rulers had already experimented with both forced labor and taxation as a way of inducing Africans (especially men) to join the colonial work force.

According to Margaret Jean Hay, wage labor for men took some time before it began to affect women's role on the land. Hay's own work was among Luo women in Kenya:

> By 1930 a large number of men had left Kowe at least once for outside employment. . . . More than half of this group stayed away for periods of fifteen years or more. . . . This growing export of labor from the province might be thought to have increased the burden of agricultural work for women. . . . As early as 1910, administrators lamented the fact that Nyanza was becoming the labor pool of the entire colony. . . . Yet the short-term migrants of the 1920's were usually unmarried youths, who played a relatively minor role in the local economy beyond occasional herding and the conquest of cattle in war. Furthermore, the short-term labor migrants could and often did arrange to be away during the slack periods in the agriculture cycle. . . . Thus labor migration in the period before 1930 actually removed little labor from the local economy and did not significantly alter the sexual division of labor.[2]

Margaret Jean Hay goes on to demonstrate how the Great Depression and the Second World War changed the situation, as migrant labor and conscription of males took a bigger and bigger proportion of men away from the land. This was compounded by the growth of mining industries like the gold mining at Kowe from 1934 onwards:

> The long-term absence of men had an impact on the sexual division of labor, with women and children assuming a greater share of agricultural work than ever before. . . . The thirties represent a

transition with regard to the sexual division of labor, and it was clearly the women who bore the burden of the transition in rural areas.[3]

Women, from the 1930s onwards, became more deeply involved as "custodians of earth." In southern Africa the migrations of men to the mines became even more dramatic. By the 1950s a remarkable bifurcation was taking place in some southern African societies — a division between a male proletariat (industrial working class) and a female peasantry. South Africa's regulations against families' joining their husbands at the mines exacerbated this tendency towards gender apartheid, the segregation of the sexes. Many women in the Front Line States had to fulfill their triple custodial role of fire, water, and earth in greater isolation than ever.

The wars of liberation in southern Africa from the 1960s took their own toll on family stability and traditional sexual division of labor. Some of the fighters did have their wives with them. Indeed, liberation armies like ZANLA and ZIPRA in Zimbabwe and FRELIMO in Mozambique included a few female fighters, but on the whole, the impact of the wars was disruptive of family life and of the traditional sexual division of labor.

After independence there were counter-revolutionary wars among some of the Front Line States. The most artificial of the postcolonial wars was that of Mozambique initiated by the so-called Mozambique National Resistance (MNR or RENAMO). The movement was created originally by reactionary White Rhodesians to punish President Samora Machel for his support for Robert Mugabe's forces in Zimbabwe. After Zimbabwe's independence the Mozambique National Resistance became a surrogate army for reactionary Whites in the Republic of South Africa, committing a variety of acts of sabotage against the fragile postcolonial economy of Mozambique.

Again, there have been implications for relations between the genders. In addition to the usual disruptive consequences of war for the family, the MNR, by the mid-1980s, had inflicted enough damage on the infrastructure in Mozambique that many migrant workers were not able to get home to their families in between their contracts with the South African mines. The miners often remained on the border between South Africa and Mozambique, waiting for their next opportunity to work in the mines, without ever having found the transportation to get to their families in distant villages of Mozambique.

It is not completely clear how this situation has affected the doctrine of "dual fertility" in relation to the role of the African woman. One possibility is that the extra-long absences of the husbands reduced fertility rates in communities, such as was the case in parts of Mozambique. The other scenario is that the pattern of migrant labor in southern Africa generally initiated a tendency towards de facto polyandry. The woman who is left behind acquires over time a de facto extra husband from among the men who either could not get mining jobs or who were not motivated to trek to South Africa on short-term contracts. These men found greater fulfillment in either local employment or in cultivating their own land. The two husbands take their turn over time with the woman. The migrant laborer from the mines has conjugal priority between mining contracts if he does manage to get to the village. He also has prior claim to the new babies unless agreed otherwise.[4]

If the more widespread pattern is that of declining fertility as a result of extra-long absences of husbands, the principle of "dual fertility" has reduced the social functions of the fertility of the womb and increased the woman's involvement in matters pertaining to the fertility of the soil. On the other hand, if the more significant tendency in mining communities in southern Africa is towards de facto polyandry, a whole new nexus of social relationships may be in the making in the region.[5]

THE GENDER OF TECHNOLOGY

Other changes in Africa during this period that had an effect on relationships between men and women included the impact of new technologies on gender roles. Cultivation with the hoe still left the African woman centrally involved in agriculture. But cultivation with the tractor was often a prescription for male dominance.

When you see a farmer
On bended knee
Tilling land
For the family
The chances are
It is a she

* * *

When you see tractor
Passing by
And the driver
Waves you "Hi"
The chances are
It is a he!
——— *Ali A. Mazrui*

Mechanization of agriculture in Africa has tended to marginalize women. Their role as "custodians of earth" is threatened by male prerogatives in new and more advanced technologies. It is true that greater male involvement in agriculture could help reduce the heavy burdens of work undertaken by women on the land. On the other hand, there is no reason why this relief in workload for women should not come through better technology. Tractors were not invented to be driven solely by men.

Another threat to the central role of the African woman in the economy in this period has come from the nature of Western education. It is true that the Westernized African woman is usually more mobile and has more freedom for her own interests than her traditional sister, but a transition from custodian of fire, water, and earth to keeper of the typewriter is definitely a form of marginalization for African womanhood. Typing is less fundamental for survival than cultivation. Thus in the second half of the twentieth century, the Westernized African woman has tended to be more free but less important for African economies than the traditional woman in rural areas.

The third threat to the role of the African woman in this period came with the internationalization of African economies. When economic activity in Africa was more localized, woman had a decisive role in local markets and as a trader, but the colonial and postcolonial tendencies towards enlargement of economic scale increasingly have pushed the women to the side in international decision making. It is true that Nigerian women especially have refused to be completely marginalized, even in international trade. However, on the whole, the Africans who deal with international markets and sit on the boards of transnational corporations are overwhelmingly men. At the meetings of the Organization of Petroleum Exporting Countries (OPEC) — where Muslims predominate — there are additional cultural inhibitions about having even Nigeria represented by a female delegate.

POLICY IMPLICATIONS ON WOMEN ENTREPRENEURS

What are the policy implications of all these trends? One central imperative, indeed, is to arrest the marginalization of women and to cultivate further their entrepreneurial potential. *Cultural adjustment* is the imperative.

Women as custodians of earth traditionally emphasized food cultivation. From now on, greater involvement of women in the production of cash crops for export is one way of linking tradition to modernity. This will also prevent Africa's economic internationalization from resulting in the marginalization of African women.

Support for traditional market women in food production and local trade need not suffer as a result of the new androgynization of cash-crop production. Credit facilities should be made available in such a manner that there is equity not only between men and women but also between Westernized and non-Westernized females. As matters now stand, traditional, non-Westernized women are often at a disadvantage when assessed for credit worthiness.

On the other hand, a higher proportion of non-Westernized women are involved in agricultural production than are their Westernized sisters. Indeed, cultural Westernization of women — though improving their credit worthiness — tends to decrease women's direct economic productivity. A balance has to be struck between these two categories of women (Westernized and non-Westernized) in relation to both credit and production.

Preventing technology from marginalizing women is yet another imperative. Special programs offering technical training — from driving tractors to repairing a lorry engine — need to be inaugurated, but it will not happen on its own. Such shifts in the cultural aspects of technology need to be addressed purposefully. Effective participation of women in the world of economic entrepreneurship requires advancing them in the world of technical and mechanical skills as well.

Women's traditional role as custodians of fire makes them the greatest users of firewood in the continent. But shouldn't women also be centrally involved in forest management and reforestation? Wood should be approached as an integrated industry, sensitized to the needs of environmental protection and ecological balance.

Women, as the greatest users of firewood, should also become among the leading planters of trees for reforestation.

This would not be incompatible with their involvement in the commercial aspects of wood more generally. Carpentry and furniture making are crafts which cry out for much greater female involvement than has been achieved so far. Culturally, women are often the selectors of furniture and the trustees of the domestic infrastructure of the family. Thus it is contradictory that African women have played such a limited role in designing furniture or making it. This is an area of entrepreneurship that beckons the female participant to become more involved.

As traditional custodians of water, do women have any special role in this era of faucets and dams? Africa's women, as we have indicated, still trek long distances in some rural areas for their water, but water-related industries are, surprisingly, still male dominated. This includes the whole infrastructure of water supply in urban areas. Even commercialized laundries and dry cleaning facilities for the elite and for foreigners in African towns are still usually owned and managed by men, even when women do most of the washing and ironing. The soap manufacturing industry is also male owned and male managed, even when the consumers are overwhelmingly women. One question which arises is whether these water-related industries are appropriate areas of linking tradition to modernity in Africa's gender roles.

What is at stake is the tapping of female talent where it was previously underutilized. What is at stake is also the androgynization of entrepreneurship. Once again the imperative is *cultural adjustment.*

Can the traditional custodian of fire be the innovative consumer of hydroelectric power? Can the traditional trustee of water be the new creative user of the high dam? Can the traditional trustee of earth take control of a new (and more creative) green revolution?

The future of the continent depends upon a new sexual equation in the whole economic process. The future of the continent depends more fundamentally on a cultural, as opposed to a structural, adjustment.

Still, none of those measures of cultural adjustment regarding gender would be feasible without a pronounced role by the state. Classical privatization and laissez faire strategies would simply permit worsening conditions of marginalization for women. Progress towards female entrepreneurialization would be aborted or retarded.

This is one reason why the cause of androgynous entrepreneurship in Africa needs an activist and enlightened state. The economy under such intervention would become less private — but the market could be released from some of the shackles of tradition and cultural prejudice.

NOTES

A shorter version of this essay appeared as "The Economic Woman in Africa," in *Finance and Development* (Publication of the World Bank and the International Monetary Fund, Washington, D.C.) vol. 29, no. 2 (June 1992), [Translated into seven languages] pp.42-43.

1. I am indebted to the late Okot p'Bitek, the Ugandan anthropologist and poet, for stimulation and information about myths of womanhood in northern Uganda. Okot and I also discussed similarities and differences between African concepts of matter and the ideas of Empedocles, the Greek philosopher of the fifth century B.C. Consult also Okot p'Bitek, *African Religions in Western Scholarship* (Nairobi: East African Literature Bureau, 1971).

2. Margaret Jean Hay, "Luo Women and Economic Change during the Colonial Period," chapter in *Women in Africa: Studies in Social and Economic Change*, ed. Nancy J. Hafkin and Edna G. Bay (Stanford, California: Stanford University Press, 1976), pp. 98–99. For a feminist perspective, consult also Maria Rosa Cutrufelli, *Women of Africa: Roots of Oppression* (London: Zed Press, 1983).

3. Hay, ibid., p. 105.

4. There is no doubt that such arrangements occur in Mozambique. What is not clear is how widespread de facto polyandry is becoming in southern Africa.

5. I am indebted to the field research and interviews in southern Africa which accompanied the BBC/WETA television project *The Africans: A Triple Heritage* (1985–86). I am also grateful to the work associated with the *UNESCO General History of Africa*, vol. 7, ed. Ali A. Mazrui.

THIRTEEN

TECHNOLOGY TRANSFER IN THE COMPUTER AGE

BY ALI A. MAZRUI
AND ROBERT L. OSTERGARD, JR.

INTRODUCTION

The significance of the computer in Africa has to be seen in relation to three processes with much wider implications: modernization, development, and alien penetration. Much of the literature on modernization conceives it as a process of change in the direction of narrowing the technical, scientific, and normative gap between industrialized western countries and the Third World. Partly because the industrial revolution first took place in the West, modernization until now has largely been equated with westernization, in spite of rhetorical assertions to the contrary.[1]

Because modernization has connotated a constant struggle to narrow the technical, scientific, and normative gap between westerners and others, development has often been seen as a subsection of modernization. Most economists in the West and in the Third World itself have seen economic development in terms of narrowing the economic gap between those two parts of the world both in methods of production and in output. Most political scientists have seen political development as a process of acquiring western skills of government, western restraints in political behavior, and western institutions for resolving conflict.

If both modernization and development are seen as a struggle to "catch up with the West," the twin processes carry considerable risks of imitation and dependency for the Third World. That is, imitation may engender vulnerability to continuing manipulation by western economic and political interests.

While we have chosen the computer as an example of technology with tremendous potential benefits to Africa, we see the computer in a broader sense as representative of information technology that has consequences for modernization and dependency. The computer in the Third World has to be seen in this wider context. In using the computer, is Africa enhancing its capacity for development? Is it facilitating the modernization of management, planning, analysis, and administration? Or is Africa instead adopting a technology that is inappropriate to its current needs, expensive in relation to other priorities, detrimental to job creation, and vulnerable to external exploitation?

The answer to these questions are mixed. We see great potential for the computer to play a larger role in Africa; however, the current development status of many nations there leads us to conclude that the haphazard introduction of the computer can be the source of many ills suggested by our final question, particularly as the world has moved toward a more globalized economy.

Framing the Debate

The debate has been under way in parts of Africa for decades now. Indeed, as early as 1976 the leading intellectual weekly journal in East Africa, *The Weekly Review*, carried an article which tried to balance the then-present costs of computers to a country such as Kenya with the potentialities and presumed benefits in the days ahead. Although computers have probably adversely affected Kenya's economy in the fields of job creation and outflow of foreign exchange, it is obvious that their potential has not been exploited to the full for the benefit of society.

But even this relatively guarded statement was soon taken up by another writer as being excessively optimistic about the utility of computers for a country such as Kenya:

> One understands . . . that over 100 such [mini] machines have been bought in Kenya: fifty million shillings for the mini-computers alone. Add to this the cost of the 40 or 50 larger computers, and

one must reach a figure of at least Shs. 100 million. Much of the greater part of the work done by these machines could be carried out by human beings. There are large numbers of adequately educated people who with a little instruction could do most of this work, and to whom a job at over a thousand shillings a month is a dream. Think how many of these could be employed with a fraction of Shs. 100,000,000![2]

The debate has not changed over two decades. Put another way,

Scarce foreign currency has been spent on equipment which is not used. The dependency on multinational corporations and expatriate personnel has increased, and sociocultural conflicts introduced. Moreover, what Africa has experienced for the most part so far is not IT [information technology] transfer but transplantation, the dumping of boxes without the necessary know-how . . . (Odedra et. al. 1993, 26).

Stripped of the rhetoric, the authors' analyses charge that computers are, first, a waste of scarce resources; secondly, their purchase aggravates balance-of-payments problems; and thirdly, they are detrimental to the struggle to reduce unemployment and underemployment.

The first author carries the attack further. He sees the type of technology symbolized by the computer as one which perpetuates the neglecting of the countryside, versus enhancing the city, while aggravating the status of African countries themselves as peripheral appendages to developed industrial states. Inappropriate technology, when introduced into a Third World country, both maintains the peripheral, rural status of the country as a whole in its dependent relationship with the northern-hemispheric metropolis, and deepens the neglect of the domestic countryside as against the new urban "civilization." There is indeed a case against the computer when it attempts to invade an economically poor and technologically underdeveloped country. In its most compelling form, that case centers around the problem of Third World, and particularly African, dependency, which means that the computer, and information technology in general, must once again be examined in relation to those wider processes previously mentioned: modernization, development, and alien penetration. But these in turn have to be redefined if Africa is not to be misled into the dark alleyways of technological robbery.

DEVELOPMENT IN THE THIRD WORLD

We define development in the Third World to mean modernization minus dependency. In this sense, we expand the traditional concept "development" from one of a strictly internal process, to one with an international dimension. Conceptually, the internationalization of development has been hastened along within the process of globalization, with significant consequences for Africa and the rest of the Third World. Information technology exerts tremendous influence over the globalization process, and in turn the patterns of winners and losers that globalization can induce (James 1999, 2). Indeed, some of the gaps between the West and the Third World must be narrowed — but this narrowing must include the gap in sheer power. To narrow the gap in, say, per capita income in a manner which widens the gap in power is to pursue affluence at the expense of autonomy. To narrow the gap in the use of computers while increasing western technological control over the Third World is to prefer gadgetry to independence. The chasm between north and south cannot be filled with the latest technological fads that produce a sensation of matching the north device for device while increasing the reliance on the north for those products. The implications of this differentiation are wide reaching.

Somehow each African society must strike a balance between the pursuit of modernization and the pursuit of self-reliance. Some African countries have and will continue to promote one of these goals more successfully than the other. It may well be that Tanzania under Julius Nyerere, for example, realized greater self-reliance than modernization in the first thirty years of independence (1961–1991). Tanzania is still falling short of an adequate developmental balance. Kenya, alternatively, arguably achieved greater success in promoting modernization than in realizing self-reliance. Yet Kenya, too, currently falls short of genuine development. In other words, just as self-reliance on its own can never give Tanzania development, neither can modern techniques on their own give Kenya an adequate progressive thrust. The formula for development in Africa is both modernization and decolonization.

But what is modernization? And how do the two processes relate to the technology symbolized by the computer? For our purposes in this chapter the three most important aspects of modernization are

- Secularization, or a shifting balance in the science of explanation and in the ethic of behavior away from the supernatural to the temporal.
- Technicalization, or a shifting balance in technique from custom and intuition to innovation and measurement.
- Future orientation, or a shifting balance between a preoccupation with ancestry and tradition to a concern for anticipation and planning.

With respect to these three processes, the role of the computer is to some extent related to the role of transnational corporations generally. But here an important distinction needs to be drawn between the technology of production and the technology of information. The technology of production ranges from the manufacture of shoes to the processing of petroleum. Most transnational corporations are primarily involved in the technology of production. The technology of information, however, ranges from radio and television to computers and the Internet. If modernization consists of the three subprocesses of secularization, technicalization, and future orientation, then the two technologies of production and information relate differently to each.

Historically in Africa it was transnational corporations concerned with the technology of production that helped to facilitate the process of secularization. But it may well be those transnational corporations which have specialized in the technology of information that have gone furthest in promoting the third aspect of modernization — i.e., future orientation. Here the radio, television and the computer are involved. Between these two — secularization and future orientation — lies the intermediate subprocess of technicalization as part of the modernizing process. Technicalization involves both production as well as information technologies. And transnational corporations become intimately involved in these aspects of modernization, with all the risks of dependency.

MODERNIZATION: SECULARIZATION AND THE TRANSNATIONALS

Positive contributions of western firms to the process of secularization in the Third World include their role in the two subprocesses — secularization of education, in the sense of reducing a religious focus, and practicalization of education, in the sense of promoting greater relevance to concrete social needs. In most societies, education was initially closely connected to religion. For instance, Oxford University in England even insisted well into the nineteenth century that academic appointments be based in part on religious affiliation. And one of the oldest universities in the world, Al-Azhar University in Cairo (more than a thousand years old), still harbors a preoccupation with religion. And, of course, Qur'an schools continue to be widespread in the rest of the Muslim world. This process was no different in Africa, especially with the introduction of colonial rule.

In Africa during the European colonial period, Christian missionaries took the lead in establishing schools. Education and salvation were closely allied under the imperial umbrella. On the whole, one of the consequences of this alliance was to make education more "literary." But when transnationals arrived, education was pushed in a different direction. The impact of transnationals on colonial schools was in the direction of both reducing schools' focus on religion (secularization), and increasing their interest in teaching practical skills (practicalization). More specifically, multinationals contributed to these two trends in the following ways:

• They helped to create a labor market in which practical skills were needed.
• They operated like a secular lobby, influencing colonial policy makers, and counterbalancing the influence of the missionaries.
• They demonstrated the impact of some of their own training programs, especially those designed to educate lower-level manpower.
• They promoted a "consumer culture" in the colonies, one that characteristically emphasizes materialist tastes as opposed to religious preoccupations.
• They fostered urbanization and general labor migration.

As a result, tensions between economic forces and the missionaries in the colonial territories were sometimes inevitable. Those colonies which had extractive (mining) industries experienced special types of tensions. There were times when the missionaries favored alternative forms of practical orientation in education, especially the development of those skills which would help to keep young Africans in their own villages. From the missionaries' point of view it seemed that the African who remained in his farming community was more likely to remain faithful to spiritual values than the migrant in search of work with multinational mining industries.

A Commission of Inquiry was set up in 1933 by the Department of Social and Industrial Research of the International Missionary Council, which had as its terms of reference, at the narrowest, the "effects of the coppermines of Central Africa upon Native Society and the work of the Christian Missions." The Commission recommended that the "educational emphasis of Missions should be directed towards preparing Bantu youth to serve the needs of Bantu rather than European society." There was indeed sincere anxiety that "Bantu labor" for the copper mines could in certain circumstances be at the expense of "native society." The Commission recommended that

> the mission societies of the Territories study together the goal towards which their education is directed, define its purpose and visualize the results which they are aiming to achieve. If such study is to be of ultimate value, the cooperation of the Government must be secured (Davis 1933, 338–339).

No less significant was the Commission's recommendation that for the sake of rural stabilization "the [syllabi] for the mission schools should be drawn to dignify farming as a vocation" (Davis 1933, 338–339). But the cleavage between missionaries' emphasis on the religious and the transnational corporations' push toward secular did not always result in conflict.

In the Belgian Congo (now Democratic Republic of Congo) multinational interests, missionaries, and the state gradually evolved a working alliance, and much of the emphasis in both missionary and state schools was, over time, directed toward practical training. The very readiness of the missionaries in the Belgian colony to promote vocational training helped to satisfy transnational enterprises and to consolidate a relative missionary monopoly of education in the country until the last decade of Belgian rule. And yet the products of these schools were often more vocationally oriented than those of schools in British and French colonies. A major reason was the more successful relationship in the Belgian Congo between the multinationals, the missionaries, and the colonial authorities. The practicalization of education could therefore take place without "excessive" secularization. The emergence of a new semi-skilled African class in the Congo was thus facilitated by the tripartite alliance. In the somewhat exaggerating but still pertinent words of one observer at the time:

The encouragement given in the Congo to African skilled workers is turning an African proletariat into a lower middle class. [The
gulf between "trade" and "profession"] will inevitably narrow
(Bartkelt 1953, 98).

Even the materialism of consumer culture could be used to justify the direction of imperial policy. The emphasis on vocational
training was deemed relevant for spiritual salvation itself. The ratio-
nale was that the "pursuit of moral and social well-being is closely
linked with the development of material well-being, the one being
the mainstay of the other" (de Vleeschauwer 1943, 549).

To some extent, Belgian policy merely amounted to a recognition that it paid to have certain practical skills. There was also the
fear that "excessive literary education" merely resulted in producing
"discontented political agitators." At least for a while, the Belgian
policy makers seemed to have grasped the significance of the following propositions:

• People trained in practical skills, such as mechanics and engineering, generally take longer to politicize ideologically than people trained in the
humanities and the social sciences.
• In less-developed economies, there may be a higher risk of occupational
redundancy for those with a purely literary education than for those
whose training is partly vocational. Such redundancy carries the risk of
discontent and instability.
• Those with a purely literary education are likely to want to move up the
educational ladder, all the way to university; but since opportunities
higher up the literary educational ladder are more limited than below,
the system risks producing disgruntled secondary-school dropouts. By
contrast, practical vocational trainees are more likely to want to get
into their jobs soon and start earning money.

The precise calculations and machinations which lay behind the
Belgian colonial policy notwithstanding, there was no denying the
practical results.

Transnational corporations played a major role in promoting
such changes, not least because they were often the most important
agencies for industrialization, mechanization, and commercialization in most of the colonies. What should be borne in mind is the
distinction between the transnational industries themselves and the
facilities and servicing industries which grew as a result of the

transnational presence. The Belgian colonial authorities used to boast that the Belgian Congo had the best transport facilities in Africa. The claim was an exaggeration, but there was no doubt that impressive progress had been made in this field. The construction of an infrastructure is not always in itself a multinational enterprise, but the need for such an infrastructure is, in part, often defined in response to multinational pressure.

In assessing the impact of transnationals on the diffusion of skills in African societies, one must, therefore, bear in mind both the direct and indirect consequences of a transnational presence. The transnational firms may themselves be capital intensive, but their presence helps to promote labor-intensive infrastructure developments and servicing industries. And these in turn have implications for education and training. Yet it is important to remember that building transport facilities and producing semi-skilled artisans is not *the* intended end of the task of meeting the practical needs of such societies. These developments create new problems of their own. This situation is explained in the report of the Langevin Commission,

> Mechanization, the use of new sources of energy, the development of means of transport and communication, the intensification of industry, increased production, the participation of large numbers of women in economic life for the first time, the extension of elementary education — all these factors have brought about a marked change in living conditions and in the organization of society. In 1880, because of the rate and scope of economic progress, elementary education had to be extended to the working classes. Now, for the same reason, we are faced with the problem of recruiting more and more trained staff and technicians (UNESCO 1959, 395).

The conclusion that the Langevin Commission drew from these new demands of modern economic life was that the educational system needed complete remodeling — "since its present form is no longer suited to economic and social conditions."

The transnationals have indeed contributed substantially to industrialization and commercialization; in the process they have also contributed to the secularization of education and to the trend towards giving education a greater practical component. But the precise nature of the industrialization and commercialization has itself distorted certain directions of both cultural and educational change. The need for a new adjustment becomes more urgent.

Modernization: Technicalization and Technology Transfer

At the center of that part of modernization which technicalizes society is the process of technological transfer. Again, transnational firms have in fact become the major media of technology transfer outside the military field. The transfer takes place mainly in four forms. The technology is embodied in, first, physical goods and equipment; secondly, skilled labor; thirdly, know-how which is legally recognized in patents and trademarks; and fourthly, knowledge that is either not patented or not patentable. Computers are themselves physical goods needing skilled labor in order to operate them, they contain a certain body of knowledge, and they are designed to generate further knowledge.

G. K. Helleiner sees a consensus emerging among analysts and some planners that the unpatentable know-how with respect to most forms of technology is of greater significance than the patented knowledge:

> Technology payments in licensing and collaboration agreements in which patent rights are not involved typically exceed those in agreements in which they are. Knowledge embodied in the patent is, in any case, normally insufficient by itself to permit its efficient working. [As Harry G. Johnson has put it], "In contemporary conditions, public tolerance and legal protection of commercial secrecy has become more important than the patent system.[3]

Helleiner (1975) regards the effect of patents on technology as being restrictive, but a good deal depends upon the options available in a given situation. There are certainly occasions when commercial secrecy is an inescapable de facto alternative to patented knowledge — and the secrecy can be a worse constraint on technology transfer than the patent. But as technology advanced, so too did the institutional structures needed to protect it. Globalization, fueled by information technology, has brought the issue of intellectual property rights protection to the center of international trade and investment decisions.

With the establishment of the controversial World Trade Organization, uniform standards for the minimal protection of intellectual property rights were established for all member countries. The idea behind such protection was to protect innovation from illicit duplication by those seeking a quick profit. But in doing so, the door has been left open to widen the chasm between "knowledge-rich" countries and "knowledge-poor" countries. Some have even decried the enforcement of intellectual property rights as "Western-style imperialism" (Hamilton 1997, 257). While this is debatable, it does raise an important question of access to technology and the ability of Third World countries to provide basic services to their people.[4] But where the knowledge is indeed made available for local use, an educational process may be under way.

Another substantial part of the debate about technology transfer has concerned the issue of appropriateness. And within this issue, the distinction between labor-intensive and capital-intensive technology has loomed large. Computers are once again a good illustration of that debate. The bias in technology transfer by transnationals has generally been towards capital intensity. There have been a number of reasons for this bias. Helleiner has drawn our attention to the following, with special reference to the technology of production:

- Transnational firms have access to relatively cheap capital.
- Unskilled labor is frequently of very low productivity. The wage rate may seem low, "but it is not cheap in terms of efficiency wages."
- Heavy protection, which the transnationals enjoy, reduces the incentive to change to the really efficient labor-intensive techniques.
- Transnational firms have tended to operate in industries (such as minerals processing) in which technology is both capital intensive and fixed.
- In the manufacturing sector their products — originally designed for richer markets — are standardized and subjected to strict quality control. These controls over standards "imply relatively capital-intensive and inflexible techniques of production for these particular products, although it might have been possible to meet consumer demand for the same basic characteristics through the provision of an alternative product with a more appropriate production technology and/or more flexible quality controls."
- Labor-intensive technologies tend to be associated with smaller scale production — whereas the multinationals have, on the whole, preferred to produce on a large scale.
- Shortages of skills in less-developed countries make capital a more efficient functional alternative.
- Labor relations in less-developed countries are at least as uncertain as in

the developed states. Labor-intensive techniques increase the risks of disruptions and interruptions.

•Capital-intensive techniques sometimes provide better insurance against unexpected fluctuations in demand than do labor-intensive ones.

•Governments and private purchasers of technology in less developed countries often prefer "the latest" in technological development as conferring a status of modernity, even if the latest technique is less appropriate for the particular developing country than an older method or older model of equipment (Helleiner 1975, 169–71).

From the transnational's point of view, what we should keep in mind is that capital-intensive techniques also tend to be skill intensive. Initially, the skilled personnel are imported into the developing country from outside, sometimes in response to demands for "streamlining" which are generated by computer vendors. The quest for this streamlining in administration may sometimes succeed in reducing inefficiency, but this is sometimes in exchange for increasing the importation of skilled manpower.

In such enterprises, which are capital intensive and in which the technology is complex, the training required for the indigenization of personnel may be substantial. This has implications for the whole problem of the brain drain, especially in situations where a country first adopts capital intensity and then shifts from capital-intensive to labor-intensive techniques. Both India and Nasser's Egypt had personnel who were well trained for certain highly technical roles and who then left their own countries when those skilled roles were no longer adequately used at home. A relatively sudden contraction of skill-intensive roles in the country — either because of the consequences of a change in ideology or a change in techniques of management — may result in the transfer of technology in the reverse direction as well-trained engineers, technicians, and accountants from the Third World seek the kind of employment in the industrial countries that is more appropriate to their new skills:

As soon as it is granted that some technology is embodied in human capital, and that it can therefore be transferred internationally through the movement of engineers, scientists and managers, it follows that the "brain drain" can also be viewed as part of the international technology transfer question. While it is quite customary to consider the role of the multinational firms in transferring technology through human capital from rich countries to poor, it has been less usual, though no less logical, to analyze their role in transferring it in the reverse direction. Their employment of indigenous talent for the pursuit of their own particular interests may deflect it from more socially profitable research and development activity, even if it does not physically leave the country (Helleiner 1975, 165).

Yet there are occasions when the training and education imparted go beyond the particular job with a computer and could make the recipient an innovator in his own right. In the words of Jack Baranson:

> . . . more important than the imparting of technical knowledge and manufacturing capabilities is the ability and willingness to implant indigenous engineering and design capability for continued technological transformation (Baranson 1970, 362).

This is what Kenneth Boulding would presumably describe as "knowledge which has the capacity of generating more knowledge in a single head" (Boulding 1966, 3).[5]

Where the training transmitted in engineering or computer science promotes such self-generating knowledge in a single head, it could indeed contribute to the innovative capacity of a particular sector of a developing economy. But what should continue to be borne in mind is that such a level of knowledge may as likely be diverted towards the brain drain. This particular dilemma of skill intensity continues to pose problems for the policy maker. Does it therefore provide an additional argument for shifting from mechanized efficiency to labor-intensive techniques which require lower levels of expertise? As indicated earlier, labor-intensive techniques that follow a period of sustained capital intensity could in any case aggravate the problem of the brain drain by aggravating the problem of skilled redundancy following the shift.

Under the technology of production, a distinction does need to be made between modifying factor proportions in an industry already established and selecting new industries or new products on the basis of their being more labor intensive. Whether labor can be substituted for capital in a particular manufacturing process depends substantially on the product:

> In continuous process industries (chemicals, pharmaceuticals, metal refining, oil refining) and in the production of many con-

sumers' goods and intermediate goods on an assembly line the
scope for such substitution is quite limited, except in certain ancil-
lary operations, particularly materials handling and packaging.
The main types of activity in which gain (measured in terms of
social costs) may be achieved by the substitution of labor for capital are in road-building, irrigation, housing and construction generally and in the production of woven fabrics, clothing, wood-
working, leather, some foodstuffs (including foodstuffs for local
consumption in local areas), bricks, tiles, and some of the simpler
metal products (Collings 1972, 13).

The level of training needed for the second category of
employment is usually less complex than for the first category.
Moreover, the less complex skills lend themselves better to in-service or in-plant training than the advanced technical skills. This is a
gain if one agrees with the UN Economic Commission for Africa
that "in-plant training is more effective than formal technical training in an academic atmosphere" (Collings 1972, 19). There are
times when an existing industry that is capital intensive can be
scaled down and in the process be made more labor intensive, or
research could be undertaken to develop unconventional indigenous raw materials. The development or use of new raw materials
could itself create new skills in the society. The scaling down of an
industry to adjust to the smallness of the market may alter factor
proportions in favor of labor.

One example of scaling down was the plant once specially
designed by Philips N.V. of the Netherlands for the assembly of
radios in certain less-developed countries:

> The main object of this design was to develop a low cost produc-
> tion unit for smaller volume of output than is typical in Europe;
> in the process the unit also turned out to be somewhat more
> labor-intensive. The firm also developed simpler types of equip-
> ment which can more readily be repaired or replaced from local
> stocks (Collings 1972, 15).

From an educational point of view, the following propositions
have therefore emerged from this analysis so far:

•Capital-intensive technological processes tend to be skill intensive. The
computer is a preeminent example.

• The education required for capital-intensive projects is likely to be at least partly formal, acquired in an academic atmosphere.
• Manpower trained for capital-intensive projects is subject to the temptations of the brain drain, in part because the technical skills involved have a market in the advanced economies.
• Labor-intensive processes lend themselves more easily to informal training and education, in-service or in-plant.
• Labor-intensive processes, almost by definition, spread skills more widely in the society and help to democratize education by broadening its distribution.

To the extent that computers have had a bias in favor of capital intensity, they have been a constraint on educational democratization. The skill intensity required will tend to aggravate the elitist tendencies inherited from the patterns of education under colonial rule.

Modernization: the Science of Anticipation and the Computer

The third aspect of modernization relevant to this analysis is, as we indicated, a reorientation towards the future and away from excessive deference to the past and to its ancestral ways. Sensitivity to the future includes an interest in identifying trends, both positive and negative. Positive trends may need to be facilitated; negative ones arrested. A science of anticipation, therefore, must be developed. The ability to harness information for future planning is critical in this regard.

A major obstacle to efficient planning in a new state may well be the very fact that the country is still undermodernized. Planning needs data on which to base estimates. Yet even basic data such as census figures are notoriously unreliable or imprecise in most new states. Planning in modern conditions needs the help of the technology of information, including the computer. Such a technology requires expertise. African states have a dearth of this expertise. Reliance on foreign experts has serious inadequacies and sometimes hazards for the host country (Odedra, et al. 1993, 26). Planning needs a certain local competence in implementation. The administrators, as well as their political superiors, have yet to accumulate adequate experience for the tasks which planning might impose upon them. But planning works best in an already developed economic system with reliable data, efficient managerial expertise and general technical and technological competence. An undermodernized society may well need planning most, but precisely because it is undermodernized it has a low capability for planning.

Can the computer help? As a major instrument of the technology of information, can it improve the data bases of African planning? Can it facilitate that aspect of modernization which is concerned with the future? Strictly speaking, data for African planning cannot be processed by a computer unless those data exist in the first place. The problem of planning without adequate data will not be solved simply by installing additional computers in Mali, Zambia, or the Congo.

There is little doubt that the computer can assist in the data problem in other ways. Analyzing the information which exists can itself yield further information to the planner. Data analysis typically yields inferences, conclusions, and findings. Such analyses, in turn, augment the body of knowledge available. Two pieces of information analyzed in relation to each other often result in additional pieces of information. Processing data is frequently an exercise in augmenting knowledge. It seems reasonable, therefore, to suggest that the computer should be conscripted in the war against poverty, ignorance, and disease in African countries. The computer's role as a storage system of information can also be critical for the African planner. Data can be retrieved at relevant moments for measured and well-defined purposes. The computer could facilitate efficient consultation of existing information as well as efficient processing and analysis of what is newly obtained. A computer might also aid that aspect of modernization which is concerned with identifying trends, both positive and negative. The computer may thus strengthen the science of anticipation.

But the computer's evolution, particularly in the developed countries, also makes it a valuable tool in the production and transmission of information. No longer are computers relegated to the simple tasks of processing existing information. Instead, computers have become primary instruments in producing, controlling, managing, and disseminating information. The centrality of the computer now makes it an even more attractive planning instrument than in its early days, a fact which is not overlooked by developing nations.

But a basic question arises: Does the computer help planning while simultaneously harming development? Is the science of draw-

ing up a rational and well-informed blueprint of planning strengthened by the computer, but at the cost of the actual substance of
development? There is certainly evidence to support this paradox.
Because of a number of factors, most computers in Africa are
unavoidably and grossly underused. Spending a large amount of foreign exchange to buy a single piece of expensive equipment is one
cost. Incapacity to use that piece of equipment adequately is an
additional one. It implies waste in a situation of scarce resources. As
Hayman (1993) points out, there are numerous cases of large sums
of money spent on computers and related systems without attention
to issues of compatibility, rendering unsatisfactory results. Yet the
incapacity to use computers fully is due to wider problems of underdevelopment which probably need to be solved *before* proficiency in
using computers attains adequate levels.

One example where the underdevelopment issue has become
more relevant in recent years has been in the area of telecommunications and computer technology. The United Nations' International Telecommunications Union reported in 1998 that approximately one quarter of the world's population live in countries with
insufficient basic telephone service. Sixty-two percent of all telephone lines are installed in just twenty-three industrialized countries, which also have only fifteen percent of the world's population.
As developed countries continue to push computers as a major tool
in communications, the basic format by which computers communicate — telephone lines — is insufficient to realize the computer's
full potential. While computers by themselves or centralized can be
useful, the inability of computers to communicate decreases their
potential effectiveness.

Beyond the single issue of telecommunications and the computer, the relationship between these two technologies illustrates a
more widespread issue in Africa: the lack of a proper infrastructure.
A major factor in Africans' inability to fully utilize information technology is the lack of an adequate infrastructure. Reliable sources of
energy, telecommunications infrastructure, and regulatory and pro-
cedural policies are all needed, in both rural and urban areas, in
order to take full advantage of the benefits that the computer and
information technology in general can bring (Mansell and Wehn
1998, 25–31; Metzl 1996, 716–717; Ngwainmbi 1995, 3; Odedra et.
al. 1993, 26; Lall et al. 1994, 193). In this sense, the underdevelopment of basic, reliable infrastructure services places developing

countries in the position of putting the cart before the horse, buying computers before they have the capacity to use them efficiently and sufficiently.

Related to this problem is the whole issue of high vulnerability to exploitation in an industry of high technical know-how. The relatively nontechnical buyer is often at the mercy of the highly specialized salesman (Odedra et al. 1993, 26–27). Discussing the Kenya situation, Hilary Ouma observed,

> More often than not, the idea of installing a computer originates from computer manufacturers, who are intent on increasing their sales, rather than from company executives. This has meant that feasibility studies on the equipment which are put before firms' boards are more often than not prepared by the computer salesmen themselves. The firms' executives probably do not understand technical computer jargon, leave alone have the ability to translate it into everyday language. [The resulting] excess capacity in expensive equipment can have serious consequences on the economy of a developing country (1976, 23).

This vulnerability to exploitation has a number of antidevelopmental consequences. The foreign exchange is depleted not only with the purchase of the equipment but also with the continuing costs of its use and maintenance. The expatriate specialists who are imported command high salaries, large portions of which are paid in hard currency. It is true that developing countries need to import for a while certain types of skilled manpower. But are computer specialists the most relevant expatriate engineers needed for the time being?

Also antidevelopmental in its implications is the economic stratification that takes place between expatriates and locals. In the case of computer specialists, this stratification can be particularly glaring. The employers in a developing country are faced with interrelated dilemmas. On the one hand, if the local specialist earns much less than the expatriate for the same job, the foreigner appears privileged and the citizen seems to be a victim of discrimination. On the other hand, if the local's pay is raised to something approximating what the foreigner earns, a new form of stratification is formed among the local people themselves. Again, if the local computer specialist is paid a much lower salary than his expatriate counterpart, a morale problem is created. As a result, the local may leave to seek a "less discriminatory" appointment elsewhere in another field.

The expatriate preponderance in skilled computer jobs thus becomes aggravated. Then, if scales for locals are based on international rates, and this attracts better local intellects to such jobs, would this genuinely stabilize the Africanization of personnel? Or would it increase the international mobility of the African personnel — and potentially contribute to the brain drain?

Some of these dilemmas are more real than others. What is clear is that a certain number of antidevelopmental cleavages open up as computers enter technologically underdeveloped societies. As Ouma puts it with regard to some of these dilemmas of personnel in Kenya,

> Expatriates installed the first systems, often with the understanding that they would train local people to take over. But two things happened. First, because most users were government or quasi-government bodies, there was an attempt to fix salary scales for local computer personnel on a level with the then existing salary scales without regard to world scales. While paying expatriate personnel more or less what they asked for, computer users did not seek any independent advice on the remuneration of local computer personnel. The result has been that a local programmer is often paid half the salary of a less qualified expatriate programmer, to take an example of imbalance in the salary structure prevalent in the industry (Ouma 1976, 25).

Ouma describes the effect as "disastrous." The very low salaries paid to local staff have failed either to attract or to retain "the right calibre of local people" in the computer industry. One consequence is that "while most of the junior posts — junior programmers, operators and key-punch operators — are held by Africans, there are very few senior local people in the industry" (Ouma 1976, 25).

Another antidevelopmental consequence of the computer takes us to another dilemma. Does the computer in Africa have real, "automatic" consequences? Does it reduce significantly the number of employees needed for specific tasks? If so, the computer complicates the problem of job creation, as we indicated earlier.

John B. Wallace refers to evidence obtained in interviews in Nigeria and Uganda, which suggests that computers there have no employment impact. But if there is no automatic result, is the computer in such nations a case of wasteful duplication? In the words of Wallace,

Computers are used in these developing countries almost exclusively on tasks for which clerical workers are the next best substitute. If, as the interviewees claimed, there is no employment impact, it is likely that computers are duplicating rather than substituting for clerical resources and that the countries are paying foreign exchange for no benefit, at least in the short run (Wallace 1977, 13).

Little has changed over twenty years, with computers relegated to routine data processing rather than better decision making (Odedra et al. 1993, 26).

Another antidevelopmental consequence of the computer overlaps with some of the other considerations mentioned before. The computer does aggravate structures of technological dependency between developing countries and the industrial states which produce them. Considering the continent as a whole, in 1972 there were an estimated one thousand computers in Africa. Half of these were in the Republic of South Africa. Obudho and Taylor (1977) relate this estimate to the original arrival of the computer in Africa in the late 1950s. African independence has indeed witnessed speedy computerization, but the absolute number is still modest. Obudho and Taylor's estimate for 1975 was 1200 computers in Africa. On the other hand, by 1972 the campuses of the University of California alone were using over two hundred computers (Obudho and Taylor 1977; See also El-Hadi 1975, Bussel 1972). The disparity between the developed and developing countries in terms of computers can also be seen in the most recent figures released by the World Bank. In 1995, high-income or developed countries possessed about 201 computers for every one thousand people while that figure for low and middle income countries or developing countries dropped to approximately six computers for every one thousand people.

Although the speed of computerization is modest in absolute terms, and countries such as Tanzania have even attempted decomputerization, the new culture that is coming to Africa with computers cannot but strengthen or aggravate technological dependency. The science of anticipation still has its most elaborate expertise outside Africa. The initial phases of the computerization of Africa carry the risk of a new form of colonialism. Africa could be duly "programmed." The "machine man's burden" looms ominously on the horizon as a new technological crusade to modernize Africa.

The arrival of the computer may indeed be contributing to modernization, but it is also adding dependency. The computer is probably helping to make planning more efficient, but is simultaneously making development more difficult. The science of anticipation is, for the time being, caught up in the contradictions of premature technological change.

TOWARDS DECOLONIZING MODERNITY

If development in the Third World equals modernization minus dependency and decolonization, how can the contradictions of premature technological change be resolved, and in what way does the computer illustrate these wider issues? Our answer to this lies in the process of decolonization and the careful use of the computer in this process.

The process of decolonization involves five subprocesses: 1) indigenization, 2) domestication, 3) diversification, 4) horizontal interpenetration and 5) vertical counterpenetration. The strategy of indigenization involves increasing the use of indigenous resources, ranging from native personnel to aspects of traditional local technology. But in applying this to the computer we have to relate it to the strategy of domestication as well. While indigenization means using local resources and making them more relevant to the modern age, domestication involves making imported versions of modernity more relevant to the local society. For example, the English language in East Africa is an alien medium. To domesticate it is to make it respond to local imagery, figures of speech, sound patterns, and to the general cultural milieu of the region. The promotion of Swahili as against English in Tanzania is, alternatively, a process of indigenization. It involves promoting a local linguistic resource, rather than making an alien resource more locally relevant.

With regard to western institutions in Africa, domestication is the process by which they are, in part, Africanized or traditionalized in local terms. But with local institutions, the task is partly to modernize them. Thus English in East Africa needs to be Africanized, while Swahili needs to be modernized in the sense of enabling it to cope with modern life and modern knowledge.

Clearly the two strategies of domestication and indigenization are closely related and are sometimes impossible to disentangle.

This is particularly so when we apply these strategies of decolonization to computers. The computer is of course more like the English
language in Africa than like Swahili. The computer is a piece of
alien culture. Can it be domesticated?

We believe it can, but the introduction or expansion of this
piece of technology in an African country must be much more care-
fully planned than it has been so far. The domestication of the computer would first and foremost require a substantial indigenization
of personnel. This would require, first, greater commitment by
African governments to promote relevant training at different levels for Africans; second, readiness on the part of both governments
and employers to create a structure of incentives which would
attract Africans of the right caliber; third, greater political pressure
on computer suppliers to facilitate training and to cooperate in
related tasks; and fourth, stricter control by African governments of
the foreign exchange allowed for the importation of computers.

The indigenization of high-level personnel in the local computer industry should in time help to indigenize the uses to which
the computer is put and the tasks that are assigned to it. When the
most skilled roles in the computer industry in an African country
are in the hands of Africans themselves, new types of problems will
in turn be put to computers. The cultural and political milieu of the
new personnel should affect and perhaps modify problem definition. This Africanization of computer personnel should also facilitate, over time, the further Africanization of the users of computer
services. What should be borne in mind is that the efficient indigenization and domestication of the computer requires a gradual and
planned approach.

The difficulty of this task is compounded, particularly in recent
years, as Africa braces for its second partition by transnational corporations and their respective governments. The move to conquer
the world's last great untapped consumer market in Africa has
brought concerted efforts to modernize Africa. One such effort is
on the part of the United States Agency for International Development's (USAID) Leland Initiative. The goal of the initiative is to
bring full Internet access to approximately twenty African countries
over a five-year period in order to promote sustainable development
(USAID Bureau for Africa 1998).

The trend towards greater computer technological sophistication in the underdeveloped countries of Africa carries the risk of a

commercial colonization of the continent. The evolution of the computer industry has led to increasingly rapid change in computer technology. As these changes occur, the chance to domesticate and indigenize the new technology may dissipate, given that many African countries will find it difficult to keep pace technologically and economically. The rapid pace of technological change will make a gradual and planned approach to domestication and indigenization of the computer in Africa a difficult task. The resources needed to sustain these new technologies may promote additional problems. As technology levels increase in these countries, the dependence of these countries on transnational corporations may likewise increase in order to maintain them.

Diversification, at the broader level of society, means the diversification of production, sources of expertise, techniques of analysis, types of goods produced, markets for these products, general trading partners, aid donors, and other benefactors. This approach — though often inefficient — should help an African country to diversify with respect to its dependence on other countries. Excessive reliance on only one country is more dangerous for a weak state than reliance on half a dozen countries.

But even if an African country has to deal primarily with the West when it comes to computers, it makes sense to exploit competitive tendencies between western corporations. What this implies is a trade-off between African countries and transnational corporations: access to large consumer markets in Africa could be contingent upon the transfer of knowledge and diversification of the transnational's work force. The result of such cooperation would yield a greater diversification in production techniques and skills for Africans, leading to some self-sufficiency while also diversifying their nations' external dependence. Just as international business monopolies once facilitated western imperialism, so too could international business facilitate decolonization, if the victims of imperialism can learn how to exploit the opportunities presented to them.

At least as important an element in the strategy of diversification is to find the right balance between the older manual techniques and the new computer techniques. Computerization should not be allowed to proceed too fast. Wherever possible, manual alternatives should consciously be encouraged alongside computers. Yet it would be wasteful if the computer only duplicated manual clerical work, for example. Between the hypothetical extremity of complete mechanization and the wasteful extremity of complete duplication there must lie a more viable diversified mixture of functions.

The computer is underutilized in Africa, not merely in terms of capacity or in terms of hours per day, but also in terms of the range of tasks assigned to it. Even in economic planning the computer in Africa is still greatly underutilized. We argued in the previous section that the computer can help planning, while simultaneously harming development. If the computers have already been purchased and are being used in ways which already harm development, should they not at least be made to perform their more positive functions in planning as well? Once again, diversification of usage — if handled with care — could extract certain benefits from the computer, while sustaining its developmental costs.

The next strategy of decolonization is horizontal interpenetration among Third World countries. In the field of trade this could mean promoting greater exchange among African countries themselves. In the field of investment it could, for example, mean allowing Arab or Malaysian money to compete with western and Japanese money in establishing new industries or promoting new projects in Africa. In the field of aid it must also mean that oil-rich Third World countries should increase their contribution towards the economic and social development of their resource-poor sister countries. In the field of technical assistance, it might mean that Third World countries with an apparent excess of skilled manpower in relation to their absorption capacity should not only be prepared, but also be encouraged, to facilitate temporary or permanent migration to other Third World countries. This last process is what might be called the horizontal brain drain — the transfer of skilled manpower from, say, Egypt to Abu Dhabi or from the Indian subcontinent to Nigeria.

In the field of computers, skill transfers among Third World countries are particularly promising in the short run as part of the process of decolonization. If an African country wants a computer, for now it has to buy it from Europe, North America, or a small number of Asian countries. But an African country does not have to import highly skilled computer personnel from those same industrialized states. As part of horizontal interpenetration, Third World countries must learn to poach on each other's skilled manpower, at least as a short-term strategy. President Idi Amin of Uganda learned after a while to distinguish between Indians with strong economic and historic roots in Uganda and Indians on contract for a specified period. He expelled almost all of those who had strong local roots — and then went to the Indian sub-continent to recruit skilled professional teachers, engineers, and doctors on contract terms. The wholesale expulsion of Asians with roots was basically an irrational act. But the recruitment of skilled Indians on contract was sound. Today, African nations should turn increasingly to the Indian sub-continent, instead of Western Europe, for some of its temporary needs for skilled personnel, including the need for computer personnel, pending adequate indigenization.

The final strategy of decolonization is that of vertical counterpenetration. It is not enough to facilitate greater interpenetration among Third World countries. It is not enough to contain or reduce penetration by northern industrialized states into southern underdeveloped economies. An additional strategy is needed, one which would increasingly enable southern countries to counterpenetrate the citadels of power in the north.

The Middle Eastern oil producers have already started the process of counterpenetrating Western Europe and North America. This vertical counterpenetration by the Middle East ranges from manipulating the money market in Western Europe to buying shares in West German industry, from purchasing banks and real estate in the United States to obtaining shares in other transnational corporations. Even the southern capacity to impose clear political conditions on western firms is a case of vertical counterpenetration. The Arabs' success in forcing many western firms to stop trading with Israel if they wish to retain their Arab markets was a clear illustration of a southern market dictating certain conditions to northern transnational corporations instead of the older reverse flow of power.

The possibilities of southern counterpenetration into the computer industry are modest, given the decline of OPEC's financial power and the economic problems of South East Asia. Recent events in the oil markets have brought a semblance of life back to a once moribund OPEC. Whether an increase again in OPEC financial power could make any difference in receiving countries of Africa is, for the time being, hypothetical.

Another question is how far the African computer market, as it expands and acquires greater sophistication, would be able to exert greater counterinfluence on the computer industry. This would depend at least in part upon the extent to which each domestic African market is organized internally and how far African countries using computers consult with each other, and possibly with other Third World users, on application of the computer and related issues. Obudho and Taylor (1977) tell us that there is greater awareness and organization on computer-related matters in Francophone Africa than in Anglophone Africa. Gabon, Madagascar, Côte d'Ivoire, Morocco, Algeria, and Burundi have all been experimenting with domestic institutions to coordinate informatics. Such consultations on computer applications should still be encouraged as part of horizontal interpenetration among African systems of informatics. But the greater sophistication which will in time be acquired should increase the influence of the African market on the computer industry itself.

Yet another element in the strategy of counterpenetration is the northward brain drain itself. Third World countries generally cannot afford to lose their skilled manpower. But it would be a mistake to assume that the northward brain drain is completely disadvantageous to the south. Indian doctors in British hospitals are indeed recruited to some extent at the expense of the sick in India. But those emigrant Indian doctors are becoming an important sublobby in British society to increase British responsiveness to the health and nutritional needs of India itself. The American Jews that are not prepared to go to settle in Israel are not merely a case of depriving Israel of skills and possessions which they would have taken there. They also constitute a counterinfluence on the American system to balance the influence of the United States on the Israeli system. The presence of Irish-Americans in the United States is indeed partly a case of agonizing economic disadvantage for the Irish Republic. But Irish-Americans are also, conversely, an existing economic and political resource for the benefit of the Irish Republic and Catholics in Northern Ireland. This is also true of Greek-Americans, Polish-Canadians, and Algerians in France. Migration from one country to another is never purely a blessing nor purely a curse to either the donor country or the receiving country. The costs and benefits vary from case to case.

As more and more Africans become highly skilled in computer technology and usage, some of them will migrate to developed states. As matters now stand, the costs of this kind of brain drain are greater than the benefits for African countries. It is essential to understand that the intellectual penetration of the south by northern industrial states must one day be balanced with reverse intellectual penetration by the south of the think tanks of the north. Given the realities of an increasingly interdependent world, decolonization will never be complete unless penetration is reciprocal and more balanced. Part of the cost may well be the loss of highly skilled African manipulators of the science of computers.

CONCLUSION

We have attempted in this chapter to place the computer in the context of the much wider issues raised by it. The equipment is a piece of modernity in the technological sense. Its functions in a society have identifiable modernizing consequences. The computer helps to secularize the science of explanation, to technicalize analytical approaches to data, and to promote a capacity for estimating the future and planning for it.

But modernization is not development. In the northern industrialized states, development should now mean rationalization plus social justice. The rationalization should include a proper balance between social needs and ecological conditions, a proper relationship not only between the individual and society but also between society and nature. Resource depletion and ecological damage have to be moderated by an adequate sensitivity to the future. As a consequence of its waste and pollution, the West has revealed that it has not yet modernized enough in the sense of responding adequately to the future by making allowances for it. By falling short of standards of justice between classes, races, cultural subgroups and sexes, the industrial states have not attained adequate standards of development either. But while development in the north equals rationalization plus social justice, development in the Third World must for the time being mean modernization minus dependency.

The computer in Africa probably helps to promote modernization but it also aggravates Africa's technological and intellectual dependency on Western Europe and North America. The computer, were it used more efficiently, would greatly aid the process of African planning. But its consequences are antidevelopmental in such tasks as job creation, reducing dependency, conservation of foreign exchange, definition of priorities as between town and country, and devising optimal salary structures for both locals and expatriates.

Africa cannot escape the computer age indefinitely. So long as the computer is an instrument for modernization, but not for development, can it be made to contribute to both processes? How is the dependency factor to be subtracted from the modernization in order to give us a truly developmental result?

We enumerated the five strategies of decolonization. The computer has to respond to the imperatives of indigenization, domestication, diversification, horizontal interpenetration among Third World countries, and vertical counterpenetration from the south into the sites of technological and economic power in the north.

But, in the final analysis, the computer is merely a symbol of much wider forces, ranging from technology transfer to job creation, from the impact of transnational corporations to the process of national planning, from race relations in South Africa or Uganda to the quest for international economic justice.

When adequately domesticated and decolonized, the computer in Africa could become a mediator between the ancestral world of collective wisdom and personal intuition on one side and the new world of quantified data and scientific analysis on the other. The sociology of knowledge is undergoing a change in Africa. And the computer is part of the process of change.

NOTES

1. For background on modernization theory see Parson (1952) and Huntington (1968).

2. "Computers: benefit or detriment?" (1976, 25). Approximately eight Kenya shillings amounted to one American dollar at the time of the article; today the exchange rate is approximately seventy-nine Kenya shillings to the dollar.

3. Helleiner (1975). We would like to thank G. K. Helleiner for simulation and bibliographical guidance on this point.

4. On this point, see Ostergard (1999a) for a discussion on the relationship between strong intellectual property rights protection and a nation's ability to provide for basic human needs. Additionally, see Ostergard (1999b) for a clear example of how international patent protection has been hindering attempts to curb the AIDS epidemic in South Africa.

5. It has also been pointed out that the introduction of technological knowledge is not enough to make a difference; entrepreneurs must have an

active role in advancing the new technology. In some cases, the inventor and the entrepreneur are the same people; in other cases, they are different. But even the introduction of new technologies can spawn new ideas for different kinds of new businesses that have what economists call "effective demand" (Volti 1995, 35–45).

REFERENCES

Baranson, Jack. 1970. "Comment." *The Technology Factor in International Trade*, ed. Raymond Vernon, p. 362. New York: National Bureau of Economic Research.

Bartkelt, Vernon. 1953. *Struggle for Africa*. New York: Praeger.

Boulding, Kenneth E. 1966. "The economics of knowledge and the knowledge of economics." *American Economic Review* 56 (May): 1–13.

Bussel, C., ed. 1972. *Computer Education for Development*. Proceedings based on the Rio Symposium on Computer Education for Developing Countries, Guambara, Brazil.

Collings, Rex. 1972. *The Multinational Corporations in Africa*. New York: UN Economic Commission for Africa.

"Computers: benefit or detriment?" 1976. *The Weekly Review* (Nairobi), 7 June.

Davis, Merle J. 1933. Modern Industry and the African, Report of Commission of Inquiry set up by Department of Social and Industrial Research of International Missionary Council. New York: Macmillan, 1933.

de Vleeschauwer, M.A., then Belgian Minister of the Colonies. 1943. "Belgian colonial policy." *The Crown Colonist* 13 (August): 549.

El-Hadi, Mohamed M. 1975. *The Status of Informatics in the African Administrative Environment*, Doc. 75-1. Tangier: CAFRAD.

Hamilton, Marci A. 1997. "The TRIPS Agreement: Imperialistic, Outdated and Overprotective." In *Intellectual Property: Moral, Legal and International Dilemmas*, ed. Adam D. Moore. Lanham, MD: Rowman & Littlefield Publishers.

Hayman, John. 1993. "Bridging Higher Education's Technology Gap in Africa." *Technological Horizons in Education Journal* 20 (6 Jan 1993): 63–69.

Helleiner, G. K. 1975. "The role of multinational corporations in the less developed countries' trade in technology." *World Development* 3 (April): 161–190.

Huntington, Samuel P. 1968. *Political Order in Changing Societies*. New Haven: Yale University Press.

James, Jeffrey. 1999. *Globalization, Information Technology and Development*. New York: St. Martin's Press.

Lall, Sanjaya, Giorgio Barba Navaretti, Simon Teitel, and Ganeshan

Wgnaraja. 1994. *Technology and Enterprise Development: Ghana under Structural Adjustment*. New York: St. Martin's Press.

Mansell, Robin and Uta When, eds. 1998. *Knowledge Societies: Information Technology for Sustainable Development*. For the United Nations Commission on Science and Technology for Development. Oxford: Oxford University Press.

Metzl, Jamie F. 1996. "Information Technology and Human Rights." *Human Rights Quarterly* 18: 705–746.

Ngwainmbi, Emmanuel K. 1995. *Communication Efficiency and Rural Development in Africa: The Case of Cameroon*. Lanham, MD: University Press of America, Inc.

Obudho, R. A. and D. R. F. Taylor, eds. 1977. *The Computer in Africa*. New York: Praeger.

Odedra, M., M. Lawrie, M. Bennet, and S. Goodman. 1993. "Sub-Saharan Africa: A Technological Desert" *Communication of the ACM* 36 : 25–29.

Ostergard, Robert L. 1999b. "The Political Economy of the South African-US Patent Conflict." *Journal of World Intellectual Property* 2: 875–888.

———. 1999a. "Intellectual Property Rights: A Universal Human Right?" *Human Rights Quarterly* 21: 156–178.

Ouma, Hilary. 1976. "The Changing World of Computers in Kenya." *The Weekly Review* (Nairobi), 17 May.

Parson, Talcott. 1952. *The Social System*. London: Lavistock Press. *The Weekly Review* (Nairobi), 17 May 1976.

UNESCO. 1959. *Chronicle* (Paris) 12 (December): 395.

USAID Bureau for Africa. 1998. http://www.info.usaid.gov/regions/afr/leland/project.htm.

Volti, Rudi. 1995. *Society and Technological Change*. 3rd Edition. New York: St. Martin's Press.

Wallace, John B., Jr. 1977. "Computer Use in Independent Africa: Problem and Solution Statements." *The Computer in Africa*, eds. R. A. Obudho and D. R. F. Taylor, 13–41. New York: Praeger.

FOURTEEN

THE MUSE
OF MODERNITY
AND THE QUEST FOR
DEVELOPMENT

Let us confront issues like culture, development, modernization, and dependency frontally. What do they all mean?
What is their significance for African societies? To answer
such questions we must be aware first of the complex role of culture
within human civilization.

Culture is relevant for development because of the seven functions it plays in society. When culture functions as *lens of perception*,
it influences how people view themselves and their environment.
For example, African cultural concepts of immortality have influenced attitudes about family size and population growth. Many
Africans believe that no person is really dead as long as the person's
blood flows in the veins of the living. Having many children, therefore, improves a parent's chances of immortality.

Translated into modern terms, no person is really dead as long
as the person's genes are still among the living. It is therefore rational to maximize one's genetic legacy by having many children. This
conception of immortality has contributed towards making population growth in Africa the fastest in the world, with implications for
development — for better or for worse.

Another function of culture is that of a *spring of motivation*.
What people respond to as incentives or disincentives for certain
patterns of behavior is a phenomenon greatly influenced by culture.

It is for this reason that the *work ethic* is very often a product of such cultural configurations as Max Weber's concept of "the Protestant ethic" and the more recent phenomenon of workaholic behavior among Japanese executives.

Is the work ethic in Africa cultivated or stifled by culture? Has it been damaged by the consequences of the colonial experience? Is the work ethic among African women stronger than among African men? Have African men been more culturally damaged than African women? Needless to say, the work ethic has enormous implications for development and, in the final analysis, is a cultural imperative.

Culture also serves as a *standard of judgment*. What is right or wrong, what is virtuous or evil, what is beautiful or ugly are all greatly conditioned by culture. What constitutes corruption? Why is taking a chicken to a chief in traditional society acceptable as a form of salutation but rejected as bribery in modern society? Is the problem of corruption in Africa compounded by the clash of standards of judgment between the traditional and the modern? Is moral fluidity itself a consequence of a clash of cultures?

The fourth function of culture is in terms of its role as the *basis of stratification*. Rank, caste, and class are all profoundly conditioned by — if not created by — culture. There is in addition traditional *gender* stratification. We have seen that in most sub-Saharan traditional cultures, women were supposed to have a triple custodial role — as custodians of fire, water, and earth — and that, to a large degree, this belief still dictates the gender distribution of economic and social roles in many African societies. It is considerations such as these that make cultural awareness indispensable for effective development planning.

The fifth function of culture is as *means of communication*. Culture provides all sorts of nuances in communication and intimation. But above all culture provides language in the literal sense of the legacy of words and lexicon. We shall return to this function of culture more fully in relation to the potential of indigenous African languages in development later in this article, as there are important questions that have to be answered. For example, can any country approximate first-rank economic development if it relies overwhelmingly on foreign languages for its discourse on development and transformation? Will Africa ever effectively "take off" when it is held hostage so tightly to the languages of its former imperial powers?

The sixth function of culture is precisely in defining *production and consumption* and influencing them. Cultures differ widely in productivity, not only in the world as a whole, but also within Africa. But are these facts or merely perceptions? Are the Kikuyu in Kenya really more productive than the Maasai? Are the Igbo in Nigeria really more productive than the Tiv? If so, are the differences between these groups cultural? Clearly development planners cannot ignore such considerations.

This brings us to the final function of culture, by which it functions as a *basis of identity*. Culture is crucial in defining the "we" and the "they" and marking the frontiers of solidarity. Indeed, what constitutes a Kikuyu or a Maasai, an Igbo or a Tiv, is preeminently a function of such cultural variables as lineage systems, kinship, and language. How can development tap into the fountains of identity to achieve results?

These, then, are the seven functions of culture: lens of perception, spring of motivation, standard of judgment, basis of stratification, means of communication, defining factor in patterns of production and consumption, and basis of identity. Whether those in charge like it or not, development is caught up in the complex configuration of these cultural factors. But our conceptual problems are by no means over. We still have to grapple with what the process of development is all about. There are issues of definition, process, and goals involved that require further consideration.

BETWEEN DEVELOPMENT AND MODERNIZATION

What is development? We can respond that development is modernization minus dependency. But what, then, is modernization? For our purposes we can define modernization as change that is compatible with the present stage of human knowledge, that seeks to comprehend the legacy of the past, that is sensitive to the needs of the future, and that is increasingly aware of its global context. This is the positive interpretation of modernization.

If development equals modernization minus dependency, and we have defined modernization, what then is dependency? Dependency could mean either surplus need or deficit control. Country B is dependent on country A if country B needs country A more than the other way round (surplus need). On the other hand, country B is also dependent on country A if country B has less control over their relationship than country A has (deficit control).

Where does culture enter into this? If development equals modernization minus dependency, there is no doubt about the relevance of African culture in at least that part of the equation which concerns "minus dependency." African culture is central to this process of reducing dependency in the dialectic of modernization.

IDENTITY AND INDIGENIZATION

One strategy of transcending dependency is *indigenization*. This includes greater utilization of indigenous techniques, personnel, and approaches to purposeful change. Indigenized modernization would include greater use of African *languages* in the pursuit of economic and constitutional change. As stated earlier, no country has ascended to a first-rank economic power by excessive dependence on foreign languages. Japan rose to dazzling industrial heights by scientificating the Japanese language and making it the medium of its own industrialization. Korea has approximately scientificated the Korean language and made it the medium of its own technological take-off. Can Africa ever "take off" technologically if it remains so overwhelmingly dependent on European languages for discourse on advanced learning? Can Africa look to the future if it is not adequately sensitive to the cultural past? Culture as communication and culture as production need to converge.

When two Japanese physicists meet to discuss a problem in physics, it is now possible for them to discuss it in the Japanese language. When two African economists (let alone physicists) meet to discuss economics, even if they come from the same linguistic group in Africa, the chances are that they can only discuss advanced economics in a European language. This lingo-cultural gap may be disastrous for reducing dependency in Africa's experience.

But languages are not enriched only by their capacity as a medium for scientific discourse. The soul of each language is ultimately in creative literature — among the poets and dramatists, among the writers and storytellers. Taking African languages seriously would have to include a patronage of the literary arts and an effort to sustain the infrastructure of publishing in indigenous languages, as well as in international languages. Modernization needs some degree of "ancientizaton" in the form of a return to tradition.

In the twentieth century no language is automatically a scientific language, but every language is automatically a poetic language. African languages need to be made purposefully more scientific. But with poetry, the focus should not be on the language of poetry but on the poets themselves — not on making the language artificially more poetic, but on making the poets more naturally productive and engaged. The two policies of scientification of African languages and support for African poets and writers have to be jointly pursued as part of long-term national development. Culture as communication and culture as identity should find a meeting point in literature.

Three Africans have won the Nobel Prize for literature since 1986. It was possible for an Arab, Najib Mahfouz, to win it for literature written in his native Arabic, and it was possible for a White South African, Nadine Gordimer, to win it for books written in her native European language, English. But it was not possible for the only Black laureate, Wole Soyinka, to win the Nobel Prize for literature written in his native Yoruba. Soyinka could only be in the running for the prize through the imperial language of the Other. Europe's linguistic domination of sub-Saharan African cultures is more uncompromising than Europe's domination of, say, the Arab world. Is this a case of culture as stratification? Is this a rank order of races, or a stratification of cultures?

Outside the African continent, a French writer may win the Nobel Prize for literature as a result of works written in French; a Japanese for works written in Japanese; and a South Asian for masterly use of Bengali, Urdu, or Hindi. Rabindranath Tagore won the Nobel Prize in 1913 when India was still decidedly a British dependency. The works for which he won the Nobel Prize were in Indian languages, especially Bengali. He created from his linguistic womb. Even after making allowances for the influence of W. B. Yeats behind the Nobel scenes, even after allowing for the fact that the award of the prize was probably aided by the fact that Tagore had personally translated a number of his own works into English, the award signaled not a clash of civilizations but the potentialities of parity of esteem across cultural divides.

However, for the foreseeable future, the Nobel Prize for literature is unlikely to be awarded for brilliant use of an indigenous African language. Are we waiting for modernization to come, or are we waiting for dependence to leave? In this domain the linguistic

Other has precluded the linguistic Self from ever being noticed as being of literary relevance. Is this "great chain of being" racial or cultural? In Africa the Euro-Other still inhabits the Afro-Self. When does race end and culture begin? They say African languages are not modernized enough. Or is this a case of Africa itself not being independent enough?

When Tagore won the Nobel Prize for literature written in Bengali before the first intra-civilizational war (World War I) it must have looked like a major step towards a Concert of Cultures and a partnership of civilizations. Unfortunately, progress in cultural parity since then has been slow and painful. The functions of culture in almost every society continue to feel the hegemony of Western power and the omnipresence of Western civilization. Has the stumbling "bloc" been Western racism? Linguistic dependence continues to be particularly severe in Africa. We need to elevate African languages. The global culture of *stratification* needs to be challenged.

THE IDIOM OF RELEVANCE

Next to *indigenization* as a strategy for transcending dependency is the related strategy of *domestication*. This second strategy involves making imported institutions more relevant to Africa. For example, the Western-style university is basically a foreign institution in Africa, and yet every African country has attempted to reproduce it, often in unabashed imitation. Some of those African campuses were previously overseas extensions of European universities. Makerere in Uganda, Legon in Ghana, and Ibadan in Nigeria started as overseas colonial extensions of the University of London, producing graduates with degrees of the British university. Université Lovanium in Belgian Congo was conceptually an extension of Louvain University in Belgium.

The strategy of domestication involved trying to make those African extensions more and more relevant to Africa in terms of the subjects they taught, the methods they used, the goals they sought to realize, and the actual people who taught the courses and made policy. In reality it has not been easy to Africanize universities in Africa. In fact, many of them are now decaying, partly because they were not adequately relevant to the needs of their societies, and partly because they were not culturally designed in the image of their societies. In our terms, they remained "undomesticated."[1]

If indigenization includes greater use of indigenous languages, domestication includes making the Euro-imperial languages in Africa more relevant for African needs. The imperial culture of *perception* needs to be changed. Instead of using the French language to promote French culture and civilization, domestication would make the French language a servant of African culture and literature. Great African novels in French are achievements in domestication.

There are times when the achievements of domestication are at the expense of indigenization. In the second half of the twentieth century it was often much easier to let the Euro-imperial language be the main language of national journalism, national politics, and national education — without bothering to develop indigenous languages for the same roles. Domestication becomes the soft option as compared with the tough alternative of indigenization. In such situations domestication may cease to be a method of transcending dependency; it may result in deepening that dependency. In former French colonies the French language is still much more part of the problem (dependency) than it is part of the solution (transcending it).

The muse of modernity is elusive in conditions of acute dependency. Is *negritude* in Senegal a case of using the French language to serve African needs? Or has it been a case of deepening that country's cultural dependence on France? The poetry of Leopold Senghor has been both a garland of African negritude and a chain of cultural dependency. The deep Senegalese dialectic between cultural dependency and cultural liberation continues. Perception is affected by culture conflict.

In secondary schools in Africa the literature taught to many African children is sometimes still European literature. But what is more to the point is that the African literature taught to African school children is almost never in indigenous languages. The European Other haunts the African Self from a young age in a postcolonial school. Have we been witnessing a clash of civilizations in African schools? Or does literature provide a cover for dependency?

The format of the literature is also often heavily European-derived. The novel is of course a European invention in any case, but even other literary genres in Africa have been profoundly affected by the legacy of colonialism.

Felix Mnthali of Malawi once wrote a poem about "The Stranglehold of English Lit." — a poem dedicated to Molara Ogundipe-Leslie:

> Your elegance of deceit,
> Jane Austen,
> lulled the sons and daughters
> of the dispossessed
> into calf-love
> with irony and satire
> around imaginary people.
>
> When history went on mocking
> the victims of branding irons
> and sugar plantations
> that made Jane Austen's people
> wealthy beyond compare!
>
> Eng. Lit, my sister,
> was more than a cruel joke —
> it was the heart
> of alien conquest.[2]

Is this a clash of cultures in the classroom? Is it racism in disguise, or a hopeful beginning of cultural convergence? Alamin M. Mazrui has reminded us that three of Shakespeare's plays have been translated into Kiswahili: *Julius Caesar, The Merchant of Venice* and *Macbeth*.[3] Shakespeare is being "domesticated."

What has not been translated, however, is at least as significant. Still untranslated into Kiswahili is the only play by Shakespeare with a Black hero, albeit a tragic hero. Why has it not been translated? Perhaps because in the play a Black man was married to a White woman, Desdemona. What is more, the Black hero killed the White woman in a fit of jealousy. The villain of the play is a White man, Iago, who manipulated Othello's jealousies. The play is, of course, *Othello*.

Why did not Julius Nyerere translate the only Shakespearean play with a Black hero into Kiswahili? Why was Nyerere's compatriot and fellow translator, Samuel Mushi, not fascinated by the fair Desdemona, Othello's wife?

Without realizing it, neither Julius Nyerere nor Samuel Mushi had confronted what colonial education had left out of their Shakespearean agenda — *Othello*. This play virtually never featured in the syllabus of Cambridge School Certificate for the British colored Empire. Nyerere and Mushi did not translate it mainly because it was not part of the Shakespeare to which they were exposed in their colonial textbooks. "Domesticating" Shakespeare in Africa has had its colonial limits. The subtle censorship of imperial racism had censored a tempestuous love affair between a White woman and a Black man.

If Alamin Mazrui's research findings are correct, these Swahili translations of *Julius Caesar, The Merchant of Venice* and *Macbeth* have now become legitimized as part of Swahili literature itself (rather than simply as Swahili translations of foreign literature).[4] Is this a deeper domestication of Shakespeare and a hopeful trend towards cultural synthesis? Is this another arena where the Euro-Other inhabits the Afro-Self? Why should translated Shakespeare become Swahili literature proper?

Here a comparison is appropriate with the *Rubaiyat of Omar Khayyam* by Edward Fitzgerald (1859). Although Khayyam was a Persian, the *Rubaiyat* is definitely part of *English* literature. Is this the equivalent of Nyerere's translation of *Julius Caesar* becoming part of Swahili literature? Of course, the main difference was that the *Rubaiyat of Omar Khayyam* was not a translation. Fitzgerald breathed his own literary genius into an independent interpretation of the world view of the Persian poet of the twelfth century. "A jug of wine, a loaf of bread and thou . . ." "The moving finger writes, and having writ moves on . . ."

A mere translation of *The Merchant of Venice*, on the other hand, does not give us a piece of Swahili literature. Only an indifference to Shakespearean literary authenticity and a readiness to engage in a drastic Swahili reinterpretation of the play would have justified enlisting the work within the corpus of Swahili literature. Only then would it have been cultural synthesis — and a deeper domestication of Shakespeare.

Nevertheless a great area for cultural domestication is precisely such translations of distinguished foreign works into African languages. Civilization has grown out of mutual intellectual and cultural stimulation. Under another strategy we shall later refer to the need to make African cultural achievements available abroad, but under this strategy of domestication, the most relevant translations are from foreign to indigenous languages. Machiavelli has already been translated into Kiswahili, but the translation is not widely available. Much more widely used are those Swahili translations of Shakespeare's *Julius Caesar, The Merchant of Venice*, and *Macbeth*. If modernization includes the trend towards globalization, the Africanization of Shakespeare is part of the process of wider modernization.

DIVERSITY AND INTEGRATION

A third strategy for transcending dependency is that of *diversification*. In agricultural production, that could mean diversifying the range of crops which a country cultivates for both domestic consumption and export. It could also mean diversifying a country's markets abroad, to make sure that the country is not too dependent on one or two overseas outlets for its products. Multilateral aid is a form of diversification as compared with bilateral aid. During the Cold War, nonaligned countries were even able to diversify their "masters," playing one against the other. Competitive imperialism like that of the Cold War can sometimes give smaller countries more space to manoeuvre than monopolistic imperialism allows.

Africa must also diversify the foreign cultures from which it seeks to learn. There is excessive reliance on the West as the only Other. And yet what is there in Japanese culture which enabled Japan to beat Westerners at their own industrial game?

In 1868, after the Meiji restoration, the Japanese asked themselves, "Can we modernize economically without westernizing culturally?" They embarked on a crusade of selective industrialization under the slogan of "Western technique, Japanese spirit." Fifty years later they had become an industrial power to reckon with. Their culture of *motivation* was highly stimulated. What was there in Japanese culture additionally, which enabled them to remain so Japanese culturally and still pull off an industrial miracle before World War II? How did culture as identity and culture as production converge?

Subsequently, Japan was briefly occupied by the Americans following the country's surrender as a result of the bombing of Hiroshima and Nagasaki with atomic weapons. When the occupation ended Japan started its second industrial miracle — less culturally selective than the first, but even more technologically triumphant. What was there in Japanese culture that made such miracles happen?

Of course, Japanese industrialization has not been without its costs. The culture of production has been allied to Japan's culture of stratification. The environment has often paid dearly, Japanese women have remained marginalized, ethnic minorities in the country have been exploited without adequate recognition. Still, Africa needs to look eastward towards the Japanese experience, as well as northwards towards Europe and westward towards North America, for cultural insights relevant to modernization and development.

Africa should also swallow its pride and look more closely at countries like South Korea, Malaysia, Indonesia, Singapore, and others in Asia. Such nations had the same per capita income as Ghana in 1957, but have since left most of Africa far behind in terms of both per capita income and industrial growth. To what extent are the economic achievements of the Asian "Tigers" due to cultural factors? Can foreign cultures be studied for lessons that are relevant for others?

Of course Africa has been studying Western culture for decades in the hope of stimulating its development. It is time that Africa diversified the cultural models it examines for developmental lessons. Such diversification may help reduce Africa's dependency upon the West in other areas of endeavor as well.

A fourth strategy in the fight against that dependency is that of *horizontal integration.* This involves not only national integration within each country but regional integration as well. Pan-Africanism therefore becomes an instrument of horizontal integration, and Pan-Africanism is partly rooted in cultural and racial identification.[5] The culture of identity is central.

In reality, such movements are born out of a combination of nightmare and dream, anguish and vision. What nightmare and dream released the forces that culminated in the formation of the European Union as a success story?

Pan-Europeanism had two parents: poetry and war. Poetry provided the vision and the sensibilities of being European; war provided the practical impetus either through conquest (as European nations expanded and contracted) or through a desire to avoid some future war. That was the combination of nightmare and dream.

After World War II, the Schuman Plan and the European Coal and Steel Community illustrated the creation of deliberate Pan-European interdependence to avoid the future risk of war. The Cold War both divided Europe (between east and west) and united

Europe within each camp. Once again nightmare and dream played their paradoxical integrative roles.

The poetry of Pan-Europeanism goes back at least to the European Renaissance as Europeans were stimulated by a new sense of shared civilization. By the time of the French Revolution from 1789 onwards, William Wordsworth, across the Channel in England, could proclaim passionately:

> Bliss was it in that dawn to be alive
> But to be young was very heaven.

However, the French revolution was a combination of both poetry and war — the two major stimuli of Pan-Europeanism. The French revolution was both nightmare and dream.

Does Pan-Africanism have a comparable stimulus of poetry and war? The real stimulus for Pan-Africanism has been the combined power of poetry and imperialism, rather than poetry and war. The poetry includes legends of past heroes and makers of history. More recently there have been two schools of Pan-African cultural nationalism: *romantic primitivism* and *romantic gloriana.*

Romantic primitivism celebrates what is simple about Africa. It salutes the cattle-herder rather than the castle-builder. On the other hand, romantic gloriana celebrates Africa's more complex achievements. It salutes the pyramids of Egypt, the towering structures of Aksum, the sunken churches of Lalibela, the brooding majesty of Great Zimbabwe, the castles of Gonder. Romantic gloriana is a tribute to Africa's empires and kingdoms, Africa's inventors and discoverers, great Shaka Zulu rather than the unknown peasant. Culture as identity and culture as stratification are intertwined.

Both forms of Pan-African cultural nationalism were a response to European imperialism and its cultural arrogance. Europeans said that Africans were simple and invented nothing. That was an alleged fact. Europeans also said that those who were simple and invented nothing were uncivilized. That was a value judgment. Romantic primitivism accepted Europe's alleged facts about Africa (i.e., that Africa was simple and invented nothing) but rejected Europe's value judgment (that Africa was therefore uncivilized). Simplicity was one version of civilization. Romantic gloriana, on the other hand, rejected Europe's alleged facts about Africa (that Africa was simple and invented nothing) but seems to have accepted

Europe's values (that civilization is to be measured by complexity and invention).

An African country can produce both types of Pan-African nationalists. Senegal's Leopold Senghor has been a major thinker and poet in the negritude school. Negritude is associated with romantic primitivism. Senghor's most hotly debated statement is "Emotion is black . . . Reason is Greek."

On the other hand, the late Cheikh Anta Diop, Senegal's Renaissance Man who died in 1986, belonged more to the gloriana school. He spent much of his life demonstrating Africa's contributions to global civilization. And he was most emphatic that the civilization of Pharaonic Egypt was a Black civilization. This was all in the grand Pan-African tradition of romantic gloriana.

What of the reality of Africa? It was a fusion of the simple and the complex, the cattle-herder and the castle-builder. It was more than romantic primitivism and romantic gloriana. Real Pan-Africanism must go beyond the twin stimuli of poetry and imperialism.

The Pan-Africanism of *economic* integration will be led by Southern Africa with the new community that has added South Africa to the old fraternity of the Southern African Development Coordination Conference (SADCC). The success of this economic subregional integration will be partly because one member of the new economic fraternity (Southern African Development Community — SADC), the Republic of South Africa, is more equal than the others. A pivotal state often helps to assure the success of regional integration, but a shared sense of Africanity will also be needed to sustain SADC. The culture of identity needs to be allied to political stratification in the quest for economic development.

In the period immediately after 1958, the old European Economic Community survived partly because some members were definitely more "equal" than others. Again, here was political stratification. The Franco-German axis was, under Charles de Gaulle, more "Franco" than German. But now German economic might has restored the balance in the new European Union. However, a shared European culture was also needed all along to sustain unification. The culture of identity was invoked.

The situation in Southern Africa is comparable with the Republic of South Africa being indisputably "first among equals." The pivotal power is the premise of regional survival. But a regional identity has to be strengthened culturally to sustain long-term unity.

The Pan-Africanism of *linguistic* integration will probably be led by East Africa, which enjoys the good fortune of a region-wide indigenous language. That language, Kiswahili, plays a role in binding Tanzania, Kenya, to some extent Uganda, Somalia, and potentially Rwanda, Burundi, and Eastern Zaire. Northern Mozambique and Malawi are also feeling Swahili influence. The language is spoken by more people than any other indigenous language of Africa. It will hit its first one hundred million people early in the twenty-first century, if not sooner, and is expanding more rapidly than any other lingua franca in the continent.

The Pan-Africanism of *political* integration will probably be led by North Africa. There is already a kind of economic cooperation fraternity binding five countries — Libya, Tunisia, Algeria, Morocco, and Mauritania — but it has been limping along. However, Egypt has now expressed an interest in joining this movement towards greater North African regional integration. The subregion is still a long way from political integration, but it is the best placed in Africa for such an adventure — since it shares a religion (Islam), a language (Arabic), a culture (Arabo-Berber), and a substantial history across centuries.

Part of the stimulus for North Africa's integration will be European integration. The economies of North Africa and Southern Europe are to some extent competitive. The deeper integration of countries like Spain, Portugal, and Greece into an enlarged European Union is ringing economic alarm bells in North Africa. This could help Pan-Africanism in Arab Africa.

The Pan-Africanism of military integration is likely to be led by West Africa, with the precedent set by ECOMOG under the Economic Community of West African States (ECOWAS). In spite of the difficulties and inconclusiveness of ECOMOG's attempted rescue operation in Liberia, the effort has been a major pioneering enterprise in the history of Pax Africana.

The peacekeeping issue is precisely the Achilles' heel of Pan-Africanism as a whole. Who will keep the peace in Africa as we enter the new millennium? Many institutions will be needed, and sustaining those institutions will require greater horizontal integration and cultural synthesis. Again a culture of identity needs to be tapped for regional cooperation.

COUNTERPENETRATION: A GLOBAL STRATEGY

The fifth strategy for fighting dependency is that of *counterpenetration*. This strategy involves infiltrating the infiltrators — counterpenetrating the citadels of power. Since we have defined modernization partly in terms of sensitivity to the global context, counterpenetrating the powerful is a search for a more balanced globalization. It is a quest for a more symmetrical interdependence.

In the second half of the twentieth century Japan so convincingly counterpenetrated European and North American markets that it is no longer clear who is exploiting whom. South Korea's counterpenetration of the American economy has also been impressive, though still on a much smaller scale.

It is also possible for a Third World country to use its raw materials as a source of influence in the world rather than as a basis of dependency. For a brief decade (1973–1983) the Organization of Petroleum Exporting Countries (OPEC) exerted some leverage on the world economy on a significant scale. Petro-power from the Third World briefly counterpenetrated the commanding heights of the world economy.

Then there is demographic counterpenetration. Irish-Americans are a demographic lobby for Irish interests in the United States; Jewish-Americans are a demographic lobby for the state of Israel. Some African-Americans, like those who support TransAfrica, are a demographic lobby for Africa on Capitol Hill. All of these are cases of demographic counterpenetration, as is the case of African professors teaching young Americans in US colleges and universities.

Making African culture available on equitable terms to the wider world could also be not only counterpenetrative but also modernizing for that wider world. The globalization of African culture is a modernizing imperative, provided it is done without exploiting Africa.

Progress is being made in the teaching of courses on African literature, African art, African philosophy, and African aesthetics in Western colleges and universities. One day, particular African works will no doubt be included in courses on world civilization, and not merely in courses on African culture.

CONCLUSION

We have redefined the once discredited concept of *moderniza-tion* to mean change which is consistent with the present stage of human knowledge, which seeks to comprehend the legacy of the past, which is sensitive to the needs of future generations, and which is responsive to its global context.

We have defined *development* as modernization minus dependency, and we have defined *dependency*, in turn, as either surplus need or deficit control. The two kinds of dependency do not always pull in the same direction. For example, in the history of imperialism, the imperial power often needed the colonies more than the colonies needed the imperial power, yet the colonies had deficit control over the relationship.

If development equals modernization minus dependency, how is dependency to be removed from the modernization process? We have suggested five strategies for ending or reducing dependency: indigenization, domestication, diversification, horizontal integration and counterpenetration. Underlying them all is the continuing salience of culture and its seven functions: lens of perception, means of communication, basis of stratification, spring of motivation, standard of judgment, pattern of production and consumption, and foundation of identity. This essay has ranged from poetry to Pan-Africanism, from sculpture to the "scientification" of African languages. The Muse of Modernity is trying to articulate a stanza vibrant with Alexandrian echoes:

A little modernity is a dangerous thing
Drink deep or taste not the Western spring.[6]

What is needed is more of modernity and less of "the Western spring." A non-Western route to modernity is possible for Africa — provided African culture is fully mobilized as an ally in the enterprise.

NOTES

A version of this essay appeared as an introductory chapter for the book, *The Muse of Modernity: Essays on Culture as Development in Africa*, ed. Philip G. Altbach and Salah M. Hassan (Trenton, NJ: Africa World Press, 1996), pp. 1–18.

1. See Ali A. Mazrui, "The African University as a Multinational Corporation," *Harvard Educational Review*, May, 1976. See also Ali A. Mazrui, "Afrocentricity Versus Multiculturalism?: A Dialectic in Search of A Synthesis," James S. Coleman Annual Lecture, University of California, Los Angeles, May 5, 1993. (A revised version of this last essay appears as Chapter 3 of the present volume.)

2. Felix Mnthali, "The Stranglehold of English Lit.," in *Modern African Poetry*, ed. Gerald Moore and Ulli Beier (London: Penguin, 1989), pp. 139–140.

3. Alamin M. Mazrui, "Shakespeare in Kenya: Between English and Swahili Literature." Paper presented at the annual meeting of the African Literature Association of the United States, Columbus, OH, March 17, 1995.

4. Ibid.

5. The section on Pan-Africanism in this paper is indebted to the author's paper "Pan-Africanism: From Poetry to Power," first delivered as the closing address to the conference on "Africa in the Contemporary World," sponsored by Espace Afrique and Centre de Recherches, Entreprises et Sociétés (CRES), Geneva, November 13–17, 1994.

6. This is a paraphrasing of Alexander Pope's famous thought:
A little knowledge is a dangerous thing
Drink deep or taste not the Pyrean spring.
(Essay on Criticism, 1711).

INDEX